The Professional Baseball Trainers' Fitness Book

By The
Professional Baseball Athletic Trainers' Society (PBATS)
with Lee Lowenfish

WARNER BOOKS

A Warner Communications Company

Copyright © 1988 MBKA Inc.
All rights reserved.
Warner Books, Inc., 666 Fifth Avenue, New York, NY 10103
A Warner Communications Company

 An MBKA Production
MBKA Inc., 1725 York Avenue, New York, NY 10128

Printed in the United States of America
First Printing: April 1988
10 9 8 7 6 5 4 3 2 1

Library of Congress Cataloging-in-Publication Data

Professional baseball trainers' fitness book.

1. Baseball—Training. 2. Physical education and
training. 3. Exercise. I. Lowenfish, Lee, 1942-
GV875.6.P76 1988 796.357'.07 87-21704
ISBN 0-446-38751-07 (pbk.) (USA)
        0-446-38752-5 (pbk.) (Canada)

To
Aspiring Trainers
and
Players
Everywhere

Acknowledgments

Matthew Colello, exercise physiologist and director of 21st Century Training Facility in New York City

Tom DiPace, V. J. Lovero, and *Fred Thornhill,* photographers

Mel Minter, copy editor

Pat Cash, Lou Cucuzza, Jr., and *Harvey Greene* of the New York Yankees and *Dennis D'Agostino* of the New York Mets

and

Tab Blackburn

David Falkner

Greta Minsky

Virginia Rosick

Kevin McGill

Each and every one of the trainers and assistant trainers of major league baseball have contributed to this endeavor, taking time from their busy schedules and endless duties.

Cover design by Mike Stromberg

Cover photo by V.J. Lovero

TABLE OF CONTENTS

The Official Trainers' Fitness Book

Foreword by Frank W. Jobe, M.D.

This is the first effort by baseball trainers to set down in writing what has been learned over many years' experience. The trainers have reached the pinnacle of their careers through countless hours of dedicated work. They accompany the players during spring training and the long baseball season. They travel with the teams, keep the same schedule, and share the same food and lodgings. They even give of themselves during the off-season. From this nearly constant association with the players and from observing them performance after performance, the trainers, perhaps more than anyone else, have learned what it takes to play consistently well at the major league level. This is the knowledge that they would like to share with aspiring recreational and professional baseball players.

The origins of baseball have been traced to many countries and time periods. One researcher has even attributed the first "batting contests" to the Egyptians over 5,000 years ago. These bat-and-ball-type games evolved over the centuries into a game similar to modern baseball, which was played in America in the early 19th century.[1] Alexander J. Cartwright and Abner Doubleday are generally credited with organizing the first formal clubs and game rules around the time of the Civil War. The next milestone was passed in 1869 when Cincinnati became home to the first professional baseball team.[2]

Just as the game of baseball has evolved over time, so has baseball training. Whereas in the past trainers were more in charge of equipment and refreshments for the team, they now help the players get into shape using the latest knowledge and techniques. They also help keep the players healthy over the long, grueling season and, hopefully, bring them in at peak condition for the playoffs. Their contributions to the athletes' well-being—and ultimately to a team's success or failure—should not be underestimated.

The evolution of baseball training also parallels the development of the sports medicine specialty. Before 1930 there were no such things as specialties in medicine or in sports training. Now sports medicine physicians, orthopedists, and trainers have accumulated a great deal of knowledge about athletic injuries, much of which has been invaluable to the training of baseball athletes. As a result, most of the trainers' recommendations in this book are soundly based in science as well as experience.

[1] *From:* Hy Turkin and S. C. Thompson, *The Official Encyclopedia of Baseball.* 10th ed. (New York, A. S. Barnes and Co., 1979), p.11.

[2] *From:* Joseph L. Reichler, ed., *The Baseball Encyclopedia* (New York, Macmillan Publishing Co., Inc., 1982), p.9.

Baseball trainers are equipped with special knowledge and skills because the requirements of the game are unique. Baseball is a game of individual skills in a team sport in which good hand-eye coordination is a necessity. In addition, the psychological aspects are very important and are often key to winning and losing. If a pitcher does not really believe that he can strike out a batter, then he probably won't. If a batter does not really believe that he can hit the ball, then he probably won't.

The characteristics of this sport require that baseball trainers acquire different skills than, for example, football trainers. The training needs, goals, and plans of the two sports differ significantly. Throwing and pitching are high-stress repetitive activities that, in conjunction with inadequate rest, can cause a breakdown in the muscles. This is called microtrauma, or overuse syndrome, in contrast to macrotrauma, which is a sudden, disabling injury. Football trainers must know how to care for the random, severe injuries that occur frequently in their sport. Baseball trainers, on the other hand, know how to recognize and treat overuse syndrome, which is more common in baseball. They are specialists in the care of overhand athletes, the rehabilitation of which, either before or after surgery, is often not understood by the general population.

The baseball trainers' goal—the same as the players—is to produce excellent athletic performance within safe physiological and psychological limits. Both know the disastrous consequences of athletic achievements produced at the expense of the body or mind. To successfully balance these two needs, the trainers have developed a close relationship to the sport and the players. They have participated in research into exercise physiology and biomechanics. They have helped sports medicine physicians with the care and rehabilitation of overhand athletes. Most importantly, they have used their knowledge and experience to develop exercise programs that improve performance and endurance and reduce injury. The effectiveness of these programs is evidenced by the trust that professional athletes place in them and by the respect that sports medicine physicians give them. I am confident that this book will serve as an invaluable resource for all those who desire to excel at any level in this sport.

About the Trainers of PBATS
American League

Ralph Salvon, 60, head athletic trainer of the *Baltimore Orioles,* has served in that capacity since 1966, the year of the modern Orioles' first world championship. Previously he had worked in the Orioles' minor league system and at American International College in Springfield, Massachusetts.

Richie Bancells, 32, assistant athletic trainer of the *Baltimore Orioles,* received his master's degree in 1981 from Eastern Kentucky University, where he was a graduate assistant trainer for EKU sports teams. He then joined the Baltimore system and arrived in the big leagues in 1984.

Charlie Moss, 40, head athletic trainer for the *Boston Red Sox,* has held his job since the pennant-winning year of 1975. He did graduate training at the University of Arizona and worked at Northeastern University in Boston prior to joining the Red Sox' organization. In 1980 he served on the Winter Olympics Athletic Therapy Staff in Lake Placid, New York.

Rick Smith, 34, head athletic trainer for the *California Angels,* was a trainer in his hometown while a student at the University of Texas at El Paso (UTEP). After graduation, he became trainer for the El Paso Diablos, the Angels' affiliate in the double-A Texas League. He joined the parent club in 1978.

Ned Bergert, 33, assistant athletic trainer for the *California Angels,* started in the Angels organization at Quad Cities, Iowa, after receiving a bachelor's degree in adaptive (rehabilitative) physical education from Saint Ambrose College in Davenport, Iowa. He joined the Angels in 1979. Since 1986, he has been the assistant trainer representative on PBATS' executive board.

Herman Schneider, 36, head trainer for the *Chicago White Sox* since 1979, is the first of the "Monahan Three," assistants to New York Yankee head trainer Gene Monahan who have earned head posts themselves. Herman grew up in Rochester, New York, across the street from Silver Stadium, home base for the Rochester Red Wings of the International League, where he later received his first baseball experience as a trainer.

Mark Anderson, 28, assistant athletic trainer for the *Chicago White Sox,* spent his entire tenure at the University of Nebraska as one of the Cornhuskers' student trainers. After graduating in 1981, Mark served for five years as a trainer in the Toronto Blue Jays' minor league system before joining the White Sox in 1986.

Jim Warfield, 46, head athletic trainer of the *Cleveland Indians,* began his career working as an assistant in the Philadelphia Eagles' summer camps during his high school and college years. In 1969, Warfield joined the Cleveland organization as trainer for the club's double-A team in Waterbury, Connecticut. He joined the parent club in 1970.

Paul Spicuzza, 35, assistant athletic trainer of the *Cleveland Indians,* has worked with Cleveland's double-A teams in San Antonio, Texas, and Williamsport, Pennsylvania. In 1980/81, he was the head trainer of the Cleveland Cavaliers of the National Basketball Association. He joined the Indians for the 1982 season.

Pio DiSalvo, 49, head athletic trainer of the *Detroit Tigers,* started his career in 1962 while serving with the United States Army. After his release from the service, he worked for 12 years in the Detroit minor league system before joining the parent club in 1980.

Bill Armstrong, 39, assistant athletic trainer of the *Detroit Tigers,* worked for the Toronto and Montreal organizations as a minor league trainer before joining Detroit's Southern League franchise in Birmingham, Alabama, in 1981. He joined the big club in 1985.

Mickey Cobb, 46, head athletic trainer of the *Kansas City Royals,* joined the big club in 1978 after spending six years in the Royals' organization. He served as trainer for the Royals' unique baseball academy in Florida from 1971 to 1975.

Paul McGannon, 34, assistant athletic trainer of the *Kansas City Royals,* served eight years of minor league apprenticeship at every level from Rookie League to triple-A. He joined the Royals' major league squad in 1984.

John Adam, 33, head athletic trainer of the *Milwaukee Brewers,* started his baseball career as a sixth-round choice of the Baltimore Orioles in the 1972 draft. He started his athletic training professional career in 1978 in Burlington, Iowa, for the Brewers' Midwest League club. He arrived in the big leagues in 1981.

Dick Martin, 38, head athletic trainer of the *Minnesota Twins,* started his professional training career in his hometown with the Lynchburg team of the Carolina League in 1969. He joined the Twins as an assistant to veteran trainer George Lentz in 1972, and has been head trainer since 1983. He is both American League representative and an executive committee member of PBATS.

Gene Monahan, 43, head athletic trainer of the *New York Yankees,* celebrated his silver anniversary as a trainer in 1987. He started as a Yankee trainer with Fort Lauderdale in the Florida State League in 1963. Since 1976, three of his assistant trainers have become head major league trainers: Herman Schneider, Barry Weinberg, and Mark Letendre. Currently, he heads up the PBATS' scholarship committee for the American League.

Steve Donohue, 31, assistant athletic trainer of the *New York Yankees,* started in the Yankee organization in 1979 and reached the majors in 1986. From 1974 to 1978, he served as summer assistant trainer for the New York Jets. In 1980, he was an assistant trainer for the national championship University of Louisville basketball squad.

Barry Weinberg, 35, head athletic trainer of the *Oakland Athletics,* worked in the Pittsburgh Pirates' minor league system before joining the Yankees as an assistant trainer in 1979. Following the 1981 season, he was named head trainer in Oakland. In terms of service, he is the middle member of the "Monahan Three."

Larry Davis, 37, assistant athletic trainer of the *Oakland Athletics,* spent 11 years as a minor league trainer with Oakland's Tucson, San Jose, Vancouver, Ogden, and Tacoma clubs. In 1984 he attained his present position.

Dave McKay, 38, in 1987 served as fitness instructor for the *Oakland Athletics.* He has been an Oakland coach since 1984, previously having enjoyed an eight-year major career with the Minnesota Twins, Toronto Blue Jays, and Athletics.

Rick Griffin, 33, head athletic trainer of the *Seattle Mariners,* was a minor league trainer in the Cincinnati organization from 1978 to 1981. He became a full-time trainer at the nationally recognized Ballard Sports Medicine Clinic in Seattle in 1981 and joined the Mariners as head trainer in 1983.

Bill Zeigler, 42, head athletic trainer of the *Texas Rangers,* started his big league career with the Washington Senators in 1970 and remained with the team when it moved to Texas in 1972. Ted Williams was both his idol and the first manager he worked under as a trainer. His oldest son is named Ted Williams Zeigler.

Danny Wheat, 36, assistant athletic trainer of the *Texas Rangers,* started with the Rangers when they had a double-A club in San Antonio, Texas. He worked for two years with the Ranger triple-A affiliate in Oklahoma City and joined the parent club in 1985.

Tommy Craig, 31, head athletic trainer of the *Toronto Blue Jays,* started in pro baseball in the Cincinnati organization but has been with the Blue Jays since 1980. He worked for several of Toronto's minor league affiliates, reaching the major leagues in 1985. During the off-season, he is a basketball official and works as a physical therapy technician for a local rehabilitation clinic in Palm Harbor, Florida.

Jon Woodworth, 30, has served for the past eight years as a trainer in the *Toronto Blue Jays* organization. In 1987, he completed his third season as head athletic trainer for the Syracuse Chiefs in the International League.

National League

Dave Pursley, 51, started his career in the minor league and college ranks in 1954. He came up to the Milwaukee Braves in 1961 and moved with the club to Atlanta in 1966. He holds a U.S. patent on a rotator cuff exercise machine. He currently serves as the secretary/treasurer of PBATS.

Jeff Porter, 32, assistant athletic trainer of the *Atlanta Braves,* has worked extensively as a student and minor league trainer beginning with his college days at the University of North Carolina–Wilmington. He joined the Atlanta Braves in 1985.

John Fierro, 31, head athletic trainer of the *Chicago Cubs,* started in baseball in 1977 as a minor league trainer in the Philadelphia Phillies' organization. He joined the parent club in 1984 as an assistant trainer and moved to the Cubs' organization in 1986. In 1987 he completed his first year as head athletic trainer of the parent club.

Dave Cilladi, 25, assistant athletic trainer of the *Chicago Cubs,* joined the big league club in 1986. A 1984 graduate of Penn State, he was trainer for the Nittany Lions' football, basketball, and gymnastic teams.

Larry Starr, 42, head athletic trainer of the *Cincinnati Reds,* started his career at Ohio University, serving as assistant trainer to the late Alan W. Hart. He actually got a head start taking correspondence courses while still in high school. After only a few months in the minor leagues, he joined the Cincinnati Reds' major league team in 1971.

Dave Labossiere, 36, head athletic trainer of the *Houston Astros,* started out in the Boston Red Sox' organization in 1973 and spent six years with three different Boston minor league clubs. He joined the Astros' organization in 1980 and has been the head major league trainer in 1984.

Bill Buhler, 60, head athletic trainer of the *Los Angeles Dodgers,* arrived in the major leagues in 1957 as assistant trainer on the Brooklyn Dodgers. He has been head trainer of the Los Angeles Dodgers since 1960.

Charlie Strasser, 37, assistant athletic trainer of the *Los Angeles Dodgers,* began his career with the Dodgers in 1972. He was a trainer for tennis teams in the mid-seventies, but returned to the Dodger fold in 1980 and has been an assistant on the parent club since 1985.

Ron McClain, 37, head athletic trainer of the *Montreal Expos,* began his baseball career in 1974 with the Cincinnati Reds' triple-A Indianapolis Indians. He served as both traveling secretary and head trainer. He joined the Expos as head trainer in 1980.

Mike Kozak, 29, assistant athletic trainer of the *Montreal Expos,* began his training career with the Royal York Junior Hockey Club in 1977. In 1980 he served as an athletic therapist at a Hamilton, Ontario, YMCA. He attained his current position in 1981.

Steve Garland, 33, head athletic trainer of the *New York Mets,* joined the Mets' organization in 1978 at Lynchburg, Virginia, where he had attended Liberty Baptist College. He joined the parent club as an assistant to Larry Mayol in 1983 and became head trainer in 1984 upon Mayol's retirement from professional baseball.

Bob Sikes, 26, assistant athletic trainer of the *New York Mets,* has been with the Mets' organization since 1980, starting at Little Falls in the New York–Penn League. He worked his way through the minor league system and joined the parent club in 1985.

Jeff Cooper, 36, head athletic trainer of the *Philadelphia Phillies,* has been in the Phillies' organization since 1970. After several minor league stops, he became an assistant to head trainer Don Seger in 1976. He became head trainer of the Phillies in 1981.

Mark Andersen, 28, assistant athletic trainer of the *Philadelphia Phillies,* began his career as a student trainer during the Philadelphia Eagles' summer camp in 1981. He worked for many Phillies' minor league clubs and also in winter ball. He became assistant to Jeff Cooper in 1986.

Kent Biggerstaff, 40, head athletic trainer of the *Pittsburgh Pirates,* had a long minor league apprenticeship with the Mets' and Brewers' organizations. He joined the Pirates in 1981 and was promoted to assistant trainer in Pittsburgh in 1972. He also works as a basketball official in the off-season.

Dave Tumbas, 29, assistant athletic trainer of the *Pittsburgh Pirates,* has been in the Pittsburgh organization since 1982. Prior to working in baseball, he worked for the San Francisco 49ers in 1981 and also during their 1982 Super Bowl year. He became an assistant on the major league level in 1986.

Dick Dent, 40, head athletic trainer and conditioning coach for the *San Diego Padres,* has held those positions since 1976. Previously he worked part-time with the San Diego Chargers of the National Football League and full-time with both San Diego franchises in the American Basketball Association—the Sails and the Conquistadors. He is the National League representative on the PBATS executive committee.

Larry Duensing, 37, assistant athletic trainer of the *San Diego Padres,* has been in the Padres' organization since 1977. He worked for seven years at the triple-A level before arriving in the big leagues in 1986.

Mark Letendre, 31, head athletic trainer of the *San Francisco Giants,* started his baseball career in the New York Yankees' organization in 1978. The youngest of the "Monahan Three" (and the youngest head trainer in the major leagues, beating out Tommy Craig by just a few months), he attained his present post in 1986.

Greg Lynn, 27, assistant athletic trainer of the *San Francisco Giants,* started in the Giants' organization in 1983. He made the jump from double-A to the parent club in 1986.

Gene Gieselmann, 41, head trainer of the *St. Louis Cardinals,* has been in the St. Louis organization since 1968. After only one year in the minor leagues, he became assistant head trainer in 1969 and head trainer in 1971. He has traveled to Japan as trainer for a group of touring American All-Stars, and he has also served as trainer for the "Superstars," "Superteams," and "Battle of the Network Stars" television programs.

About the Author

Lee Lowenfish, 45, is the author of two previous books about baseball, *The Imperfect Diamond: The Story of Baseball's Reserve and the Men Who Fought to Change It* (Stein & Day, 1980) and collaborated with Tom Seaver on *The Art of Pitching* (Morrow, 1984). Since 1982 he has produced and hosted a weekly sports feature show, "Seventh Inning Stretch," heard on WBAI-Pacifica Radio in New York City.

CHAPTER ONE

Introduction:
The Life Of A Baseball Trainer

By Charlie Moss, Head Trainer,
Boston Red Sox, and
President of the
Professional Baseball
Athletic Trainers' Society (PBATS)

Who are those men in the white uniforms who occasionally run out onto a baseball field to tend to an injured player? What is their role on a baseball team? Even more than umpires, baseball trainers are the unknown and inconspicuous men of the national game. Like umpires, when they are noticed, something bad is probably happening.

Trainers always hope that the discomfort is minor and that the player can stay in the game. In their back pockets they carry supplies for immediate relief, including Band-Aids, adhesive tape, cotton swabs, ammonia capsules, and an ethyl chloride spray that numbs the immediate pain. Sometimes, however, it is not momentary pain that a player faces but the prospect of serious injury. The trainer must then urge the player to control the fierce competitive instinct that made him a major leaguer and to retire from the day's fray in order to return a healed and healthy player later on. With experience, the trainer and the player learn the important difference between playable pain and threatening injury.

There is much more to the trainer's job than his duties during the game. You might even describe the job as a "calling" because the duties are enormous and the hours long. A trainer works from dawn to dusk during spring training, and if night games are scheduled (as they frequently are these days), a trainer is on call from dawn to midnight. Once the regular season starts, the trainer lives the life of a player, traveling half of the season and sharing the jet lag, irregular sleeping and eating hours, and other stresses of men constantly on the move.

The job does not end with the completion of the regular season. Before a team disbands in October, the modern baseball trainer makes certain that all the players on his team's major roster as well as its promising prospects know what is expected of them for off-season conditioning. The old days of getting out of shape in winter because of laziness or the demands of a nonbaseball job are over. There is too much money available in today's baseball for a player to fall foolishly out of shape.

I worked closely with Jerry Remy, a former California Angels and Boston Red Sox second baseman, who struggled valiantly to rehabilitate an injured knee. Jerry said it best when he declared, "The secret to staying in shape is never to get out of shape." Major leaguers now perform until their early forties, and the major reason is their conscientious improvement of playing shape. Carlton Fisk, catcher for the Chicago White Sox, went on a strenuous off-season weight program, and he continues to perform effectively at age 39. Pitcher Don Sutton, age 42, is an avid jogger and exercise bicyclist in the off-season, and he still gets batters out. These are but two current examples.

Today's baseball trainer oversees a player's off-season conditioning. (Appendix A suggests a general off-season conditioning calendar, which can always be adjusted to an individual's particular strengths and weaknesses.) The trainer suggests fitness centers near a player's home where he can maintain his playing shape. If a player is rehabilitating from an injury, many a modern trainer will visit him in the off-season to monitor his progress and keep up his spirits.

The baseball trainer's calling thus requires a commitment throughout the calendar year, but you will find few of us complaining. We share a love of the great national game of baseball and a sense of pride when our players stay healthy and are able to exhibit their great skills with consistency. The true sign of a major leaguer is the ability to excel day in and day out, and trainers realize that they must be on permanent call to aid their players in their pursuit of excellence.

Who are the trainers of major league baseball and how did we get there? All of us have played baseball on some level and know how hard it is to play this game well. I was an enthusiastic but average catcher in my hometown of Kimball, Nebraska, a tiny hamlet of four thousand near the Wyoming border. Barry Weinberg, head trainer of the Oakland Athletics, was good enough to play four years at Springfield College in Springfield, Massachusetts, and even got onto a double-A roster for ten days when he was working for the Pittsburgh Pirates as a trainer for the Shreveport, Louisiana, franchise in the Texas League.

John Adam, head trainer of the Milwaukee Brewers, had the highest ranking as a player among today's trainers. (A retired Pittsburgh Pirates trainer, Tony Bartirome, played first base for Pittsburgh in 1952.) John was a sixth-round choice of the Baltimore Orioles in 1972. From Gardena, the southern California town that produced two former major leaguers, pitcher Dock Ellis and infielder Enos Cabell, John was a promising pitching prospect until he hurt his arm on the Fourth of July, 1973, in a game at Idaho Falls, Idaho. John looks back at that day and recalls that he was insufficiently warmed up. In the pages ahead, you will find many appeals to the young player to warm up well, but of course, human beings sometimes will not practice what is preached. There is always risk in disobeying a fitness command, as John Adam learned.

Some of us have gained valuable experience as trainers for other sports. Kent Biggerstaff, head trainer of the Pittsburgh Pirates, was a student trainer at Southern Illinois University when the future Hall of Fame basketball player Walt Frazier was enrolled. During a season when Frazier was academically ineligible, Biggerstaff remembers how

Frazier honed his great defensive skills by playing on the second team in team scrimmages. Ron McClain, head trainer of the Montreal Expos, has great championship memories of being a trainer on coach Bobby Knight's Indiana University basketball team of 1972.

Tommy Craig, head trainer of the Toronto Blue Jays, has a lot of football in his blood, hailing from the same New Hanover High School in Wilmington, North Carolina, that produced quarterbacks Roman Gabriel and Sonny Jurgensen. (Basketball superstar Michael Jordan went to *another* high school in the same town!) Tommy got valuable experience as a college football trainer at East Carolina University, in Greenville, North Carolina, where Ronnie Barnes, current head trainer of the New York Giants, was a fellow student.

Some of us trainers became interested in athletic training after experiences as participants in individual sports. Jeff Cooper, head trainer of the Philadelphia Phillies, was a high school gymnast in Wilmington, Delaware, who turned to athletic training at the University of Delaware after an injury forced him to give up a competitive career. Dick Dent, head trainer of the San Diego Padres and one of baseball's first strength and conditioning coaches, wrestled in high school in Berwick, Pennsylvania, and later in college. After service as an infantry platoon leader in Vietnam, he pooled his experience as a competitor and a soldier and became devoted to athletic training.

The trainers of major league baseball hail from all four corners of our land as befits the national game. (And Herman Schneider, head trainer of the Chicago White Sox, was born in Amsterdam, Holland, although he was raised in Rochester, New York.) We come from as far north as Manchester, New Hampshire (Mark Letendre, head trainer of the San Francisco Giants); as far east as Providence, Rhode Island (Dave Labossiere, head trainer of the Houston Astros); as far south as El Paso, Texas (Rick Smith, head trainer of the California Angels); as far west as Eugene, Oregon (where Rick Griffin, head trainer of the Seattle Mariners and a native of Utah, did some pioneering graduate studies at the University of Oregon on the biomechanics of elite runners).

Pennsylvania has spawned the greatest number of today's head trainers: Dick Dent; Pio DiSalvo, Detroit Tigers; John Fierro, Chicago Cubs; Jim Warfield, Cleveland Indians; and Bill Zeigler, Texas Rangers. But the South and the Midwest are very well represented, too.

Within our ranks we have developed two impressive lineages. Since Gene Monahan, head trainer of the New York Yankees, started taking on full-time assistants in 1976, three of his aides have become head trainers themselves: Herman Schneider, Barry Weinberg, and Mark Letendre. And Larry Starr, head trainer of the Cincinnati Reds since 1971, has seen three of his organization's minor league trainers become head men in the big leagues: Tommy Craig, Rick Griffin, and Ron McClain.

Minor league apprenticeship, some of it lengthy, is the rule for trainers just like players. The years in the minor leagues produce friendships that last a lifetime—a wonderful product of the baseball life—but the conditions in the minors can be grueling. The schedule is almost as long and incessant as the major leagues, without any of the comforts. All of us who have endured endless bus trips will testify to this.

Kent Biggerstaff recalls starting out as a trainer for the New York Mets' farm team in Marion, Virginia, in the Appalachian League. He not only was the home team's trainer but served as trainer for all five of the other clubs in the league. Barry Weinberg remembers life in Thetford Mines, Quebec, where he started his baseball career with the Pittsburgh Pirates' organization in the Provincial League. "There was no clubhouse for the home team," Barry recalls, "so we had to dress in a hockey rink three hundred yards from the ballpark, and then walk fully uniformed to work!"

One day during the off-season of 1981/82, Jeff Cooper and I were reminiscing about the struggles and discomforts of minor league life. We noted that although minor leaguers are the future stars of tomorrow, they often work under conditions hardly conducive to good professional play. Bad lighting and erratic field conditions are common, and players have to fuel their athletic bodies on $11- to $14-a-day meal money, less than one-third of what their major leagues counterparts receive.

We understand the problems major league baseball faces in operating its minor league system. Football and basketball do not have the costs of development because the colleges serve as a free minor league system. The junior hockey system in Canada serves similarly to remove the burden of development from owners of major league clubs, but baseball organizations must meet the payroll of at least five minor league franchises. While many players today have college baseball experience, only the very rare exceptions, like Dave Winfield of the New York Yankees and Bob Horner, formerly of the Atlanta Braves and now with the Yakult Swallows in Japan, can come to the major leagues without minor league seasoning.

Jeff Cooper and I pondered the problem and agreed that as beneficiaries of the major league baseball life-style, we wanted to give something back to the game we loved by helping our brothers below us, the minor league trainers. Wouldn't it be useful if we shared the knowledge we had gained at the major league level from team doctors, other medical specialists, and fellow trainers? Wouldn't helping the minor league trainers in their work have a salutary effect on the minor league players?

We sought out opinions from other trainers, who greeted our ideas enthusiastically. We all consider ourselves baseball fans who remember vividly championship moments in our teams' seasons, but I think Jeff Cooper speaks for all of us when he says, "My most memorable moments are the moments people don't see, when an injured player like Joe Lefevbre or Darren Daulton makes it back to active major league duty because he knew in his heart that he could recover and I helped him do it." We trainers of major league baseball thought that the time had come to share our knowledge about fitness, injury prevention, and rehabilitation with all the minor leagues.

Thus, in 1983 the Professional Baseball Athletic Trainers' Society (PBATS) was chartered. I was proud to be elected its first president. I am happy to report that today we have, in addition to the major league trainers and assistant trainers, over 125 minor league trainers in our ranks. We meet during baseball's annual winter meetings in December, and because we all remember our days as struggling students, we have regularly dispensed scholarships to rising young trainers. We know how nice it is to get funding and to be recognized for our talents.

Starting with spring training 1987, PBATS started a new program, a series of seminars for minor league trainers which were so widely attended and successful that they will become a regular part of PBATS' spring training program. Choosing central locations in Phoenix, Arizona, and Orlando, Florida, we arranged for panels of team doctors, nutritionists, and public health and other medical specialists to share their expertise with the trainers.

The grueling season with its constant travel makes it difficult for any group of baseball professionals to meet in one place. But because minor league camps usually do not open until mid-March, these conferences will meet before the minor league players have reported for their spring training.

PBATS has been very gratified at the response to its educational work. Baseball as an institution has often been resistant to change and suspicious of cooperative endeavors. This is understandable since every one of the 26 major league teams is competing to become the one and only World Series winner. There is also an historic rivalry between the American and National leagues, which contributes to the sense of division within the game.

Happily, however, major league teams today have come to understand that the health and fitness of their players is a good in itself. Team doctors increasingly share their knowledge about the correct procedures in rehabilitation and prevention of injuries. Front offices share medical histories of a traded player with his new team's trainer and doctor so that the player will feel confident that his unique physical constitution will be understood in his new surroundings.

And now, with this book, *The Professional Baseball Trainers' Fitness Book,* we want to share with you our combined learning and knowledge about fitness. There is a commonly held view that baseball players are the least-conditioned and least-professional athletes. We disagree. While there are exceptions (players who can get along on great God-given skills without proper conditioning), we believe that the modern player is far more conscious of proper training, nutrition, and mental attitude than his counterpart in the past. You just do not see today's players coming into spring training to lose weight and get into shape. If anything, players today may *add* good muscle weight before the start of a season. To repeat Jerry Remy's wisdom: "The secret to staying in shape is to never get out of shape."

We hope that this book will be a useful guide to the aspiring player who wants to know how the big leaguers train. For the baseball fan who can never learn enough about his favorite sport, we hope this book will shed light on the role of the man in the shadows, the baseball trainer. And for every reader who hopes to be fit and live a long happy life, we hope that the following chapters will help you become a healthier, happier person.

CHAPTER TWO

The New World Of Baseball Testing

By Larry Starr,
Head Trainer, Cincinnati Reds

Virtually every American male has dreamed at one time or another of becoming a major league baseball player. Oh, to slug the game-winning home run over the fence in the bottom of the ninth! Or to dive through the air to make the game-saving circus catch, or to fly around the bases after a line drive into the gap! The sad truth of the matter is that only a few hundred can qualify as major leaguers—624, to be exact, in these days of 24-man rosters for the 26 major league teams. Thousands may be waiting in the wings in the minors, but only a few will be able to harness their skills and attain the consistency to qualify for the major league elite, to make "The Show," as the players call it.

Major league talent is a rare commodity, and it stands to reason that everything that can be learned about it is a benefit to club and player. My Cincinnati organization has been in the forefront in applying modern fitness techniques to baseball. After the 1974 season in which the Reds finished a close second to the pennant-winning Los Angeles Dodgers, Cincinnati became the first major league team to install Nautilus strengthening equipment in its clubhouse. We thought that off-season conditioning might cut down on injuries, and after reviewing the equipment on the market, we decided that Nautilus best met our needs. The Midwest division of the Nautilus company is based in Cincinnati, which made it convenient to try their equipment both at home and in spring training. In 1975 and 1976 we were fortunate to stay away from injuries, and these world championship teams, which became known as "The Big Red Machine," dominated baseball.

One never knows if any conditioning program is the reason injuries are prevented, but we think that the Nautilus system more than proved its worth. Our goal was to develop a program that would prevent injuries and delay the onset of fatigue in a long, arduous season. Injuries often occur because of a muscle weakness, imbalance, or lack of flexibility. Nautilus-type conditioning is based on providing equal work for each muscle group, making sure that the front and back muscles of each joint are strengthened equally and that the both sides of the body are equally engaged. It seemed obvious to us in the Reds' organization that this type of balanced, progressive-resistance program was a major step forward in our conditioning needs.

A few years later, the Reds again became involved in a pioneer project, with the assistance of many of our players who live the year round in the Cincinnati area. We have always been an organization that has courted local talent. On our current roster are Cincinnati natives Buddy Bell, Barry Larkin, Ron Oester, Dave Parker, and of course, manager Pete Rose. Before players headed south for the start of spring training in 1981, we decided to give a series of tests to Cincinnati-based players that would establish guidelines for evaluating their general physical condition. As a graduate of Ohio University in Athens, Ohio, I was familiar with the work of the Exercise Physiology Laboratory on the Athens campus. With the approval of the Reds' organization, the laboratory's director Dr. Fritz Hagerman and I worked out a pilot program for fitness evaluation.

The aim of the testing was two-fold: (1) to determine the overall physical condition of the player, and (2) to offer suggestions to improve his training and conditioning program during the season and off-season. We hoped that the tests would give the player important information about possible injury and fatigue identification, prevention, and rehabilitation. The tests would also provide important indications about a player's nutrition and his life and work habits.

Baseball is often resistant to change, and neither the strength training introduced in the mid-seventies nor the fitness evaluation of the early eighties caught on immediately. But just as strength training in baseball is now an accepted norm (in chapter 4, Barry Weinberg, head trainer of the Oakland Athletics, will give you an insider's guide), testing in some degree is done by virtually every major league organization. It obviously makes sense to understand the strengths and limitations of every player's body. The player gets to know the areas of the body he must improve lest he run the risk of injury. The club gets to know if a certain player's physiological makeup will make it unlikely that he can perform at peak efficiency for an entire season. Such data helps an organization to make plans for a roster.

Testing gives important baselines for players and clubs. If a player gets injured, his recovery period can better be determined by comparing the results of the initial tests to his present level of fitness. Since today's players stay in good condition throughout the calendar year, there should not be too much variance in the test results.

Players want to "get in shape" as quickly and easily as possible. However, high levels of fitness cannot be accomplished overnight, and it is a never-ending process. In addition, every individual is different and thus requires a unique program.

The point to stress constantly is that these tests are just baselines, they are not designed to provide immediate feedback. And even if a player doesn't grow leaner or aerobically and anaerobically stronger on the basis of the test results, we feel that establishing a baseline and a guideline are reasons enough to continue testing. We are concerned not just with making a more productive player but also with helping an individual to live a healthy and happy life after baseball. An added benefit of the testing is that it has created an excellent vehicle for dialogue. This communication is so vital for a successful program!

One last caution about testing is in order, and it needs to be emphasized. *For testing to produce meaningful results, it must be done at regular intervals by the same personnel on the same testing devices.* The qualities and conditions of testing laboratories vary dramatically; this is the reason they must be performed on the same equipment by the same personnel.

There are five specific fitness areas that we test: body composition, aerobic endurance, anaerobic capacity, muscular strength and power (the Cybex test), and flexibility.

The following is the pattern most major league teams use for testing:

1. Before the start of the preseason, usually the day before spring training begins —complete testing.
2. Toward the end of the preseason, usually about a week before the trip north—everything but the muscular strength and power test (Cybex test). A player may show significant improvement unless he already arrived in playing shape.
3. Sometime in May—the body composition test only.
4. Early August, the post–All-Star Game test—everything but the Cybex test.
5. A final test at the end of the season—everything but the Cybex test. This is an important time to test because an athletic season grinds players down, mentally and physically, and the results of this last procedure afford important data on how much the wear-and-tear of major league baseball has affected the player's conditioning. In addition, this information is used to set up a specific, individualized program for each player.

BODY COMPOSITION TEST

The first test, the body composition test, which calculates the percentage of body fat, is somewhat controversial because most people, especially professional athletes, are sensitive about their shape, and therefore need objective information. Some baseball players *seem* to be pudgy and out of shape when, in fact, they are not. That is why we need to test them, for to say that someone "looks" fat is as meaningful as to say that someone "looks" Canadian.

Often what appears to the naked eye is large muscle mass. Take, for instance, our Cincinnati outfielder Dave Parker. When the Reds acquired Parker as a free agent in 1984, the media of the Pittsburgh area, where he performed for years for the Pirates, suggested that Dave's best playing weight was around 215 to 220 pounds. Parker has since become an avid advocate of year-round fitness—he is a fierce off-season racquetball player and conditioning devotee. When he reported to spring training for Cincinnati in 1987, he weighed in at 255 pounds with a body-fat composition of slightly over 10 percent, an excellent ratio.

Since we started testing, we have seen the team body-fat average drop from 14 percent (1981) to 11 percent (1987), and we happily note that the figure continues to drop. Too much body fat will simply fatigue a player over the course of a long season and thereby increase the chance of injury. Too much fat also indicates improper nutrition or a lack of caloric expenditure, either one of which will ultimately affect performance negatively, not to mention impair the enjoyment of life (a subject that New York Yankees head trainer, Gene Monahan, will explain fully in chapter 5). On the other hand, we do not encourage an extreme loss of fat/weight in a player because that could lead to dehydration and predispose him to injury. In addition, some fat is necessary to line and protect all the vital internal organs (about 3 percent). For the general population, body fat in the range of 14 to 16 percent for males and 22 to 24 percent for young women is considered acceptable. Professional athletes, however, should strive for percentages in the low-teens range. Actually all active men and women should seek to lower their body-fat percentage to help their laymen's skills and, more importantly, their appearance, self-image, and general good health!

The body composition test measures the subcutaneous fat (located beneath the skin) to determine what percentage of our body weight is fat and how many pounds of fat we have on our body. A Lange skin-fold caliper is applied to six areas of the body: subscapular, triceps, chest, umbilicus, supra-iliac crest, and anterior thigh. The measurements in millimeters are placed in the following formula to give us the percentage of fat:

subscapular measurement x 0.0746

triceps measurement x 0.0769

chest measurement x 0.1483

umbilicus measurement x 0.1524

supra-iliac measurement x 0.1602

thigh measurement x 0.1020

% body fat = the sum total of the six measurements + 3.314

Pinch calipers cannot measure the fat around the internal vital organs, but the number 3.314 is an approximate estimate of the amount of body fat located in those regions the calipers cannot reach. We have done underwater weighing measurement, and there is a high correlation with the method outlined above. Once we know the body fat of a player, we have an excellent baseline to provide for his conditioning and his nutritional goals. Body fat composition is a much more exact measure than simply placing a player on a scale. Body fat percentage will give the club and the player a more objective evaluation of his physiological makeup.

Rick Griffin, head trainer of the Seattle Mariners, a former Cincinnati minor league trainer, and a widely published young scholar in the field of athletic training, has conducted recent body composition studies of both major leaguers and minor leaguers in the Seattle organization. The object was to trace, by field position, body fat change over the course of a season. The results of one study, of course, cannot be deemed definitive, but the findings were interesting. Starting pitchers gained the most fat over the course of a year as gauged by four separate tests. Relievers tended to remain stable or lose fat, probably a product of working in games more often than starters. Everyday infielders and outfielders tended to remain stable or lose fat, probably for the same reason as the relievers.

Catchers, on the other hand, tended to show increase in fat and weight. Two factors are probably working to keep catchers' fat percentage high. First, though catchers work very hard during the course of a game and over the length of a season, it is mainly the work of squatting and not the kind of aerobic running and sprinting of the other players, which burn up more fat. Second, catchers usually have large lower torsos, thickly muscled thighs and buttocks, which is also a factor in low fat-loss.

Studies of the minor leaguers revealed an almost universal loss of fat and weight during the season. Minor leaguers' paltry per diem food allowance of between $11 and $14 a day suggests that baseball's fledglings are not receiving enough valuable calories.

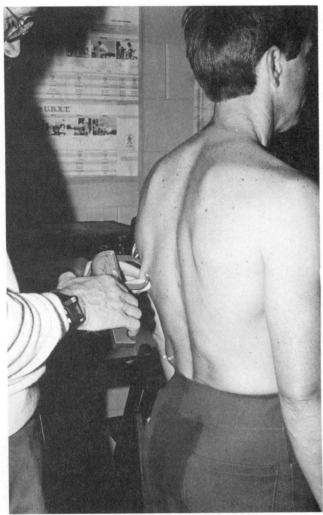

Body composition test, subscapularis. Dr. Fritz Hagerman with calipers on Larry Starr, head trainer of the Cincinnati Reds. On location: Redlands complex, spring training home of the Cincinnati Reds, Tampa, Florida, March 1987. (Tom DiPace)

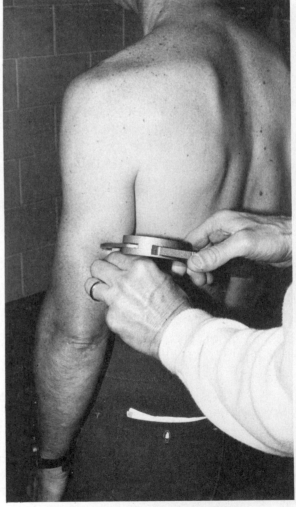

Body composition test, triceps. Dr. Fritz Hagerman with calipers on Larry Starr. On location: Redlands complex, March 1987. (Tom DiPace)

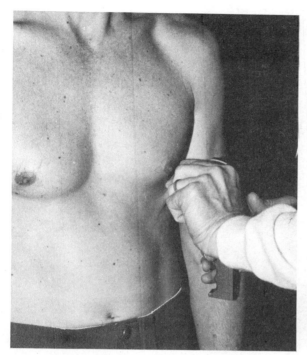

Body composition test, chest. Dr. Fritz Hagerman and Larry Starr. On location: Redlands complex, March 1987. (Tom DiPace)

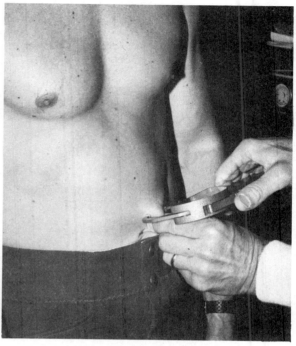

Body composition test, umbilicus. Dr. Fritz Hagerman and Larry Starr. On location: Redlands complex, March 1987. (Tom DiPace)

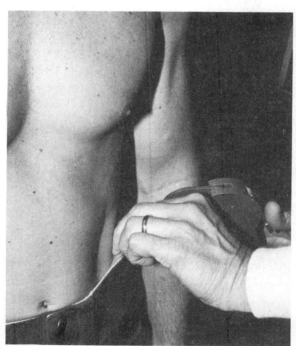

Body composition test, iliac crest. Dr. Fritz Hagerman and Larry Starr. On location: Redlands complex, March 1987. (Tom DiPace)

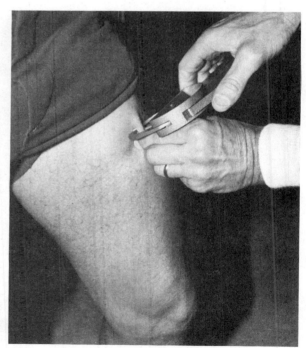

Body composition test, anterior thigh. Dr. Fritz Hagerman and Larry Starr. On location: Redlands complex, March 1987. (Tom DiPace)

It is the ardent hope of trainers of PBATS that professional baseball in the near future sees that the minor leaguers, baseball's hope of the future, are afforded increased nutritional allotments.

AEROBIC ENDURANCE TEST

It is true that baseball players do not need the endurance of marathon runners or basketball players, but they do need a minimum level of stamina to withstand the rigors of a full season: the constant travel, irregular hours, doubleheaders, extra-inning games, and the general pressures of a pennant race. We use the Monarch 868 bicycle ergometer to test for the heart, blood vessel, and lung function of the player. The player rides the bicycle for five minutes, and his heart rate is measured first at rest and then for each succeeding one-minute interval. The heart rate is measured by biotelemetry, using

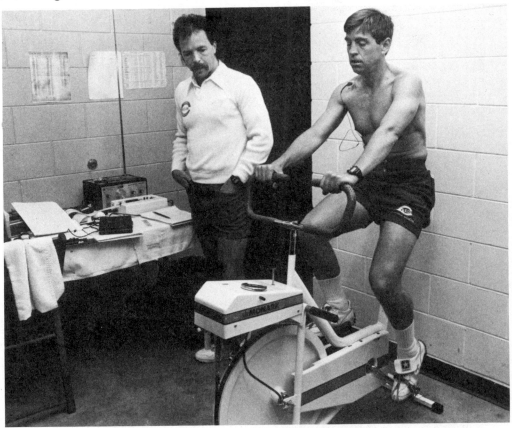

Aerobic endurance test. Larry Starr on stationary bicycle as physiologist Thomas Murray observes. On location: Redlands complex, March 1987. (Tom DiPace)

a biotelemeter transmitter-receiver system and recording the signal on an electrocardiograph. The steady power output is 150 watts, which is an easy work load for most players. Based on the relationship between the exercise heart rate and the work load of 150 watts, a predicted maximal VO_2 (volume of oxygen consumption) can be determined. This value gives us an indication of the player's cardiovascular fitness.

This is the formula used for establishing the player's *absolute* maximal volume of oxygen consumption (VO_2 max) in the aerobic endurance test:

VO_2 max absolute[1] (in liters per minute) = 6.13 − (0.0193 x 5-minute heart rate)

This is the formula used for establishing the player's *relative* VO_2 max, taking into account his body weight:

$$VO_2\ relative^2\ \text{(in liters per minute per kilogram)} = \frac{VO_2\ absolute}{weight\ in\ kilograms \times 1,000}$$

Although baseball is a game where most of the running is sudden and short, aerobic conditioning leading to cardiovascular endurance is very important. All trainers and baseball organizations today include running (both sprints and distances) as part of their off-season conditioning program.

Most coaches and young players will not have access to sophisticated aerobic-endurance testing equipment. Therefore, we want to give you inexpensive alternatives for coaches to test their teams before the start of a season. These tests include the following:

A timed mile-and-a-half run

A 12-minute run for distance (Dr. Kenneth Cooper, a leading practitioner of aerobics, warns that any person unable to complete a mile in 12 minutes should be restrictive in his conditioning program.)

The results of these runs will give coaches and trainers an idea of the range of fitness among their players. For us trainers in the big leagues, the results of aerobic endurance testing give us an idea of the kind of work a player may need to do in the off-season. Some may need speed work for better strength, while others may need to build up their stamina by longer runs.

ANAEROBIC POWER TEST

Measuring the muscular power and endurance of any athlete is obviously an important test. In baseball, however, it takes on special importance because this is a game with explosive activity from a starting point, unlike the continual activity in such sports as cross-country running and swimming.

The test we use for anaerobic power is called the modified Wingate test (modified in terms of work load and resistance). The same stationary bicycle used in measuring aerobic endurance can be used here.

After the fifth minute of aerobic testing, we increase the power output according to the player's weight:

THE RESISTANCE TABLE[3]	
Resistance	Athlete's Weight
3.0	130 to 150 pounds
3.5	151 to 170 pounds
4.0	171 to 190 pounds
4.5	191 to 210 pounds
5.0	211 to 230 pounds
5.5	231 and above

For 30 seconds the player pedals as hard and as fast as he can. The number of pedal revolutions are counted every 5 seconds during this 30-second exhaustive period. The highest 5-second output is an index which reflects peak power generated by the muscle

[1,2]*From:* Donald K. Mathews and Edward L. Fox, *Physiological Basis of Physical Education and Athletics,* 3rd ed. (Philadelphia: Saunders College Publishers, 1976), pp. 628–29.

[3]*From:* D. K. Mathews and E. L. Fox, p. 630.

groups involved in the test and is referred to as maximal anaerobic power. The difference between the highest and lowest 5-second periods divided by the elapsed time is an index of fatigue. This is very important information to the player and the club regarding the potentiality of injury in a fatigued muscle.

We have found that the vigorous cycling in these five-second intervals gives a good approximation of the kind of explosive leg power required in baseball. These test results have been very predictive of possible injury dangers.

This is the formula used for establishing a player's sprint power in the anaerobic power test:

$$\text{Revolutions after 30 seconds} \times \text{resistance in kiloponds (kp)} \times 6$$
$$= \text{absolute sprint power in watts}$$

To convert from kiloponds to watts, go first to kilopond meters, which are derived from the braking power measured in kiloponds times the distance pedaled in meters; 100 kilopond meters equals 16.35 watts.

The formula for sprint power relative to body weight:

$$\text{same formula as above} \div \text{weight in kilograms}$$
$$= \text{sprint power relative to body weight}$$

For those lacking access to expensive and sophisticated computerized bicycles, there are again inexpensive alternatives to measure the anaerobic power of your athletes. They include:

A timed 40- or 60-yard dash, a distance similar to the short bursts of running a baseball player does.

A standard step test, running up the steps as fast as you can with your heart rate measured at the end.

A "sergeant" jump test—as in, "Hey, soldier, how high can you jump?" —an excellent measure of your explosive anaerobic power and horizontal and vertical lift

MUSCULAR STRENGTH AND POWER

It is obvious that baseball players require strength and power for successful performance. Testing players for muscular capabilities and limitations is thus very important. The tests reveal not only the current level of conditioning in the muscles but, equally important, the state of balance or imbalance among the groups of muscles that are paired throughout the muscular system of the body. If a front thigh muscle (quadriceps) is strong, for example, but the back thigh muscle (hamstring) is weak, a nagging hamstring pull can occur and a player can lose weeks of effectiveness, if he is not outright disabled. Or, to take another common example, a pitcher may overdevelop his front shoulder muscles while the posterior muscles, used to decelerate his arm in the violent motion of throwing, remain weak. He, too, is at high risk of injury.

The Cybex II dynamometer is the machine commonly used to test muscular strength and power in athletes. No machine has yet been developed that truly approximates the speeds which the joints of the body attain in the act of throwing and hitting a baseball, but the Cybex II comes the closest, allowing a prediction of muscular strength and weakness.

The Cybex II is a safe machine; in 10 years of using it, the Reds have never incurred any injury to muscle, soft tissue, or tendon from using it. But because it is a strenuous and demanding test, this is the only one of the five testing procedures that is limited to one time a year, at the start of spring training. An exception might be made if a player had been injured and we wanted to reevaluate him. Like the other tests, the results give a baseline for the player and the club to judge muscular strength and power. It is compared from year to year and also as a guide to rehabilitation from an injury.

The dynamometer is an isokinetic machine, meaning that the player controls the resistance. He can move it harder or easier depending on his strength. The test is done in the two key areas for baseball performance, the legs and the throwing shoulder.
The Leg Test. We examine flexion and extension at three different speeds, 30 degrees per second, 180 degrees per second, and 300 degrees per second. The player is urged to perform two maximal contractions at each speed and the highest one is recorded. After the 300-degree-per-second contraction, the player is given a short rest and then is asked to perform an endurance test: at 180 degrees per second, he is asked to do as many knee flexions/extensions as he can in 30 seconds. This rapid contraction and all-out effort reveals the ability of a localized muscle group to contract repeatedly over a given time period and measures muscular power and local muscular endurance in the group.

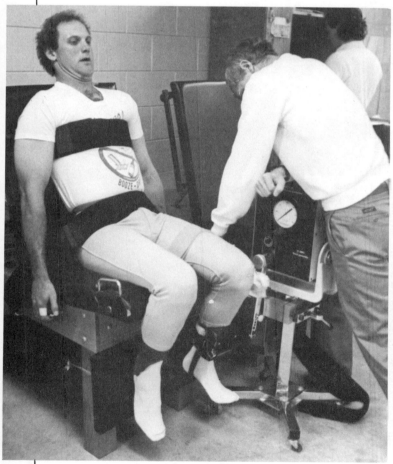

Cybex II leg strength test, starting position. Dr. Fritz Hagerman and Ron Oester, Cincinnati Reds second baseman. On location: Redlands complex, March 1987. (Tom DiPace)

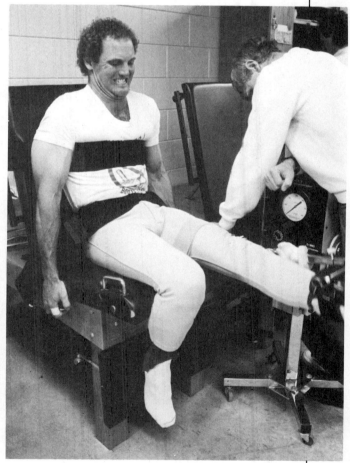

Cybex II leg strength test, exercise position (extension). Ron Oester and Dr. Fritz Hagerman. On location: Redlands complex, March 1987. (Tom DiPace)

The Shoulder Test. The throwing-shoulder tests (these tests are not done on the non-throwing arm) are done at the high speeds of 180, 240, and 300 degrees per second. Tests at lower speed with high resistance from the machine might cause injuries to the delicate shoulder joints and adjacent muscles. The tests are straight-arm shoulder flexion/extension from a supine position; flexion/tension from a supine position on an incline; and finally, internal/external rotation from supine and standing positions.

Inexpensive alternatives to Cybex II testing are counting the number of pull-ups (chins), push-ups, bent-knee sit-ups, and dips that a player can perform in one minute. To test upper body strength or weakness, a player can perform a one-time, maximum-resistance bench press. To test lower body strength or weakness, a player can perform a one-time, maximum-resistance squat or leg press. Be sure that the proper safety and assisting mechanisms are in effect.

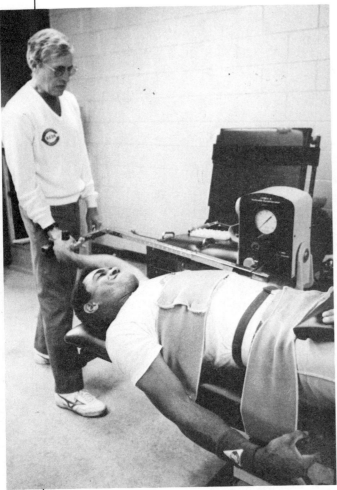

Cybex II straight-arm shoulder-flexion test, starting position. Dr. Fritz Hagerman and Leo Garcia, Cincinnati Reds outfielder. On location: Redlands complex, March 1987. (Tom DiPace)

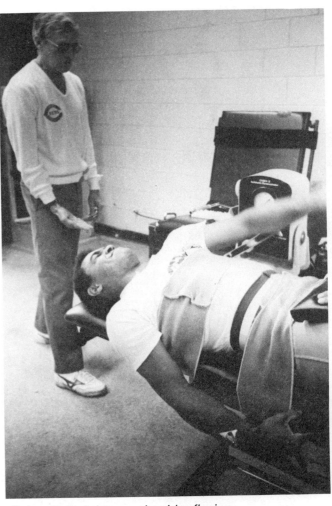

Cybex II straight-arm shoulder-flexion test, exercise position. Leo Garcia and Dr. Fritz Hagerman. On location: Redlands complex, March 1987. (Tom DiPace)

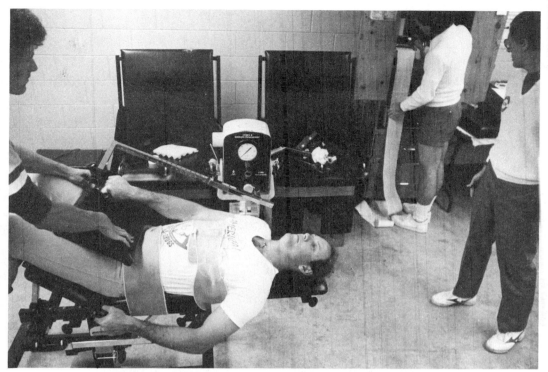

Supine flexion-extension test on incline, starting position. Dr. Hagerman aided by Cincinnati Reds pitcher Bill Scherrer and Ron Oester. On location: Redlands complex, March 1987. (Tom DiPace)

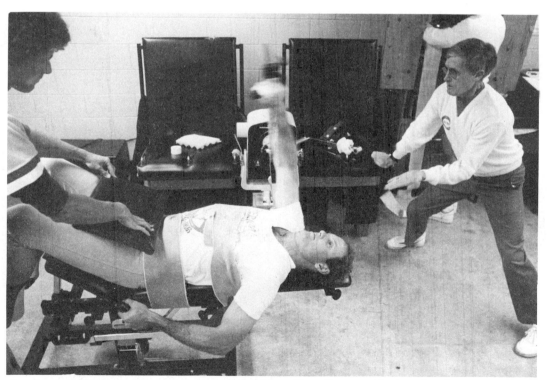

Supine flexion-extension test, exercise position. Ron Oester aided by Bill Scherrer (holding down Oester's midriff) and Dr. Fritz Hagerman (keeping Cybex bar from overextending). On location: Redlands complex, March 1987. (Tom DiPace)

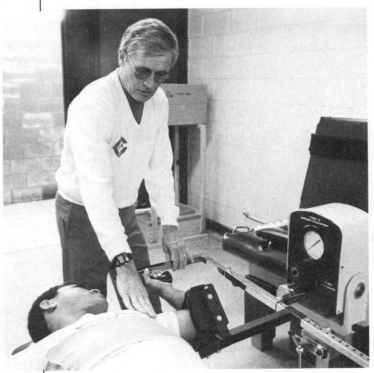

Supine internal rotation shoulder test, starting position. Dr. Fritz Hagerman and Leo Garcia. On location: Redlands complex, March 1987. (Tom DiPace)

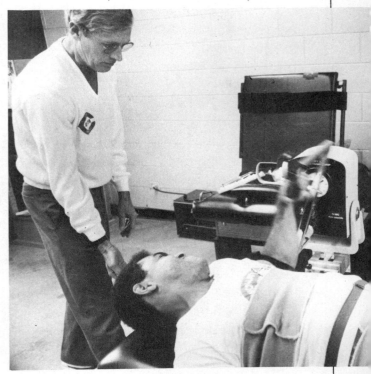

Supine internal rotation test, exercise position. Leo Garcia and Dr. Fritz Hagerman. On location: Redlands complex, March 1987. (Tom DiPace)

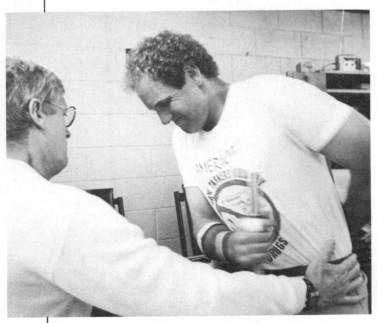

Standing external rotation shoulder test, starting position. Dr. Fritz Hagerman and Ron Oester. On location: Redlands complex, March 1987. (Tom DiPace)

Standing external rotation shoulder test, exercise position. Ron Oester and Dr. Fritz Hagerman. On location: Redlands complex, March 1987. (Tom DiPace)

FLEXIBILITY TESTS

All the great actions of baseball—the spectacular catch, the unhittable pitch, the game-breaking hit—require superior flexibility. In the next chapter, you will see how major leaguers do the warm-ups, stretches, and cool-downs that enable them to stay flexible. Here we are trying to establish, via testing, the flexibility baseline of our players. We perform five tests to evaluate both the specific joint flexibility and the all-important range of motion. The tests are sit-reach, back extension, shoulder flexion, adductor stretch, and trunk flexion.

1. The Sit-Reach. This test utilizes a special box, the sit-reach box, which is a foot wide and 20 inches long. (The box can be made out of wood by a high school shop class or even constructed out of cardboard using tape as a measuring device.) A measured track runs down the center of the top of the box with zero at the point where the player's soles rest. A wooden ruled extension is fastened to the box, indicating negative numbers. Keeping his head down, the player reaches forward with his hands, keeping arms and knees straight. It is a gradual movement since neither in testing nor in actual stretching do we ever want a player to bounce his way through a movement. That is the surest road to injury. A reach beyond the toes is registered as a positive score and a failure to touch the toes is a negative score. This test measures the flexibility of the hamstrings, the gluteals (in the buttocks), and the lower back muscles.

2. Back Extension. The player lies on his stomach with head down and hands held behind his head. His hips and legs are held to the floor or a mat with the aid of an assistant. He raises his upper body very slowly until it reaches maximum height and is held momentarily. Using either a tape measure or shoulder-width caliper, the measurement is taken from the floor or mat to the mid-chin of the player.

3. Shoulder Flexion. This test is done with the player again lying prone. With arms extended out above his head on the floor or mat, he holds a three-foot rod of wood or metal. Keeping his forehead down, the player lifts the rod as high as possible with arms and elbows straight. The best of three attempts is taken as measured from the floor or mat to the middle of the rod.

4. Adductor Stretch. This test measures the flexibility of the groin muscle, a common area of injury in baseball players, and particularly the strength of the groin adductor, that muscle which draws itself toward the midline of the body (as opposed to the abductor, which draws itself away from the body center). Before the player assumes the "split" position with his legs resting against a wall, a mark is made on the round end of the tibia (the medial condyle) of each leg. At the point of maximum expansion of his legs, a measurement is taken from upper tibia to upper tibia, from an area on the inside of each knee. Take this measurement quickly because upper leg muscles can cramp when held too long in this uncomfortable "split" position.

5. Trunk Flexion. This test is similar to the adductor stretch except that the legs are not completely apart but spread at a prescribed distance of 42 inches from the inside of one ankle to the other. With his back against the wall and the fingers of both hands clasped behind his head, the player slowly brings his forehead forward—again, slowly not choppily—in an attempt to place it on the mat or floor. The caliper measures the lowest descent of the forehead in three tries.

It is important that all these tests be performed after the player has been adequately warmed up. Testing the flexibility of a cold muscle can lead to serious injury. A player gives a clear sign of readiness for testing when he has broken out in a sweat from such warm-up exercises as jogging, bicycling (either stationary or moving), calisthenics, or a combination of all of these. It takes only a few minutes and it is time vitally well spent.

So there you have the story of how major league organizations start the training season by testing players, both the major leaguers and the prospects for the future. It is an encouraging sign to me that more and more players are reporting to spring camp in fine shape. They can actually add lean muscle weight during preseason preparation rather than, as in the old days, working to remove unwanted fat. One of the advantages of today's high salaries in baseball is that the conscientious player does not have to hold down an off-season job; so he can seriously devote himself to staying in shape. (Of course, there is a counterargument that with the decline of farming and many manual labor trades, much valuable off-season labor has been lost.)

Many clubs turn testing in spring training into a competitive situation. They stimulate the juices of the players by making an Olympics out of the test results. My organization and several others give out awards for the best performances, and even more important, for the most improved in all categories. I also award shirts to the leanest players in body composition, the most flexible, the best heart-lung endurance, fastest 30-second bicycle rider, the greatest leg strength, and the greatest endurance. Two of the Cincinnati awards are named in honor of our devoted physiologists, Dr. Fritz Hagerman and Mr. Thomas Murray, who have worked for years on developing and improving these tests.

Sometimes a minor leaguer wins an award, and it serves to keep him going if he has not made the major league squad during spring training. Outfielder Tracy Jones, who emerged in 1987 as a major leaguer and enjoyed considerable playing time, frequently won testing awards during his years of development. Who is to say that his superior conditioning did not play a major role in his emergence? As we noted earlier, injury prevention is not a headline-making concept. But if you have the talent and dedication, staying away from injuries by good conditioning is an almost guaranteed formula for success.

CHAPTER THREE

Flexibility Exercises For Baseball:
Warm-Ups, Stretches, And Cool-Downs

By Larry Starr,
Head Trainer, Cincinnati Reds
Herman Schneider,
Head Trainer, Chicago White Sox

Professional baseball players and pro athletes in general make their sports look easy and almost effortless. Watch a fleet outfielder gobble up yards of ground and dive for a catch. Observe a pitcher's graceful coordination of upper and lower body as he delivers a ball toward a batter. Or look at a home run hitter going down for a pitch, the quick flick of his wrists propelled by powerful forearms, and watch the ball sail in a beautiful trajectory over the fence.

All these feats may look easy, but in fact they are the product of superior coordination as well as strength and talent. In this chapter, we are going to analyze and explain flexibility, a trait that all pro athletes must possess. You have undoubtedly heard the truism from a doctor or physical therapist: "You don't play sports to get into shape; you get into shape to play sports." This wisdom is especially true for the professional baseball player, who plays the most demanding kind of baseball day in and day out for more than half the calendar year. When faced with a 90-mile-per-hour fastball or a batted ball traveling twice as fast or the flying spikes of major league speedsters, you cannot think about your response. Your body must be conditioned for maximal reaction to the stresses and the challenges of the sport. The best way to achieve this state of readiness is to attain peak physical condition.

Flexibility is a major component of conditioning (as are strength and nutrition, subjects which will be explained in the following two chapters). Flexible muscles will have greater range of motion in the joints and greater overall elasticity. Flexible muscles will be easier to coordinate. Psychologically, flexible muscles will make you more confident in performing your skills. You will also be less likely to get injured.

Stretching is a principal way of attaining flexibility in your muscular system. *But before you begin to stretch your muscles, it is vitally important to have your body warmed up.* Your muscles do not exist in isolation, they are just one of the many systems in your

Warm-up jog prior to group stretching. Larry Starr leads the morning run. On location: Redlands complex, March 1987. (Tom DiPace)

body. A warm and accelerated cardiovascular system is absolutely necessary before you start any kind of serious exercise. Your heart rate and your blood flow must be elevated before you start to stretch. At rest, 85 percent of your blood is concentrated in your abdomen and thorax; only 15 percent of your blood is in your extremities.[1] One purpose of warm-up is to reverse this ratio: to get the majority of your blood cells into the arms, legs, and entire lower body, which will be functioning during exercise. Another purpose of warm-up is to raise your body temperature 2 to 4 degrees above its normal level of 98.6 degrees. At the higher temperature, you will begin to sweat, a clear signal that you are ready for serious work.

You can choose several kinds of warm-up. Running in place for 5 minutes is one option. Or you can jog 40 yards four to five times. Riding a bicycle, either stationary or moving, for 10 minutes is an excellent warm-up. Or you can jump rope for 5 minutes, one of the finest of all warm-ups.

You are now ready for a series of flexibility exercises, starting with the head and working down the body to the feet. In the off-season, these exercises should be performed every day. Maintaining proper flexibility should be a year-round goal for any serious athlete. These exercises should become second nature to you. You will feel better after doing them. There may be occasions during the season when the grind of everyday baseball may cause you to miss a day or two of serious exercising, but never allow too much time to pass without exercising. *It is much easier to stay in shape all the time than to fall out of shape and have to work your way back to fitness.*

OK, you are now warmed up and have broken a good sweat from jogging or cycling or jumping rope or some other good exercise to elevate your heart rate and body

[1] *From:* Kenneth Forsythe, M.D. and Neil Feinman, *Athletics for Life: Optimal Fitness through Recreational Sports* (New York: Simon & Schuster, 1985), p. 35.

temperature and to stimulate a good blood flow throughout the body. It is time for the flexibility exercises and stretches, starting from your head downward. Remember three key principles throughout these exercises:

Always demonstrate proper form and technique. It is better to do fewer repetitions well than the prescribed number with bad form.

Relax all the muscles that your are not stretching or exercising.

Don't go beyond your limits. If you feel pain, you have stretched too far.

1. Side-to-Side Neck Rolls. Drop chin to chest and roll head slowly to the right and then back through center and to the left. Repeat in the opposite direction, five repetitions each. Notice that my arms are down in front of me and that my knees are bent slightly to enable relaxation throughout the rest of the body, which remains stationary during this exercise.

Side-to-side neck roll, head back. Larry Starr. On location: Redlands complex, March 1987. (Tom DiPace)

Side-to-side neck roll, to the right. Larry Starr. On location: Redlands complex, March 1987. (Tom DiPace)

2. Shoulder Rolls. Shrug the shoulders, then move them upward (trying to touch your ears), then backward, downward (trying to touch the ground), and forward. Hold one to two seconds in each direction because this is not a constant stretch. Do five repetitions in the four directions.

Shoulder roll, starting position: shrug. Larry Starr. On location: Redlands complex, March 1987. (Tom DiPace)

3. Arm Circles. With arms slightly bent to the sides and at shoulder level, rotate the arms in large circles forward, then in reverse. Then rotate the arms in smaller circles across the front of the body first inward and then outward. Ten repetitions in each direction.

4. Across-the-Arm Stretch. With knees slightly bent, bring your left arm across your chest, holding the left elbow with your right hand until you feel a stretch. Hold for 15 to 20 seconds. Repeat to the opposite side.

All these stretches have been static, which is the safest and most effective way to stretch. However, it helps to vary the kinds of stretches, and so some of the exercises will be more dynamic in nature. But we still stretch gradually, *never bouncing through an exercise, and always short of pain.*

Across-the-arm stretch, left arm. Larry Starr. On location: Redlands complex, March 1987. (Tom DiPace)

Across-the-arm stretch, right arm. Larry Starr. On location: Redlands complex, March 1987. (Tom DiPace)

5. Windmill. With feet wide apart, stand with arms extended to the sides with hands open. Bend forward at the hips and touch the right hand to the left toe. Return to the standing position and touch the left hand to the right toe. Repeat 10 times in alternate directions.

Make sure that the knees are slightly bent to avoid lower back strain. Also, if you are not particularly flexible in your stage of conditioning, don't force yourself. Reach down as far as you can without undue discomfort.

You are now ready to stretch the biggest part of your body, the area from which all your throwing and batting motions derive, the trunk.

Windmill stretch, right hand to left toe. Larry Starr. On location: Redlands complex, March 1987. (Tom DiPace)

Windmill stretch, left hand to right toe. Larry Starr. On location: Redlands complex, March, 1987. (Tom DiPace)

6. Trunk Twists. Stand with feet apart and arms extended to the sides with hands open. Twist the body as far to the left as possible and then as far to the right as possible. Repeat five times each way.

Advanced exercisers can repeat these twists halfway forward, completely bent over, and halfway backward. But people with back problems should avoid these complicated variations.

Trunk twist, to the extreme left. Larry Starr. On location: Redlands complex, March 1987. (Tom DiPace) For maximum benefit from the trunk twists, do them also from bent-forward positions, both halfway and completely forward, and from a bent-backward position.

Trunk twist, to the extreme right. Larry Starr. On location: Redlands complex, March 1987. (Tom DiPace)

7. Palm Pushes. These are isometric exercises designed to strengthen your forearms. Start with your arms straight in front with palms down and pull back with your hands, keeping your arms straight. Then pull in to your chest, then push away. Repeat each motion 20 times. Then do the same exercises with the arms extended to the side, arms extended in front at chest level, and finally, with the arms slightly bent overhead. Twenty times in each position.

It is now time to move to lower extremity stretches.

Palm push, arms straight in front and palms down. Larry Starr. On location: Redlands complex, March 1987. (Tom DiPace)

Palm push, arms extended to the side. Larry Starr. On location: Redlands complex, March 1987. (Tom DiPace)

Palm push, arms extended in front at chest level. Larry Starr. On location: Redlands complex, March 1987. (Tom DiPace)

Palm push, arms slightly bent overhead. Larry Starr. On location: Redlands complex, March 1987. (Tom DiPace)

8. Straight-Leg Toe Touch. This is a familiar stretch. You slowly bend at the waist and reach as close to the ground as you can without bending your legs. Then straighten and reach as high as possible. Repeat 10 times. Don't worry if you cannot touch your toes. Go as far as you can *without pain.*

Straight-leg toe touch, starting position. Larry Starr. On location: Redlands complex, March 1987. (Tom DiPace)

Straight-leg toe touch, extended position. Larry Starr. On location: Redlands complex, March 1987. (Tom DiPace)

9. Head-to-Knee Stretch. Standing with legs straight, feet together, and hands behind the thighs, bend your head toward the knee and hold for 10 to 20 seconds.

Head-to-knee stretch. Larry Starr. On location: Redlands complex, March 1987. (Tom DiPace)

10. Head-to-Knee Stretch with Hands behind Back. Stand with your feet spread apart and your hands clasped behind your back. Bend toward your left knee, while raising hands behind your back, and hold 10 to 20 seconds. Return to the starting position and bend toward your right knee, again raising your hands, and hold for 10 to 20 seconds.

Head-to-knee stretch with hands behind back, toward left knee. Larry Starr. On location: Redlands complex, March 1987. (Tom DiPace)

Head-to-knee stretch with hands behind back, toward right knee. Larry Starr. On location: Redlands complex, March 1987. (Tom DiPace)

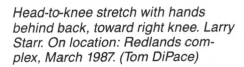

11. Foot-Out/Toe-Up Stretch. Stand with your feet considerably apart. Keeping your left leg straight and right leg bent, bring both your hands clasped together to your left toe. Hold 15 to 20 seconds. Return to the starting position and alternate: keep right leg straight and left leg bent and bring both clasped hands toward right toe. Hold 15 to 20 seconds. The toe-up position enables the less flexible person to experience a good stretch. It also affords the excerciser the opportunity to stretch the calf as well as the hamstring muscle.

Toe-up stretch, left foot. Larry Starr. On location, Redlands complex, March 1987. (Tom DiPace)

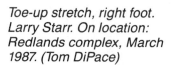

Toe-up stretch, right foot. Larry Starr. On location: Redlands complex, March 1987. (Tom DiPace)

12. Standing Calf Stretch. To stretch my right calf, I place my left foot out with my left knee bent; then I stretch my left calf with my right foot out and right knee bent. Hold for 10 to 15 seconds on each leg. Note that both feet are facing directly forward with the weight on the bent leg; the heel of the back foot is flat on the ground. My upper body is supported by both hands on the bent leg.

Standing stretch, right calf. Larry Starr. On location, Redlands complex, March, 1987. (Tom DiPace)

Standing stretch, left calf. Larry Starr. On location: Redlands complex, March 1987. (Tom DiPace)

13. Groin Stretch. The groin is a vital and often troublesome area for any athlete. This stretch is thus very important. With your right knee bent, your right hand hanging straight down toward the ground, and your weight on your heel, stretch out your left leg to a point short of discomfort and hold 10 seconds. After the hold, turn your upper body to the right, and hold 10 seconds with your weight on your toe. Reverse and with your left knee bent and your left hand extended, stretch out the right leg to a point short of discomfort. Hold for 10 seconds. After the hold, turn your upper body to the left, with weight shifted to your toe and hold for 10 seconds.

Left groin stretch, feet wide apart, hands out in front of body. Larry Starr. On location: Redlands complex, March 1987. (Tom DiPace)

Right groin stretch, feet wide apart, hands out in front of body. Larry Starr. On location: Redlands complex, March 1987. (Tom DiPace) In both these groin stretches, imagine that you are holding glasses of water. Don't spill them!

14. Kick-Ups. Standing with legs and knees slightly apart, kick the right foot to the left hand which is outstretched slightly above the shoulder level. Repeat 10 times and then shift to the left foot, kicking to the right hand, which is extended outward slightly above the shoulder level. Repeat 10 times. *Do not overextend!* This is a dynamic exercise and should be done under control! (Notice that my left leg is much more flexible than my right leg; if I were a professional athlete, I diligently would strive to correct this imbalance.)

Kick-up, right foot. Larry Starr. On location: Redlands complex, March 1987. (Tom DiPace)

Kick-up, left foot. Larry Starr. On location: Redlands complex, March 1987. (Tom DiPace)

FLOOR OR SEATED EXERCISES

15. Double Groin Stretch. This works both sides of the groin. You sit in a yogi position with your hands clasping the outside of both feet. Hold for 20 seconds. To increase your range of motion, push down with your elbows on your knees, breathe deeply, and relax the upper body.

Double groin stretch, yogi position, feet held together. Larry Starr. On location: Redlands complex, March 1987. (Tom DiPace)

16. Ankle Cradle. This exercise loosens up the ankle joint and stretches the buttocks and upper thigh. Seated on the ground with your left leg extended, bring your right foot toward the left knee, cradling the right ankle in your hands. Hold for 10 to 20 seconds. Reverse, extending your right leg and bringing the left leg toward the knee; cradle the left ankle.

Right ankle cradle. Larry Starr. On location: Redlands complex, March 1987. (Tom DiPace)

Left ankle cradle. Larry Starr. On location: Redlands complex, March 1987. (Tom DiPace)

17. Alternate-Toe V-Spread Stretch. Seated on the ground with your legs spread apart and straight, stretch your left arm to reach your right foot. Then reverse to reach your left foot with your right arm. The ideal is to perform 20 toe touches in 20 seconds, but some players in a group may not have the flexibility to reach this goal. The basic rule applies: Do as many as you can with proper form and technique. Don't force or bounce through a stretch improperly.

Flexibility varies from player to player, but with proper understanding and the establishment of a routine, you can certainly improve on your flexibility and thereby make yourself a more durable and consistent player.

Alternate-toe V-spread stretch, left arm to right foot. Larry Starr. On location: Redlands complex, March 1987. (Tom DiPace)

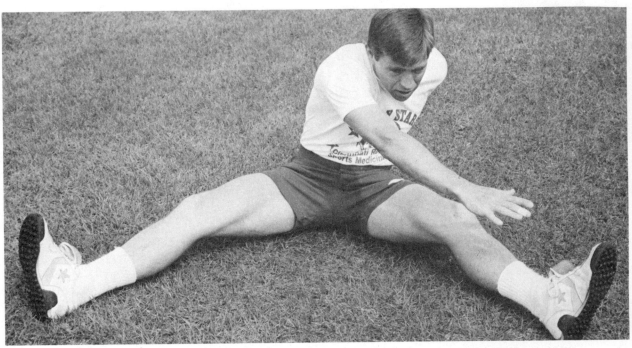

Alternate-toe V-spread stretch, right arm to left foot. Larry Starr. On location: Redlands complex, March 1987. (Tom DiPace)

STANDING EXERCISES
18. Three-Quarter Squats (an excellent strengthening exercise, too). Start with your hands outstretched and imagine you are holding two glasses of water. Move to a three-quarter squat position and hold for 1 second. Repeat 10 times, then hold in down position for 10 seconds. You will feel the stretch in the quadriceps and the groin. Keep your back straight and your head up! Don't spill your water!

Three-quarter squat, starting position. Larry Starr. On location: Redlands complex, March 1987. (Tom DiPace)

Three-quarter squat, exercise position. Larry Starr. On location: Redlands complex, March 1987. (Tom DiPace)

The preceding exercises are a good sampling of the flexibility and stretching work that the modern baseball player must constantly perform in-season and off-season to enable him to perform at the peak of his craft. Bench players must particularly keep up on this work because they never know when they will be rushed into action. A good bench usually means the difference between a good and a pennant-winning team. On "The Big Red Machine" teams of the mid-seventies, infielders Doug Flynn and Junior Kennedy, and backup catcher Bill Plummer (now a manager in the Pacific Coast League at Calgary) made key contributions off the bench because they were always physically and mentally prepared.

There are many innovative methods being used in today's baseball that constantly encourage players to work on their flexibility and readiness for action. Kent Biggerstaff of the Pittsburgh Pirates has instituted a stretching period for all of the players on the bench, excluding pitchers. It happens either in the bottom of the fifth inning of a road game or the top of the sixth inning of a home game, with Kent's assistant, Dave Tumbas, leading a stretching period of about five minutes in the clubhouse. Cincinnati's batting instructor, Billy DeMars, has done something similar by setting up a batting tee in our clubhouse for our pinch hitters to loosen up on.

It is time now to go into more depth on flexibility exercises for one of the most important parts of any athlete's body, the legs. Herman Schneider, head trainer of the Chicago White Sox, will be our guide, with the assistance of two Chicago players, All-Star outfielder Harold Baines and veteran pitcher Richard Dotson.

V-stretch on the ground, starting position. Richard Dotson, Chicago White Sox pitcher. On location: Payne Park, spring training home of the Chicago White Sox, Sarasota, Florida, March 1987. (Tom DiPace)

V-stretch to the right. Richard Dotson. On location: Payne Park, March 1987. (Tom DiPace)

V-stretch to the left. Richard Dotson. On location: Payne Park, March 1987. (Tom DiPace) Notice that the toes of the stretched leg's foot are up to maximize the stretch throughout the entire leg.

Double groin stretch. Richard Dotson. On location: Payne Park, March 1987. (Tom DiPace)

Upper right quadriceps stretch, starting position. Richard Dotson. On location: Payne Park, March 1987. (Tom DiPace)

Upper right quadriceps stretch, exercise and hold position. Richard Dotson. On location: Payne Park, March 1987. (Tom DiPace)

Over-the-head stretch, right arm. Richard Dotson. On location: Payne Park, March 1987. (Tom DiPace)

Perpendicular stretch, left arm. Richard Dotson. On location: Payne Park, March 1987. (Tom DiPace)

Bilateral arm stretch, starting position. Richard Dotson. On location: Payne Park, March 1987. (Tom DiPace)

Bilateral arm stretch, exercise and hold position, arms up and back. Richard Dotson. On location: Payne Park, March 1987. (Tom DiPace)

Left calf/right quadriceps stretch. Richard Dotson. On location: Payne Park, March 1987. (Tom DiPace)

Right calf/left quadriceps stretch. Richard Dotson. On location: Payne Park, March 1987. (Tom DiPace)

Seated trunk twist, to the left. Richard Dotson. On location: Payne Park, March 1987. (Tom DiPace)

Seated trunk twist, to the left. Richard Dotson. On location: Payne Park, March 1987. (Tom DiPace)

Modified sit-up, right elbow to left knee. Richard Dotson. On location: Payne Park, March 1987. (Tom DiPace)

Modified push-up (also called press-up), upper thigh and groin resting on the ground. Richard Dotson. On location: Payne Park, March 1987. (Tom DiPace)

Standing hamstring stretch, hands against fence. Richard Dotson. On location: Payne Park, March 1987. (Tom DiPace)

Standing hamstring stretch, hands against fence. On location: Payne Park, March 1987. (Tom DiPace)

Standing hamstring stretch, hands against fence. Richard Dotson. On location: Payne Park, March 1987. (Tom DiPace)

Standing hamstring stretch, one hand on fence. On location: Payne Park, March 1987. (Tom DiPace)

Standing hamstring stretch, one hand on fence. On location: Payne Park, March 1987. (Tom DiPace)

Stretching for both pitchers and everyday players should be as natural as brushing their teeth. These exercises should be done every day by position players and relief pitchers and nearly every day by starting pitchers, especially the day after they have pitched. During the off-season, when the grind of a season is over and there should be no residual soreness, every player should do some form of these exercises every day.

As in every stretching sequence, the player must first be warmed up and nicely sweated. Richard Dotson demonstrates a sequence of hamstring, calf, and shoulder warm-ups that he does before the stretch and often afterward.

Now it is time for me to begin the manually assisted stretches. Manual assistance is used to educate the player's leg muscles to feel the right motion for the fullest proper stretch. A few times in clockwise motion and a few times in counterclockwise motion, I work all the leg muscles, both in the front and in the back: high and low hamstrings, hip flexors, abductors, adductors, quadriceps, calves, ankles, and Achilles tendons.

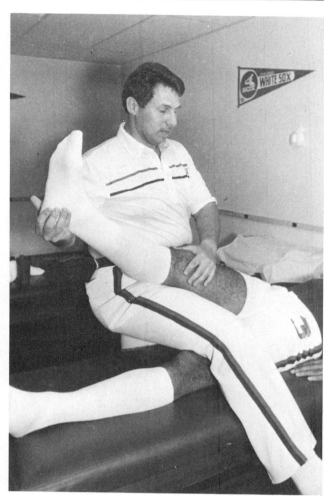

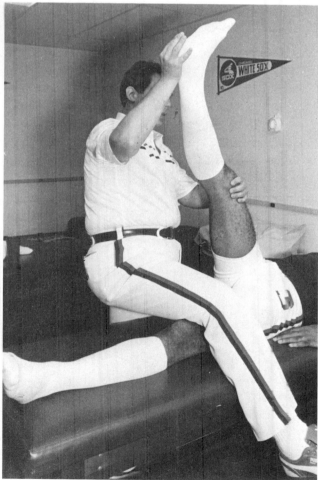

Assisted right hamstring stretch, starting position. Herman Schneider, head trainer of the Chicago White Sox, uses his right leg and both hands to isolate right hamstring of Harold Baines, Chicago White Sox right fielder. On location: Payne Park, March 1987. (Tom DiPace)

Assisted right hamstring stretch, midexercise position. Herman Schneider and Harold Baines. On location: Payne Park, March 1987. (Tom DiPace)

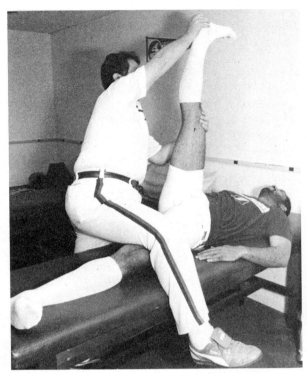

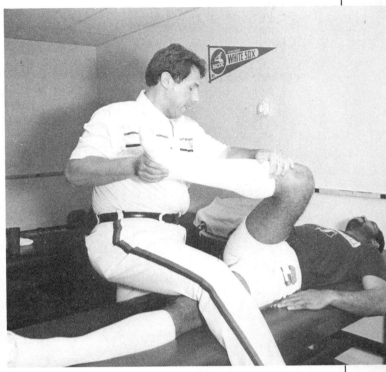

Assisted right hamstring stretch, final exercise position. Herman Schneider and Harold Baines. On location: Payne Park, March 1987. (Tom DiPace) Notice that Herman uses his right leg across the table to keep Harold's left leg stationary, and he uses his left hand to stabilize Harold's left knee, with his right hand firmly behind Harold's right foot.

Assisted right hip-flexor stretch, starting position. Herman Schneider and Harold Baines. On location: Payne Park, March 1987. (Tom DiPace) Notice that Herman's position is identical to the start of the hamstring stretch.

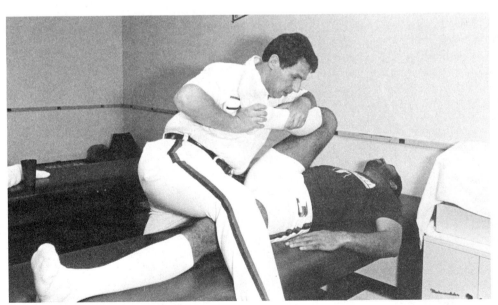

Assisted right hip-flexor stretch, rotation of flexors. Herman Schneider and Harold Baines. On location: Payne Park, March 1987. (Tom DiPace)

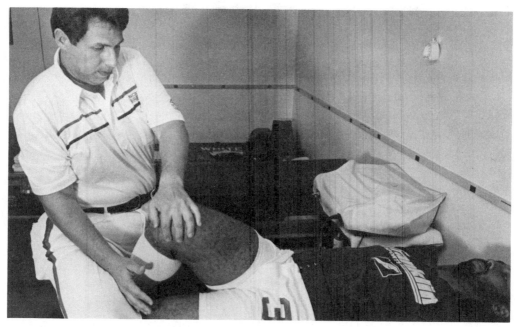

Assisted right hip-flexor stretch, adduction. Herman Schneider and Harold Baines. On location: Payne Park, March 1987. (Tom DiPace) Notice that Herman, in the same position as for the hamstring stretch, is bringing Harold's hip flexors toward the midline of his body (adduction).

I start with the player on his back, as shown by Harold Baines. I first secure his leg by resting it on my right leg, which is draped across the table. I work the hamstrings first and then move toward the hip flexors, stretching and rotating them. Then I abduct the flexors, pushing them away from the middle of the body; next, I add resistance to the adduction of the hip flexor. The sequence is important. I start with the player on his back and work from the larger muscles of the trunk down to ankles and feet. Notice that Harold's feet are on the edge of but not over the table, to assure stability.

Once both legs are stretched from the supine position, I turn the player over for the quadriceps stretch from the prone position. The movement is the same in counterclockwise and clockwise direction—several times each way to insure a good blood flow in the stretched area.

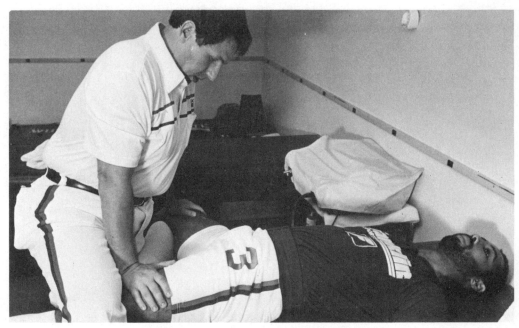

Assisted right hip-flexor stretch, abduction. Herman Schneider and Harold Baines. On location: Payne Park, March 1987. (Tom DiPace) Notice that Herman has stretched Harold's right hip flexors all the way from the midline of the body (abduction).

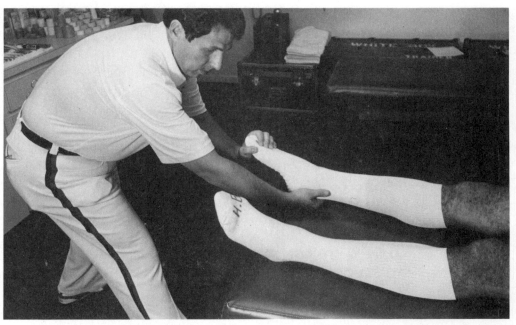

Assisted right-ankle plantarflexion stretch. Herman Schneider and Harold Baines. On location: Payne Park, March 1987. (Tom DiPace) Herman stabilizes the top and bottom of Harold's right foot, and Harold pushes down against the resistance (plantarflexion).

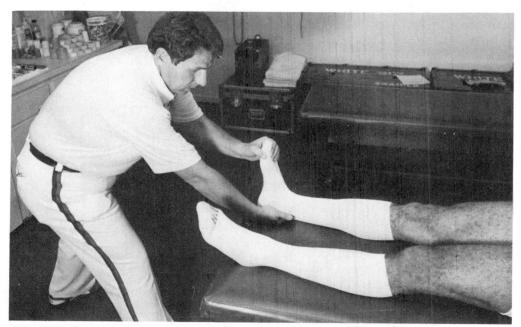

Assisted right-ankle dorsiflexion stretch. Herman Schneider and Harold Baines. On location: Payne Park, March 1987. (Tom DiPace) Herman stabilizes the top and bottom of Harold's right foot, and Harold pushes up (dorsiflexion).

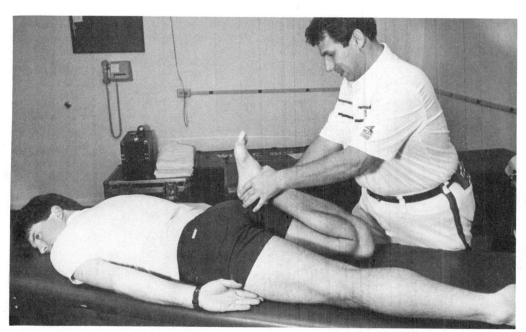

Assisted right quadriceps stretch, starting position. Herman Schneider and Richard Dotson, Chicago White Sox pitcher. On location: Payne Park, March 1987. (Tom DiPace)

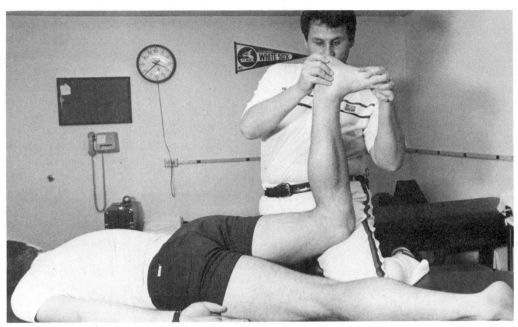

Assisted right quadriceps stretch, exercise position. Herman Schneider and Richard Dotson. On location: Payne Park, March 1987. (Tom DiPace) Notice that Herman has placed his left knee on the table to give more leverage, aiding the stretch.

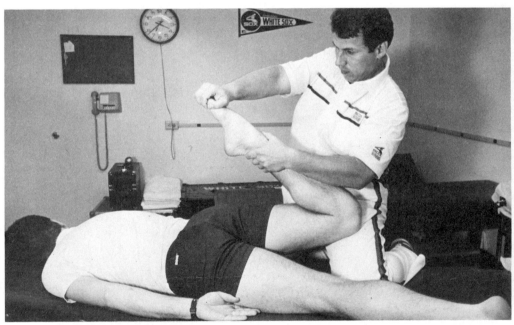

Assisted right quadriceps stretch, exercise position. On location: Payne Park, March 1987. (Tom DiPace)

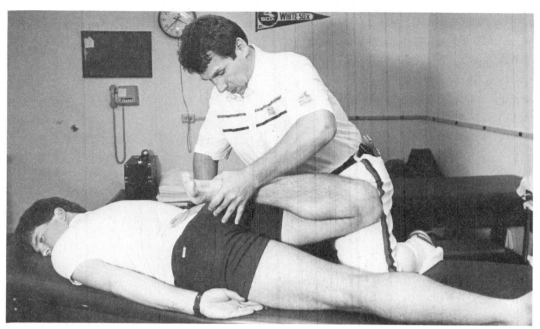

Assisted right quadriceps stretch, exercise position. On location: Payne Park, March 1987. (Tom DiPace) Richard Dotson is an extremely flexible athlete and thus can be stretched so fully. Trainers and players must exercise caution doing this stretch because most players are not this flexible. They can be injured if not aware of the difficulty of this stretch.

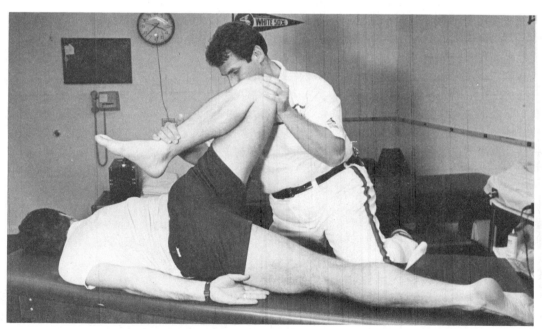

Assisted right quadriceps stretch, final position. Herman Schneider and Richard Dotson. On location: Payne Park, March 1987. (Tom DiPace)

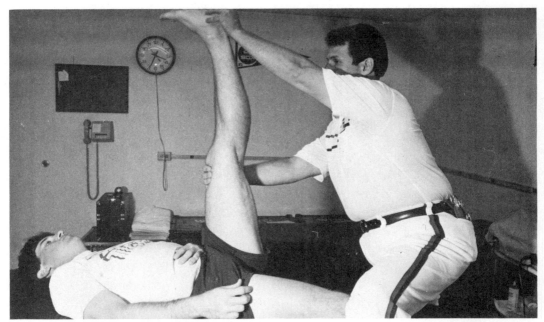

Assisted left high-hamstring stretch. Herman Schneider and Richard Dotson. On location: Payne Park, March 1987. (Tom DiPace) The high-hamstring stretch is pictured last because it is optional.

I can also perform an optimal high hamstring stretch with the player prone. Richard's leg is perpendicular to the table, and I hold his foot at a right angle to his leg. I bring the leg back as far as it can go without discomfort, rotating the foot as much as possible.

In the manually assisted stretches it is very important that the trainer have a good rapport with the player. Some of the muscles, especially the hip abductors and adductors, are not easy to identify, but once you have a feel for a particular player's idiosyncrasies, you will be able to provide the maximum benefits of your skills.

You must stabilize the muscle to be stretched with either your leg or your hand and ease the player slowly but surely through the exercise. Once you have done about 10 minutes of the assisted stretches, he then goes out to the field or to a quiet corner of the clubhouse to complete a few more minutes of the stretches on his own. A limber, flexible player like Harold Baines does these every day, rain or shine. Both he and Richard Dotson would feel that something was missing if they did not do them. These are good habits for players to develop and practice.

To conclude, manually assisted stretches are very important to a professional player's fitness. These athletes are so strong that the value of the exercises might be lost if there was not an experienced trainer to isolate the muscle groups and to apply resistance in exactly the right place during the exercise. The more the player exercises and stretches, the better educated his muscles will become, and in sports as in life, knowledge is power.

Larry Starr rejoins me now to conclude our flexibility discussion with an extremely important subject, the cool-down.

No discussion of warm-ups and stretching can be complete without a discussion of cool-downs. As important as it is to elevate your body temperature before you exercise, it is equally vital to good health and conditioning to bring down your temperature to normal at the conclusion of exercise.

There are many ways to cool-down. If you have ever been to a spring training game, you will notice that after the last out an entire team will run around the bases several times. In the minor leagues, where crowds are not often large and empty out quickly, many organizations have a group stretch and then a group cool-down, which may consist of stretching movements done slowly or the kind of jogging noted before. Another possible cool-down is simply to go in slow motion through the acts of swinging a bat or tossing a baseball.

In the big leagues, it is hard to organize cool-downs. The crowds are larger and the demands of the media for postgame interviews are intense. But while it is harder, it is not impossible. Many players go into a weight room or a corner of the trainer's room—which is off-limits to the media—and cool down by gentle stretching. One of the simplest methods is to lie down at a right angle to a wall and allow your legs to hang against the wall for several minutes. With normal nose-in/mouth-out breathing, you will experience a refreshing sensation of blood flowing back to the center of your body from the extremities, the reverse pattern from the warm-up activity.

Another common form of big league cool-down is for players to stand for a few minutes in a lukewarm whirlpool. Especially after playing in the fiercely hot temperatures of the artificial surface (which exceeds 140 degrees in the summertime!), the whirlpool water will feel very comfortable, ease the trauma from tissue microtears that may have occurred on the playing surface, and most of all, provide a gradual decrease in body temperature. As in almost everything concerning good conditioning, gradual pacing is vital. You do not want your body temperature to decrease drastically after a hard game or a vigorous session of exercising. Therefore, *never* jump into a cold shower after a workout. Practice regular and intelligent cool-downs.

CHAPTER FOUR

Strength Training For Baseball

By Barry Weinberg,
Head Trainer, Oakland Athletics,
with Dave McKay,
Strength and Conditioning Coach, Oakland Athletics

The emergence of strength training has been one of the most revolutionary developments in the conditioning of baseball players over the past few years. Baseball wisdom used to scorn weight training as work for bodybuilders. The old myth claimed that if you developed too many muscles, you would become "muscle-bound" and unable to perform the quick and supple movements necessary to swing a bat and throw a baseball.

Fortunately, today's baseball is growing to appreciate the importance of muscle toning and conditioning all year round. Wise use of conditioning equipment and free weights will make for a healthier and more durable player. Of course, we don't want players to develop bodybuilders' muscles, but we do want them to understand how important well-conditioned muscles are to successful performance. There are 620 muscles in the human body, and they are vital to the movement of the 206 bones in the body.[1] It stands to reason that understanding these muscles and using them intelligently can only help a player.

A stronger muscle will be less likely to get injured. A stronger muscle will have a better blood flow and a stronger supporting cast so that, in the event of injury, healing will be quicker and less playing time will be lost.

Strength training will not make a .300 hitter out of a .200 hitter or turn a mediocre pitcher into a 20-game winner. Charlie Moss recalls dissuading Red Sox slugger Jim Rice early in his career from pumping a lot of iron in the off-season, in an attempt to pass the barrier of 60 home runs. There is no one-to-one relationship between strength work and field performance.

[1] *From:* Michael Bisacre, et al., eds. *The Illustrated History of Human Development* (New York: Exeter Books, 1984), p. 37.

But there are many intangible benefits to strength training, not least that you will *feel* better. You will have a better command of your muscular system if you are properly conditioned, and a stronger and healthier player will have a chance to improve on his numbers. San Diego Padres trainer Dick Dent observes, "Greater strength may turn 20 ground ball outs into 15 hits that make it out of the infield." We add that a stronger pitcher may last longer on the mound, his improved conditioning enabling him to keep his "good stuff" longer. A better-conditioned fielder may gain a little extra range and more velocity on his throws, thus preventing more hits.

Strength training has become an essential part of today's baseball because of one salient truth: *You simply do not prepare yourself for baseball by taking a few batting practice swings or a few grounders and fly balls.* You must be more active to prepare yourself for the grind of a baseball season.

In this chapter, I am joined by Dave McKay, a former major league infielder and the current strength and conditioning coach of the Oakland Athletics, and Carney Lansford, the Athletics' standout third baseman. We are going to illustrate the kind of weight program practiced by many of today's major leaguers. About a third of the Athletics' 24-man roster participated in this particular program during the winter of 1986/87. Many of our younger players in the minor leagues did likewise. This is a significant number, because pitchers account for almost half of the players in any baseball organization and pitchers will not perform the heaviest part of this program because of the delicate nature of their meal ticket, the shoulder muscles. But even pitchers are increasingly seeing the advantage of work with conditioning machines and free weights.

The principles of strength training are simple. Muscles make up 42 percent of the body weight in the average human male (36 percent in the average human female, thus accounting for the comparatively weaker strength achievements of women).[2] There are three kinds of muscles in the human body: the skeletal, or striated, muscle, around the bones of the body; the smooth muscles around the body's internal organs; and cardiac, or heart, muscle. Weight training seeks to maximize the condition and performance of the smooth and striated muscles of the body.

Muscles derive their strength from contraction. The cylindrical fibers that contract within the muscle can shorten it by up to 30 to 40 percent. A muscle gets stronger only when a load is applied to it, and so we use both conditioning machines and free weights to contract the muscle. But before the muscle is contracted, it must be stretched. One of the basic principles of strength training is the following: *The more you lift, the more you must stretch.* You must always be conscious of stretching the muscle before you can successfully strengthen it through contraction.

As we learned in the previous chapter, before you stretch, you must be warmed up in order for the blood to flow to the muscles you are strengthening. You can choose any of the warm-ups described by Larry Starr in the last chapter. When properly warmed up, you can turn to the strengthening of two major complementary muscle groups in the core of your body, the abdominals and the spinal erectors. These two groups, one in the front and one in the back of the body, keep you upright, like opposing guy wires supporting a tent pole.

These muscle groups are vitally important to an athlete because all sports activities originate from the middle of your body. Without a strong central foundation, you weaken

[2]*From:* Michael Bisacre, et al., p. 37.

and make inefficient every other muscle group in the body. Think of all the movements necessary in baseball. Swinging the bat requires good hip rotation. Throwing a ball requires strong and firm back and leg muscles. Running with abandon, arms pumping and legs flying, requires coordination of the body's center and limbs.

The following abdominal exercises work the stomach muscles—upper and lower abdominals—and the spinal erectors in the back. You cannot strengthen one group and ignore the other. *One of the greatest causes of injury in sports is muscle imbalance.* You must, therefore, be diligent about working all your muscle groups equally from all possible angles—anterior, posterior, and oblique. You want a balance of strength around your joints, and you achieve it by working all your muscle fibers.

Another strength-training principle: *Always work the larger muscle group before the smaller group.* In the following exercises, the larger lower abdominal groups will be worked before the smaller upper abdominals. As in stretching, throwing, or any activity associated with baseball, strength training follows this basic principle: *Always use proper form and technique.* It is better to perform correctly fewer repetitions of an exercise than to fulfill a program's quota inaccurately. There are no strength gains from improper form, only an illusion of progress.

The following abdominal exercises are truly amazing in their effectiveness in a short period of time. Baseball players crave immediate results with minimum expenditures of time. Many times, especially in rehabilitation, impatience is very dangerous, but if you are healthy and eager to strengthen yourself, these abdominal exercises, used as a prelude to a strength training session, can produce an intense and positive sensation very quickly. They take barely more than two minutes, and provide a good burning of the muscles and a positive strengthening effect.

The sequence below is part of a program of strengthening exercises that has 10 levels of difficulty. The program pictured is one step above beginners' level. Baseball players do not need to get involved beyond this stage, although with proper understanding and supervision, they can try more advanced workouts as long as they do not forget to continue honing and polishing their basic baseball skills.

1. Six-Inch Lying Leg Raises. Start with your hands under your buttocks, your legs stretched out 12 inches off the ground. Bring your legs up to 18 inches off the ground and then lower them to the starting position. This is 1 repetition. Perform 25 leg raises without a rest at medium speed, which means 1 rep per second. Pause for 15 seconds and then do 20 reps again at the medium speed of 1 rep per second.

The legs are lifted only in 6-inch increments because at a higher height the leg and back muscles are worked. This is a *stomach* strengthening exercise, and in all strength and stretching work, the isolation of the involved muscle is the key point. That is why proper form and technique is so important. One should be careful not to substitute other muscles in this exercise by rocking back and forth, using momentum instead of the stomach muscles themselves.

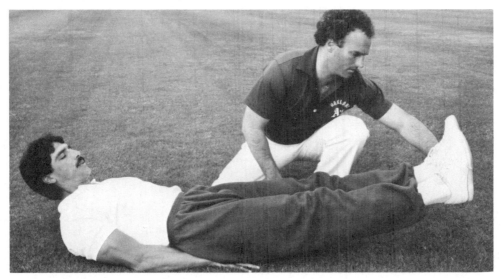

Six-inch lying leg raise, starting position. Barry Weinberg, head trainer of the Oakland Athletics, estimates height of 12 inches off the ground for start of exercise, done by Dave McKay, Oakland Athletics coach and fitness instructor. On location: Phoenix Municipal Stadium, spring training home of the Oakland Athletics, Phoenix, Arizona, March 1987. (V. J. Lovero)

Six-inch lying leg raise, exercise position. Barry Weinberg—height of 18 inches off the ground as Dave keeps his back flat on the ground. On location: Phoenix Municipal Stadium, March 1987. (V. J. Lovero)

2. Abdominal Crunches. Without pausing to rest after the second set of lying leg raises, you start these abdominal crunches. Still lying down, place your feet on the ground with your knees bent; put your hands behind your head.

Clear your shoulders off the ground with your chin and face up—focus on a spot above you. Keep your elbows back and hold for three seconds. You bring your body up only 30 degrees because that is the angle at which the abdominal muscles are getting maximal work. If you rise farther, your lower back and hip flexors start doing the work. The object of this exercise is to work the stomach to strengthen the back and not vice versa. Do 25 repetitions at slow speed, 1 rep every two seconds.

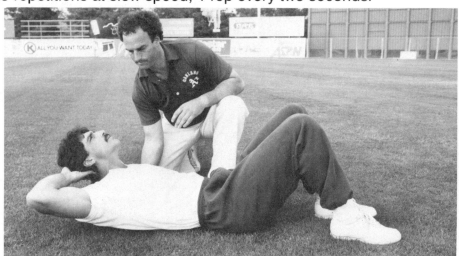

Abdominal crunch exercise, starting position. Barry Weinberg observes that Dave McKay's form is correct: knees bent, chin and face up. On location: Phoenix Municipal Stadium, March 1987. (V. J. Lovero)

3. Quarter Sit-Ups. Without pausing from the crunches, go into this exercise, which works a new muscle group, the upper abdominals. Cross your legs at the ankles, and spread your knees at about shoulder width. The legs should form a 90-degree angle at the crotch. With your hands behind your head, tuck your chin into your chest and quickly raise your shoulders and upper back. Do the quarter sit-ups 10 times at fast speed, 2 repetitions a second. You will feel an intense burning in the chest cavity.

Quarter sit-up, exercise and hold position. Barry Weinberg oversees Dave McKay's form, which is correct: hips and knees at a 90-degree angle, legs crossed at the ankle, and head up at about 30 degrees. On location: Phoenix Municipal Stadium, March 1987. (V. J. Lovero)

It is now time to enhance the strength effect by going immediately to a series of exercises with free weights and circuit training equipment. Move without pause from exercise to exercise, a process called "supersetting," which weight lifters know all about. The operating principle is: *Strength is gained through fatigue.* Be sure to follow the sequence.

Illustrating these exercises are Carney Lansford, a recent convert to strength training, and Dave McKay, who has spent years studying and trying different programs to find the right mix for the baseball player. The barbell in the accompanying pictures happens to weigh 135 pounds, a load Carney was comfortable with in the early stages of spring training 1987 when these photographs were taken. As in all the exercises in this book, the object is to attain proper form and technique. The amount of weight that you use is incidental to the purpose of strengthening yourself properly. In fact, we feel that youngsters (starting after puberty) can profit from these exercises by going through the proper motions with minimal weight or none at all.

1. Supine Bench Press with Olympic Bar. The bench press increases the strength of the chest, shoulders, and triceps. Lying on your back, take a shoulder-width grip on the barbell. When you remove the barbell from the bench, your arms should be straight and the barbell supported above your chest. Making sure that your elbows travel out to your sides, slowly bend your arms and lower the barbell until it touches your sternum. Keeping your lower back flush against the bench, push the weight straight up toward the ceiling and repeat. Do three sets of 10 repetitions with 30 seconds in between.

While the purpose of most strengthening exercises is general improvement in muscular training and not enhancement of sport-specific activities, the explosive, tight movement needed to do this exercise is reminiscent of the kind of sudden movement needed in throwing a baseball or swinging a bat.

Supine bench press with Olympic bar, starting position. Carney Lansford, Oakland Athletics infielder, and Dave McKay. On location: Scottsdale Community College, Scottsdale, Arizona, March 1987. (V. J. Lovero)

Supine bench press with Olympic bar, exercise position. Carney Lansford and Dave McKay. On location: Scottsdale Community College, March 1987. (V. J. Lovero) Carney's left arm could be straighter and parallel to his right arm, but his back form is excellent, flush against the bench. On location: Scottsdale Community College, March 1987. (V. J. Lovero)

2. Close-Grip Lat Pull-Downs. Lat pull-downs work the large muscle group in the upper back called the lats (from latissimus dorsi). Holding the "double D" grips, slowly bend your arms and pull the handle down to the sternum, keeping the chest out and the head looking up.

They are called "double D" grips because the two grips are shaped like capital letter *D*s. Each hand holds on to the straight line of one of the *D*s, which are welded together at their rounded edges.

Remember that your chest reaches out to meet the grip and that the movement in both these exercises is from sternum to chin and not chest to forehead.

The goal is three sets of 10 repetitions with a 30-second pause between each set. Three perfect sets of 10 will not be long in coming if you go about this exercise properly, but a practical goal at first is to aim for two perfect sets of 10 and then a third set of perhaps 8 or 9 good repetitions. *Remember that working muscles properly through the point of fatigue is the way muscles get stronger.* Feel satisfied if you maintain good technique while achieving only 8 reps on your last set.

By supersetting these first two exercises, the supine bench press and the close grip lat pull-downs, you are actually working two prime muscle groups in one routine. The back will be getting warmed up with the bench press, making it possible to go from one to the other with no rest or warm-up. This makes for a speedier and safer way of lifting.

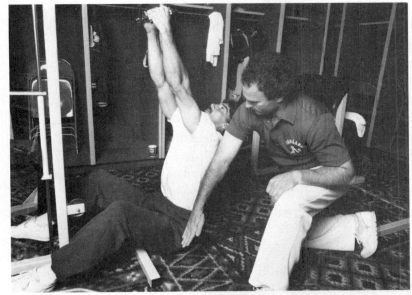

Lat pull-down, starting position. Barry Weinberg establishes the oblique angle for the exercise as Dave McKay reaches up to hold the "double D" handles. On location: Phoenix Municipal Stadium, March 1987. (V. J. Lovero)

Lat pull-down, exercise position. Barry Weinberg holds the proper angle of movement as Dave McKay pushes down to his sternum. On location: Phoenix Municipal Stadium, March 1987. (V. J. Lovero)

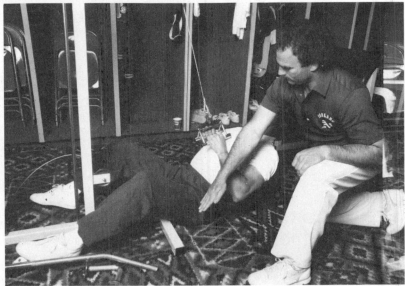

3. Spinal Erector Hyperextensions. Hyperextensions work primarily the erector spinae muscles running up each side of your spine. Secondary muscles being worked are the hamstrings and buttocks. Standing in the middle of a hyperextension bench (Roman chair), place your pelvis on the large padded surface in front of you. The upper part of your pelvis is at the front edge of the pad. Lean forward so that your torso is hanging downward. At this point the backs of your calves will rest under the rear pads. Placing your hands behind your head with elbows up, slowly lift your body upward. Do not raise your torso above a position parallel to the floor. Return to the starting position and repeat 10 or 12 times. Pause for 15 seconds, and then try for a second set if you can do it with the proper form and technique. Again, it is better to do fewer exercises properly than perform incorrectly the required number of exercises. (Advanced weight trainers can try a third set of hyperextensions, working the oblique angles by doing a slight twisting at the peak of the lift.)

N.B. Use caution if back pain exists in any form.

If you do not have access to a gym or fitness center, spinal erector hyperextensions can be done on the edge of a pliable surface such as a bed, a padded table, or the arm of a sofa.

Spinal-erector hyperextension on Roman chair. Barry Weinberg is in proper position with head and upper torso hanging down, elbows out, and calves underneath pads. Dave McKay supervises. On location: Phoenix Municipal Stadium, March 1987. (V. J. Lovero)

Spinal-erector hyperextension, exercise position. Barry Weinberg brings head up with hands behind head and elbows out. Dave McKay supervises. On location: Phoenix Municipal Stadium, March 1987. (V. J. Lovero)

4. Shoulder Exercise with Two Dumbbells (aka "Twenty-ones"). We now move our strength training program to the area of the shoulder. The dumbbells used are small in weight, ranging from 5 to 8 pounds up to a maximum of 25 pounds. Pitchers will rarely use weights above 10 pounds, but they too can profit from the strengthening this exercise gives to the many muscles in the shoulder, especially the four key muscles of the rotator cuff: the supraspinatus, infraspinatus, teres minor, and subscapularis.

"Twenty-ones," lateral shoulder (middle deltoid) raise, starting position. Dave McKay with weights held thumb down, arms slightly bent. Barry Weinberg points to part of shoulder being exercised. On location: Phoenix Municipal Stadium, March 1987. (V. J. Lovero)

"Twenty-ones," lateral shoulder raise, peak position. Dave McKay lifts weights up to near ear level. Barry Weinberg makes sure Dave keeps arms straight. On location: Phoenix Municipal Stadium, March 1987. (V. J. Lovero)

"Twenty-ones," lateral shoulder raise, "tipping glass" position. Dave McKay demonstrates the motion of tipping a glass of water on the downward movement of this exercise. Barry Weinberg illustrates the angle. On location: Phoenix Municipal Stadium, March 1987. (V. J. Lovero)

The exercise is known as "Twenty-ones" because it is divided into three sequences of seven repetitions apiece, working the middle, front, and rear deltoid muscles of the shoulder.

Lateral Shoulder Raise. This is the first of the sevens, and it works the middle deltoid. With a dumbbell in each hand, stand erect with arms at your sides, thumbs pointed downward. Your arms should be slightly bent. Slowly raise your arms out to the side until they are at ear level. Pause at the top and then lower back to starting position.

This exercise has been dubbed "the tipping glass exercise" because the movement of the weight with the thumb downward is like the action of a glass of water (or beer) being poured.

"Twenty-ones," front shoulder (anterior deltoid) raise, starting position. Dave McKay holds weights in front of body, placing them parallel to each other and slightly inside the legs. Barry Weinberg supervises. On location: Phoenix Municipal Stadium, March 1987. (V. J. Lovero)

"Twenty-ones," front shoulder raise, peak position. Dave McKay lifts weights outward until they are near ear level. Barry Weinberg supervises. On location: Phoenix Municipal Stadium, March 1987. (V. J. Lovero)

"Twenty-ones," front shoulder raise, tipping glass position as in lateral raise. Dave McKay and Barry Weinberg. On location: Phoenix Municipal Stadium, March 1987. (V. J. Lovero)

Front Shoulder Raise. This is the second set of seven repetitions, an exercise that works the anterior deltoid. Begin with arms slightly bent and resting in front of your body. Slowly raise your arms to the front until the dumbbells are at eye level. Pause at the top and then lower back to starting position.

"Twenty-ones," rear shoulder (posterior deltoid) raise, starting position. Dave McKay establishes straight-up starting position as in front shoulder raise. Barry Weinberg supervises. On location: Phoenix Municipal Stadium, March 1987. (V. J. Lovero)

"Twenty-ones," rear shoulder raise, bent-over position, arms hanging down. Dave McKay, with Barry Weinberg supervising. On location: Phoenix Municipal Stadium, March 1987. (V. J. Lovero)

"Twenty-ones," rear shoulder raise, peak position. Dave McKay brings weights up to about ear level. Barry Weinberg supervises. On location: Phoenix Municipal Stadium, March 1987. (V. J. Lovero) There is no tipping glass position for the posterior shoulder raise.

Rear Shoulder Raise. This last set works the rear deltoid. Move from a straight standing position to the bent-over starting position. Slowly raise your arms out to the side and up toward the ceiling, keeping the dumbbells forward, in line with your ears. Note that the dumbbells are brought out in front of Dave McKay's ears so that he doesn't work his back muscles. Pause at the top and return to starting position.

The goal is two full sets of Twenty-ones, with 10 seconds between each set of seven and 30 seconds between each whole series. The proper weight for you will be determined by trial and error. If you completed the second series easily, the weight was probably too light, but if you struggled through the last sequence, you probably need to ease off to a lighter weight.

5. Biceps Curls and Triceps Push-Downs (Supersetted). From the Twenty-ones shoulder exercise, we move without pause to a supersetted biceps/triceps exercise. The biceps curl is done on a preacher curl bench with your arms extended straight in front and your triceps resting on a mat. Slowly lift the bar up toward your chin, keeping your arms flexed. Lower the bar all the way down to the point where the arms are fully extended. Repeat eight times in one set.

Biceps curl on a preacher-curl bench, starting position. Dave McKay seated with arms extended straight forward. Barry Weinberg notes that Dave's head is facing straight down. On location: Phoenix Municipal Stadium, March 1987. (V. J. Lovero)

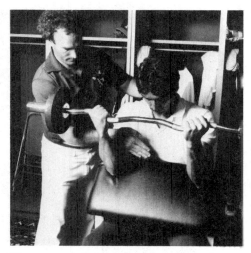

Biceps curl, flexed position. Dave McKay brings bar toward his chin. Barry Weinberg makes sure Dave's head stays down. On location: Phoenix Municipal Stadium, March 1987. (V. J. Lovero)

Biceps curl, return to starting position. Dave McKay brings the bar all the way down to the front of the bench. Barry Weinberg supervises. On location: Phoenix Municipal Stadium, March 1987. (V. J. Lovero)

You then go immediately to the triceps push-down. We use a special triceps bar to reduce the stress on the triceps tendons and to better isolate the triceps muscle. Keeping your upper arms and elbows at your sides, slowly extend your arms to push the triceps bar from the sternum down below your waist. Return to the starting position and repeat eight times. Remember to keep your upper ams and elbows at your side throughout the entire movement.

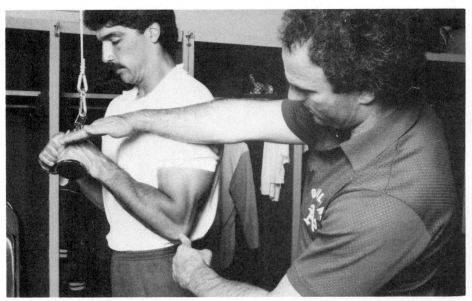

Triceps push-down, starting position. Barry Weinberg points out the forearm movement that Dave McKay will do in this exercise. On location: Phoenix Municipal Stadium, March 1987. (V. J. Lovero)

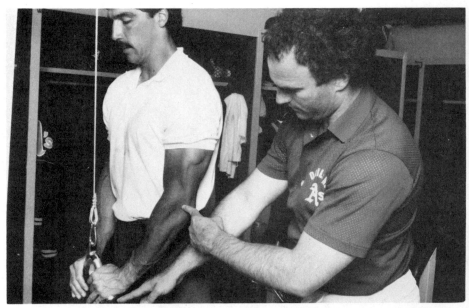

Triceps push-down, finishing position. Barry Weinberg points to forearm movement as Dave McKay brings triceps bar from sternum to below the waist. On location: Phoenix Municipal Stadium, March 1987. (V. J. Lovero)

Remember: When supersetting these two exercises, you go immediately from the biceps to the triceps for one set, eight repetitions on each movement. Rest 30 seconds and repeat the routine for three sets of 8 to 10 reps for both exercises.

Don't lean back when doing the biceps curls, because you want to work the biceps only and not the back muscles. Work smoothly with no rest, up to the forehead and back; 8 reps, or 10 reps if you can handle them with proper form and technique. Remember that the intensity of the effort maximizes biceps tension and thereby strengthens it.

5. Forearm Exercise with Barbell. This last exercise is a quick one, but it will burn your arms out thoroughly. It is done last because you could not complete the other exercises with your arms as tired as they will be once you complete this one.

Stand with your hands at thigh width and grasp the bar firmly, lifting the weight with as much wrist flexion and extension as possible.

The goal of this exercise is a sequence of 40, then 30, and then 25 repetitions with a 30-second rest in between each set.

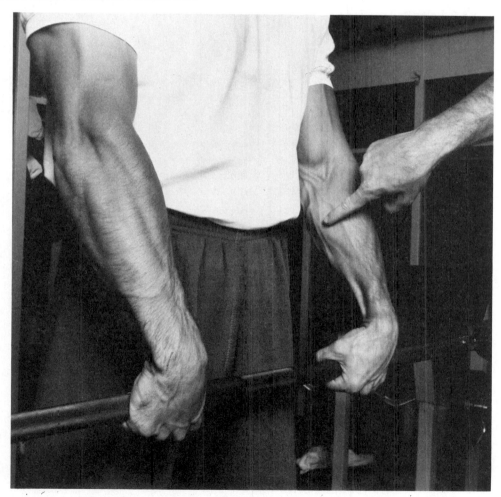

Forearm exercise with barbell, starting position. Barry Weinberg notes burning area in forearm where Dave McKay will feel this exercise. On location: Phoenix Municipal Stadium, March 1987. (V. J. Lovero)

There it is, the strength-training program of the Oakland Athletics devised by strength and conditioning coach Dave McKay, based on his wide experience and interest in developing the optimum program for the busy and impatient baseball player. During the off-season the program can be performed sucessfully in three 35-minute sessions per week. It is designed for the player who wants to see fast results, but it must be stressed that nothing will be gained if the program is not followed dutifully with proper form and technique.

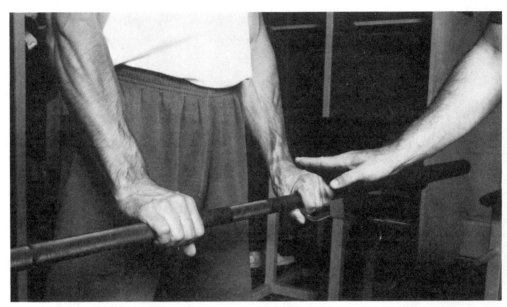

Forearm exercise with barbell, wrist flexion. Barry Weinberg and, with barbell, Dave McKay. On location: Phoenix Municipal Stadium, March 1987. (V. J. Lovero)

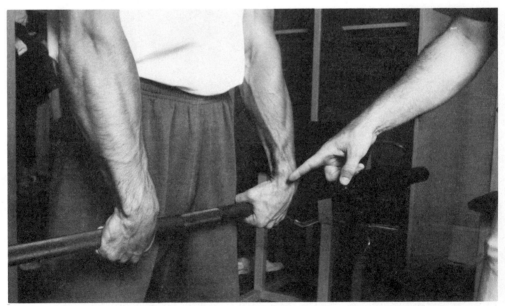

Forearm exercise with barbell, wrist extension. Barry Weinberg and, with barbell, Dave McKay. On location: Phoenix Municipal Stadium, March 1987. (V. J. Lovero)

During the season, everyday players may cut down on the extent of their weight work, but the change must be gradual. You are asking for trouble if you suddenly cease working out with heavy weights. It is a truism of conditioning that you can lose good shape in a matter of days, thereby wasting the good work of months and weeks. Specifically, the baseball player must be wary of losing the muscular balance and good muscle tone that he has obtained by a solid weight-training program. Such imbalance is the surest road to injury.

We have found that working three times a week with this program will work during the season if only a slight modification is made. Instead of working the whole gamut on a Monday, Wednesday, and Friday, arm work is done alone on Wednesday, let us say, and then the full program on Monday and Friday.

As we all know, the travel and arduous schedules of a major league season make regularity of exercise difficult. But it is not impossible to arrange a gym visit on the road, and some visiting clubhouses have strength-training equipment to share. So our final word to you on strength-training is simple: Once you are deemed physically fit, go for it!

CHAPTER FIVE

Nutrition For Baseball Players

By Gene Monahan,
Head Trainer, New York Yankees

Many myths have been broken in recent years about the best diet for athletes. There used to be a standard pregame meal of steak and potatoes, but we've learned from scientific studies that too much red meat raises the cholesterol level and cannot be easily digested before game time. We know now the virtues of carbohydrate loading before games. Carbohydrates increase the glycogen level in the bloodstream, an important consideration because glycogen is the storehouse of reserve energy that athletes draw upon during their intense activities.

Then there was the myth of the candy bar for "quick energy." There is now considerable scientific evidence that the candy bar and other artificially sugared confections and sodas actually impair athletic performance. These unnatural and simple sugars enter the bloodstream and decrease the blood sugar level. They also force blood to the stomach, thereby taking it away from the muscles and tendons that are truly vital to athletic activity.

Of course, myths linger on, and an occasional lapsing into junk foods will not automatically mark you for the bush leagues. However, I fervently believe that if you follow the nutritional program presented in this chapter, you will definitely help your chances as a baseball player. You will become better conditioned and more durable. You will feel healthier and will enjoy a higher quality of life. You will enhance by a significant percentage your chance of making the major leagues. We all know how long the odds are against anyone making the elect circle of 624 major leaguers. But why not give yourself an extra opportunity by improving your nutrition? A professional athlete's body has been compared to an expensive automobile. Doesn't it make sense to use the wisest and best available fuel?

Ballplayers, incessant travelers who spend half their season on the road, have a saying, "Dial eight," when someone hits a home run. Eight is the number in hotels to connect for long distance. For good diet, I suggest a series of numbers for aspiring athletes: 44432. This is a code to remind you to eat every day the prescribed servings of the five basic food groups: fruits, vegetables, cereals and grains, proteins (through fish, poultry, nuts, and lean red meats), and milk and dairy products. Specifically, fruits, vegetables, and cereals and grains should be taken four servings a day (444), protein three servings a day (3), and milk and dairy products twice (2).

I cannot say too much about the importance of fruits and vegetables. I have included them as two separate groups because they aid the body in so many ways. They may not be high in caloric content, but they contain many basic vitamins and minerals unavailable in other foods. Fruits and vegetables are also rich in natural sugars, which the body converts into glucose, the blood sugar that provides vital energy to both the muscles and the brain. Some glucose also is converted into glycogen, the reserve energy ingredient that, as we noted, is so important to the athlete's extra-energy burst.

Before World War II, Americans used to eat fruits and vegetables in considerable portions, not relying heavily on well-advertised artificial confections and candies. Returning to a diet heavily loaded with fruits and vegetables is excellent nutritional advice, especially for athletes. The four daily servings can be taken in a variety of ways: a half-banana in the morning, a few wedges of orange at lunch or dinner, celery and carrot sticks at major meals or snacks, and a few slices of cucumber in similar fashion. Fruits and vegetables are tasty, and since variety is the spice of life, many different kinds should be encouraged.

Now we turn to the four servings of cereal and grain daily. These foods provide essential fibers, vitamins, and minerals for the diet, and they too can be enjoyed in a variety of ways. For instance, have a bowl of cereal in the morning with two pieces of toast, and then take your fourth serving as a muffin at dinner. Or you can space four pieces of bread throughout the day. Just remember to keep unnecessary additives like jams and excess butter to a minimum. And if you have a weakness for oily substances, stick to the polyunsaturated margarines.

Let us turn to the "3" in our dietary code number, 44432. Protein remains an important part of an athlete's diet, even if not to the degree that conventional wisdom used to stress. Protein is essential to building body tissue. Protein breaks down to amino acids, the building blocks of body tissues, organs, and subsequent systems—for example, the digestive, pulmonary, and gastrointestinal systems. So your daily protein servings should include lean red meats, poultry, fish, nuts—and perhaps an occasional bacon slice in the morning.

Finally, let us explain the two servings (at least) of milk and dairy products daily. "You never outgrow your need for milk" goes the old advertising slogan, and it is true. (Youngsters who are still growing can stand to have three daily milk and dairy servings because the calcium and phosphorus in milk aids the development of the cellular growth plates in youngsters under 16.) I have found that ballplayers like the taste of 2-percent low-fat milk, but if 1-percent or skim milk is to one's taste, all the better because the less lactose (the excess fat in milk) you ingest, the better your nutrition will be.

Now that you have the special dietary code number—44432—let me illustrate how it applies to the athlete's life from spring training through the season and, if all goes well, into the postseason. There are, of course, numerous perils lying in the path to good athletic nutrition: long periods of travel, irregular hours of work, unfamiliar sleeping conditions in foreign places, and the inevitable psychological stress in a ballplayer's life. But with proper preparation and continued education of his players, a good trainer can overcome these obstacles. I am with our players daily for at least two-thirds of the year; so I get to know them well, and it is up to me to set the tone for proper nutrition. I must tell them and tell them again what is efficient and what is counterproductive for their needs.

I set the tone in spring training when all the players are gathered in one site and I can plan a special lunch for them every day. But even as the season gets hectic, players can be helped to eat wisely if they know the reasons why. Let us look at the three basic meals of the day.

BREAKFAST

Breakfast is a meal that an athlete cannot and should not want to avoid. Everyone burns calories even while sleeping; so you want to raise your caloric level at the start of the day for a morning's first workout. During the season, after a night game on the road, players should have breakfast by 10:00 A.M.

The kind of breakfast can vary widely according to taste. Whole-grain pancakes three times a week are an excellent breakfast food with high carbohydrate content. (A low-fat syrup can add to its enjoyment.) Fruit on the side can start you on your way to the four daily servings of fruit. When in doubt about any part of your daily diet, always consult the recommended dietary allowances (RDAs) published by the federal Food and Drug Administration (FDA).

You can have any kind of eggs about twice a week for breakfast. But beware the greasy oils used in preparing many kinds of eggs. Some fat is necessary in any diet, even for the athlete, because fats break down into fatty acids that are essential high-energy nutrients. But too much fat is obviously going to detract from the kind of sound muscular performance a ballplayer desires.

It is fine to end your breakfast with coffee, tea, or a low-fat milk. But it is important not to start working out for at least an hour after your meal. Your body needs the time to digest the morning's foods. Rushing into activity too soon may lead to cramping and other digestive disorders.

Once you begin your workout, however, you should not be hungry again until lunch. A sound breakfast should insure that you feel no hunger pangs and keep you from eating between meals, one of the greatest hazards to any sound diet. Eating between meals has ruined many a nonathlete's diet, and it is even more damaging to a player. You obviously don't want unnecessary foods causing digestive procedures to overwork while you are engaging in the stress of athletic activity.

Once your morning workout is over, it is important not to rush immediately into the lunchroom. You have sweated profusely under the warm sun of spring training. You need time to cool down first. Replenish yourself with fluids, and try a few cool-down stretches. For instance, lie down on the floor and slowly lift your legs to a 90-degree angle to rest against the wall. Remain in this position for about 7 to 10 minutes. You will experience a restorative sensation of your blood returning from all your extremities. Take your cool shower and ingest more fluids and then prepare for lunch.

LUNCH

I prepare a special lunch at our Yankees headquarters in Fort Lauderdale, Florida. As you might imagine, I have copious quantities of fruits and vegetables for the meal and afternoon snacks. On the vegetable tray, I have carrot and celery sticks, radishes, pepper and cucumber slices. For my fruit tray, I have bananas, pears, Washington apples, and seedless grapes (seedless because they are easier to digest than grapes with seeds).

Fluids of every imaginable kind are available: orange and grapefruit juices, diet sodas, athletic drinks like Gatorade, and plenty and plenty of water. Each day I have a different soup for lunch, usually some kind of broth. I stay away from creamed soups because I have found that as many as 25 percent of the players develop a mild digestive problem from creamy soups. Brothy soups are just as nutritious and less caloric.

Dessert consists of sherbet or ice cream, the low-fat variety. Fruit is available at all the exit doors leading out of our dining room. I encourage our players to take fruit for their midafternoon snack if they want it. But the same warning applies after lunch as after breakfast and after dinner: *Don't eat between meals.* Snacking on fruits and/or vegetable sticks is desirable, but stay away from the junk foods!

During the regular season, I cannot monitor the midday meal as closely as I do in spring training. But I can strongly recommend foods to players, and restaurants on the road that serve food properly and nutritiously. One important thing to remember is to eat your big meal before 2:00 P.M. if there is a night game ahead. Basically, you want to play on an empty stomach.

DINNER

During spring training, I urge players to eat their dinner between 5:00 and 7:00 P.M. You don't want to eat too late because it can affect your sleeping if the meal is close to bedtime. If you sleep uneasily, you're not ready for the next day's activity and you may fall prone to injury, or at least decreased performance. As the saying goes, "One thing leads to another"; so the wise practice is to develop sound habits and stick to them.

For dinner I recommend entrees of broiled chicken and broiled fish; lean red meat a couple of times a week is also acceptable. Pasta to aid in glycogen buildup is another favorite choice. Three times a week is recommended for pasta, even if it is only a side dish.

Once the season begins, meals cannot be eaten at regular hours; that is an obvious fact of the baseball life-style. But you can still eat nutritiously and intelligently on the road. I stress those restaurants where the food is fresh. I know that my advice is not always heeded, and once in a while, it won't kill you if you have a fast-food hamburger and a diet soda.

But there are controls on diet that I work on during road trips. Postgame meals in the clubhouse are now common in baseball, and I tell the visiting clubhouse man exactly what I want prepared for the postgame meal. Spaghetti with some kind of protein is a fine postgame meal. The pasta allows enough carbohydrate buildup so that the player does not gorge himself at some diner after the game. I also order plenty of fruit for a postgame snack.

I even occasionally allow for some light ice cream both at home and on the road. The key is having the player filled up enough at the ballpark so he doesn't raid the icebox after midnight at home. I constantly warn my players: "Gorge at midnight and be a dead fish tomorrow."

There is a special problem on the road for trainers to consider. Visiting clubhouse men get tipped by visiting players, and if they are not instructed otherwise, the clubhouse people will prepare saucy, spicy foods and earn nice gratuities from the players. You must give careful instructions or else this kind of food may enter your clubhouse. I have a firm rule that pastries and bulky and greasy foods *never* enter my clubhouse.

The same caution must be taken on commercial flights. Suppose you are flying cross-country at three in the morning after a tough series on the road. The stewardess smilingly wheels out stuffed pork chops and home fries for your weary players. They may drool over such a meal, but if you have a day game coming up, these are the last kinds of foods they should eat. A good trainer will always exercise a veto on the food on commercial flights and at least choose the least damaging of the menu items. On charter flights, the food is no problem because you choose the meals yourself.

CONCLUDING THOUGHTS

Every now and then, there are exceptions to these rules of good nutrition. We all remember players, such as rotund pitchers like Mickey Lolich and Terry Forster, who scoffed at exercises with standard chestnuts as "You don't run the ball across home plate" or "You don't throw with your stomach."

But clearly these are exceptions. Mind you, there is nothing wrong with the comfort and food value provided by a bottle of beer or two after a strenuous workout. But too much alcohol can obviously devastate an athletic career, and even shorten your life expectancy. Remember also that after the initial feeling of pleasure brought on by a bottle of beer, alcohol actually dehydrates you. So the more beer you drink, the more you must rehydrate yourself with water (a point that Dick Martin, head trainer of the Minnesota Twins, will expand upon in the next chapter).

I understand why athletes and people in stressful walks of life turn to excessive alcohol usage and drug abuse. After a quarter-century of experience in professional baseball, I believe that the mental aspect of the game is as crucial as any of the others—strength, flexibility, and God-given skill.

So in spring training 1987 I began a series of twice-weekly evening counseling sessions with players and their families. I believe that it is important to discuss the problems that inevitably gnaw at players and families in baseball. Start with the first major league camp for a prospect. He asks himself, "With 70 others in camp, am I good enough to make a 24-man roster at nearly three-to-one odds? If I do make it, how will my wife and kids adjust to my being away from home so long? How will I adjust to *their* absence?"

These are just a few of the immediate problems that a player faces in spring training. Once summer arrives, the family is reunited, but the player is deep into his season. The family may have a normal summertime desire to take a vacation trip. What happens when the wife and children want to go away during your home stand? Can you deal with the absence and the implied (though unintended) rejection? Experience shows that many players grow irritable in August. Is it the grind of a long season or could it also be family stresses—the kids making too much noise and other factors?

I don't know the answers to these questions, but they are important to raise. Different individuals will have different personalities and moods. But I feel that discussing these issues in the relatively relaxed atmosphere of spring training is a good start.

While on the subject of counseling, let me say a few words about drug abuse. I am active in my small town in New Jersey in a "Just Say No" antidrug group. I have talked to a lot of young people about the danger of both alcohol and drugs. I proudly wore my green button on Opening Day 1987, proclaiming my commitment to the cause of eliminating drug abuse.

Drug abuse is a difficult problem because drugs are so pervasive in our society and so easily obtained. I have seen players who could not survive in society or on the ball field without the use of stimulants. It was so sad to see them withdraw altogether if they did not have that catch of a drug.

It is hard for adults to change, though certainly not impossible. The earlier in life you start encouraging people to affirm life and not drugs, the easier it will be to lead them away from the threat of addiction. The word I stress in talks to kids is "respect": respect for others; respect for your family and friends; and respect for yourself. I tell kids that respect means respect for other people's thoughts and feelings. Respect means that if you do not have something good to say about somebody, say nothing. Respect means that you have a guideline as to what is right and what is wrong and what is neutral. Respect is something that players and families and all citizens should understand and practice.

If you can find it honestly within yourself to respect "you"—your own best friend—you will earn the respect of those who love and care for you.

Now that I've had my say on what might be called "mental nutrition," counseling, and fighting drug abuse, there is an area of nutrition, fluid replacement, which needs more discussion.

CHAPTER SIX

The Importance Of Fluid Replacement

By Dick Martin,
Head Trainer, Minnesota Twins

Baseball, "the summer game," is played mostly at a time of year when heat and humidity are at their peak. Sometimes, in the heat of battle and competitive concentration, the player neglects the importance of constantly rehydrating his body. He does this at his peril because just the slightest imbalance in the body's thermoregulatory system can lead to heat injury: heat cramps, heat exhaustion, and most serious of all, the life-threatening heatstroke. In this chapter, we want to explain the crucial processes of hydration and dehydration in the human body and spell out the best measures to insure adequate fluid replacement and consistant athletic performance. It is commonly accepted that deyhdration contributes to declining athletic performance more than any other nutritional factor.

Dr. Nathan J. Smith informs us in his classic book, *Food for Sport,* that about 60 percent of adult male body weight is comprised of water (the percentage is somewhat less in females). Of that 60 percent, 35 percent is intracellular (within the cells), 25 percent is extracellular (outside the body cells), and 40 percent is in the circulating blood. Water, water, is everywhere within your body's system and every chemical reaction takes place in a watery context. But Dr. Smith cautions, "If the distribution [of water] within and outside body cells is significantly disturbed, energy metabolism will be compromised, whether or not the total amount of body water is normal."[1]

The sweat glands normally function to keep the body at a safe temperature. But in a steamy environment when the temperature and the humidity rise above 90 degrees, the sweating process malfunctions. Instead of evaporating into the air, the sweat stays on the skin and the core body temperature of the athlete rises dangerously high.

We have seen earlier in this book how the body temperature must rise a few degrees above its normal 98.6 degrees before effective exercise can begin. But the

---

[1] *From:* Nathan J. Smith, *Food for Sport* (Palo Alto, California: Bull Publishing Company, 1976), p. 91, paperback edition.

human body's regulatory mechanisms are very delicate. If the core body temperature rises much above 103 degrees during exercise, there are great dangers of heat-related injury. Let us look at the three kinds of heat injury.

THE THREE KINDS OF HEAT INJURY

Heat Cramps   These are indicated by muscular cramping, twitching, and spasms, mostly in the arms, legs, and abdomen. The most common cause of cramps in athletes is a low body level of one or more minerals, particularly potassium and salt.

Heat Exhaustion   This injury is indicated by excessive thirst, dry mouth, weight loss, fatigue, incoordination, mental dullness, elevated body temperature, reduced sweating, headache, dizziness, anorexia, nausea, vomiting, diarrhea, muscle cramps, or a combination of some or all of these symptoms.

Heat exhaustion is really a protective mechanism to prevent heatstroke, a much more serious ailment. Heat exhaustion occurs at the point when competition for blood among your brain cells, working muscles, and skin becomes intolerable because of the heat and humidity factors during exercise. The circulatory system simply collapses, the body gives up trying to maintain an equitable distribution of blood throughout, and the blood pressure drops. The brain lacks for air in these dangerous circumstances.

The human body has a delicate and intricate thermoregulatory system designed to cope with heat production. The key to the effectiveness of this system is the difference between the core temperature in the trunk of the body and the skin temperature. The skin temperature can vary in individuals, but it must always be at least two degrees cooler than the core temperature; otherwise it starts to act like an insulating blanket, keeping the heat in.

Under normal circumstances, sweating maintains the two-degree difference. The sweat evaporates, which cools the skin. Heat from the body core is carried to the skin by the blood; the skin absorbs the heat and passes it into the atmosphere; and the blood cools and travels back to the body core. Exercise physiologist David L. Costill has noted that sweat is sometimes called "a filtrate of plasma" because it possesses many of the same minerals present in the water portion of blood.[2] All is well when the sweat glands are operating normally.

Excess humidity—i.e., dangerous levels of moisture in the air—threatens nature's creation. One hundred percent humidity means that the air cannot hold any more water, and sweat will not evaporate; it just runs off the skin without cooling the body. High percentages of humidity thus greatly affect the reactions of our bodies to heat!

Heatstroke   This most serious of heat-related injuries is indicated by hot and dry skin, irrational behavior, muscle flaccidity, seizures, involuntary limb movements, coma, rapid pulse and breathing. Also, there may be tiring sooner than usual, blurred vision, a pounding in the head, a parched throat, dizziness, and a tingling sensation over the trunk. The most telltale sign is the first noted, hot and dry skin.

When the body suffers heatstroke, the hypothalamus gland—the body's thermostat, so to speak—ceases to function. When this vital gland, located in the brain, stops working, a dangerous chain reaction ensues. The blood vessels in the skin constrict and

---

[2] *From:* David L. Costill, *Inside Running: Basics of Sports Physiology* (Indianapolis: Benchmark Press, 1986), p. 73.

sweat production stops. Heat is insulated inside the skin, and the body's core temperature increases, leading to fever. The fever interferes with blood clotting, which can lead to hemorrhage, convulsion, coma, and death. Health and fitness writer Eric Olsen has graphically described what happens to the body at core temperatures not much above 108 degrees. "The body's protein will begin to coagulate like the proteins in a boiled egg," Olsen writes. "The brain literally begins to cook."[3]

I hope I have not scared you too much with this account of the dangers of heat injury, but if I have gotten your attention, so much the better. For I will now tell you the best way to prevent any extreme heat injuries and to assure yourself of solid performance under practically every circumstance. Let me start, though, by stressing that *you should always be aware of your environment.* If heat and humidity are very high, into the 80s and 90s, and there is very little wind velocity, postpone your exercise until it has noticeably cooled off.

PREVENTION OF HEAT INJURIES

The key to safe and successful performance in hot and humid conditions is maintaining a proper balance between fluid intake and fluid loss through sweating. The body can absorb only one to two pints an hour from the stomach during exercise, so it is recommended that you drink at least a pint of water about 20 minutes before exercise or competition. Cool water is best (50 to 55 degrees) because it is absorbed into your system faster than warmer water.

Once the game or exercise has begun, a water break every 20 minutes, at least, is something that should become second nature to every coach and player. Look in major league dugouts today, and you will notice the big containers of fluid available in addition to the water fountain. Some players may like their water from a fountain, others from a cup, and still others from a squeeze bottle. It does not matter how you take your water as long as you do drink it—before, during, and after a game. *You must drink!*

I also recommend athletes weighing in before and after practice sessions on particularly hot and humid days. Weight loss can be accurately measured, and the athlete will learn whether he has a weight-loss deficit. "Individuals in excellent physical condition can perform adequately," Dr. Nathan J. Smith says, "until body water equal to four to five percent of body weight is lost."[4]

Another important principle of fluid replacement is: *Don't let thirst be your guide!* By some quirk of nature, humans are a rare mammal group that will not replace all the needed fluids that are lost under conditions of extreme exertion (unlike dogs, for instance, who will quickly drink up all the water that they need).[5] Humans may lose up to 5 percent of their body weight before thirst makes them drink. Unfortunately, the devastating effects of dehydration will have probably occurred by then, which is why it is so important to keep a 20-minute maximum interval between drinks.

"Involuntary hypohydration" is another serious condition that can result if you are not constantly rehydrated. Following a period of exercise with its resulting dehydration,

[3] *From:* Eric Olsen, "Cooling Off," *The Runner,* vol. 3, no. 9 (June 1981), p. 57.
[4] *From:* Nathan J. Smith, p. 95.
[5] *From:* Eric Olsen, p. 59.

the average thirst response will not in itself call for complete replacement of body water for a considerable period of time, often up to three days or more. This "involuntary hypohydration" can be cumulative, and as a result, after two or three days of dehydrating workouts, water deprivation can reach serious levels. To repeat, *your need for a prescribed schedule of water intake to maintain body weight is extremely important.*

There is another problem, "insensible water loss," to which ballplayers are particularly susceptible because of their constant travel on airplanes. Insensible water losses are losses we do not detect, such as the constant loss of water through the skin from the normally moist skin to the drier air. It is estimated that after a three-and-a-half-hour flight on a standard commercial jet liner, a player may lose as much as two pounds, more than a full quart of body water. To counteract the efforts of dehydration, Dr. Nathan J. Smith offers this prescription for athletes taking an airplane trip of more that an hour or two: "two or three glasses an hour immediately before, during, and after a flight."[6]

During a strenuous game on a particularly hot and humid day, it is not uncommon for baseball players, especially pitchers and catchers, and the home plate umpire to lose between 7 and 15 pounds. It is very important for an athlete to monitor his weight loss carefully. In his widely read book, *Eat to Win,* Robert Haas says that the ability to do hard work drops 15 percent with a loss of as little as 2 pounds during exercise. Haas adds that a 7-pound water loss can increase the work loss to 30 percent.[7] Any athlete who has a persistent weight deficit of more than 2 to 3 pounds from a workout should be regarded as a high risk. He must consult with a physician before risking further exercise.

How much water should you drink? Most of the studies have been done on distance runners. Their exact work load is much easier to measure than that of baseball players, whose game is one of stops and starts, with dramatic variations from game to game. But there are general fitness principles concerning water intake that apply to all athletes, especially in warm weather environments.

A good guide is to take about 10 ounces of water before the start of exercise and then 10 ounces every 20 minutes thereafter. The average individual can absorb up to 1 ounce a minute. At that rate, you can take about two quarts an hour without difficulty. You need not worry about drinking too much because the body can absorb only one to two pints an hour from the stomach during exercise. You don't have to worry about losing water through urination if you remember not to start drinking until 20 minutes or less before you start exercising. The kidneys shut down during exercise; so you should have no worries on that score if you do not drink too early.

WHY WATER IS THE BEST FLUID REPLACEMENT

Researchers from the University of South Carolina Exercise Physiology Laboratory maintain that plain, cool water always has been, and will continue to be, *the* effective fluid replacement beverage. The exception is during prolonged periods of exercise, such as distance running and marathons. In those situations, rehydration with plain water can result in a drop of blood sugar levels and forced mobilization of tissue energy stores, resulting in earlier fatigue and reduced endurance.

The findings of this South Carolina study support previous studies, which show that certain carbohydrate/electrolyte drinks can contribute to improved athletic performance

---

6 *From:* Nathan J. Smith, p. 124.
7 *From:* Robert Haas, *Eat to Win* (New York: Rawson Associates, 1983), p. 77, paperback edition.

of endurance athletes since these drinks supply energy and may help maintain plasma electrolyte balance. This is especially important for athletes who may dilute their blood sodium level by consuming large amounts of plain water during prolonged exercise. Drinks with minerals and sugars are good for runners after exercise because at that point the body can tolerate the added sugar.[8]

For the baseball player and other nonendurance athletes, most "athletic" drinks contain too many carbohydrates. Their flavor, however, makes them attractive to many athletes; so I suggest that you dilute them with water. So, too, should fruit juices be diluted with water. In a recent study, Janie Metcalf Kelly has noted that the sugar concentration in athletic drinks should be no higher than 2.5 percent.[9] Higher sugar and carbohydrate content will slow the gastric emptying rate and contribute to dehydration. Heavy concentrations of sugar can cause water to pass out of the blood plasma into the stomach, resulting in diarrhea and still further dehydration.

During exercise you want the body water to be absent from the stomach and drawn to those parts of the body that most need water, namely, the muscles. Pure water leaves the stomach and enters the bloodstream much faster than other fluids. During exercise, particularly competitive exercise, digestion virtually ceases—so the energy that the sugar in those drinks is meant to provide is not immediately available to the muscles and the brain. When large amounts of salt and sugar finally do leave the stomach and enter the blood, more water is drawn from the working muscles in order to dilute the high salt concentration in the blood. This deprives the hot, overworked muscle cells of what they need most—more water.

American College of Sports Medicine researchers have determined that the maximum concentration of sugar, salt, and potassium in any sports fluid-replacement beverage should be 5.9 grams of sugar, 55 milligrams of sodium, and 46 milligrams of potassium for every eight ounces of fluid.[10] This is a great deal less than what is to be found in sports drinks. Yet no more than this concentration of nutrients can be absorbed efficiently from your stomach and delivered efficiently to the areas of your body that require them.

As late as the sixties and early seventies, I saw athletes poping salt pills, supposedly to replenish their fluids. Actually, one popular brand of salt pill contains 15½ grains of sodium, more than enough for as much as a three-pound weight loss during exercise. And to think that athletes were carelessly popping as many as three at a time!

The cardiovascular system needs some sodium, of course, for proper functioning. Too much of this mineral however, can disturb the relationship between intracellular and extracellular fluids in the bloodstream, as well as disrupt the osmotic pressures between the various water compartments. When there are too many sodium salts in the extracellular system, the intracellular water is drawn to the extracellular system, seeking to dilute the sodium ions and maintain the normal osmotic conditions.

---

[8]*From:* "Fluid Replacement Facts," a pamphlet published by Quaker Oats Company, manufacturers of Gatorade, Chicago, Illinois, no date, no page numbers.

[9]*From:* Janie Metcalf Kelly, "Fluids for Hot Weather Exercise," *Running and Fitness News,* vol. 5, no. 8, (August 1987), p. 5

[10]*From:* Robert Haas, pp. 78–79.

But conditions are not normal. The withdrawal of intracellular water thickens the blood, making it harder to pump, and the heart's work load is thus increased. As a result of this malfunctioning, sweating decreases, and all the serious conditions of heat injury are in place, from dehydration to life-threatening heatstroke. The entire unfortunate sequence has been created by excessive salt ions that forced intracellular water into the extracellular system. Research has shown conclusively that dehydration as a cause of poor performance is attributable to a decrease in intracellular water. [11]

It should be obvious from this discussion, but I'll say it again: *Stay away from salt tablets!* Too much salt thickens the blood, which can lead to clots, strokes, heart attacks, and kidney failures. High levels of sodium also raise the body temperature, which is the last thing that you need if you are running (or playing baseball) on a hot day and are already dehydrated.

Even if you have suffered a heavy sweat loss, you rarely need a specific salt replacement during athletic activity. The salt from three regular meals a day can usually replace the salt lost in 5 to 10 pounds of exercise-induced sweat. If, however, you regularly lose that many pounds from exercise, a specific salt replacement may be in order, but it should be one containing fluids, whose concentration should not exceed 1.5 grams of sodium chloride per liter of water (or one-third of a teaspoon per quart).[12]

But for the normal, healthy athlete, a balanced diet with food salted to taste, plus a little extra fruit or fruit juice for potassium, ought to provide an athlete with all the minerals and salt lost through sweating. Potassium is an important body mineral, but its losses in sweat are negligible under any but the most extreme conditions. So potassium depletion is not a primary concern. Potassium should be obtained only through diet. Salt substitutes are very low in salt and high in potassium so they can be used as a supplement if necessary.

Some final words about diet are in order. Gene Monahan sang the praises of fruits and vegetables in the preceding chapter, and I echo that tune now because fruits and vegetables contain 90 percent or more of water and thus are very good fluid-replacement foods. Potatoes are good, too, because they contain 75 percent water. On the other hand, high-protein and high-fat foods cause dehydration and should be used sparingly.

Let me remind you of the physiological process going on in your body during exercise. Glycogen is what your muscles burn, and each molecule of glycogen holds on to three molecules of water. This water is released to the muscles when you need it most—during exercise.

Therefore, an active athlete should be aware of the need for hydration and rehydration through liquids and foods containing water.

Fluids with adverse effects to avoid are caffeine-containing beverages such as coffee, tea, certain cola drinks, and cocoa. They increase urine production and deplete the supply of body water.

Alcohol also has a very severe dehydrating effect. The cool beer may taste nice as momentary relief, and as Gene Monahan says, an occasional one will not irreparably harm you. But always think of rehydrating with water after drinking alcohol. Charlie

---

[11] *From:* Nathan J. Smith, p. 97.
[12] *From:* Nathan Smith, p.97.

Strasser, assistant head trainer of the Los Angeles Dodgers, suggests this rule of thumb: "If you insist on drinking a 6-pack of beer, you better prepare to drink a 12-pack of water, too!"

SUMMARY OF FLUID INTAKE GUIDELINES

1. Drink eight cups of water a day.
2. Drink several cups of water just prior to exercise or competition.
3. Drink at least eight ounces between innings. *Don't let thirst be your guide.*
4. Drink copious amounts of water after the game. Again, *don't let thirst be your guide.*
5. Chilled water is best (between 45 and 55 degrees) because it empties out of your stomach quickly.

I have talked at length about excess body temperature and excess salt and the importance of replenishment of water, because highly competitive athletes are most vulnerable to heat disorders in general and heatstroke in particular for several reasons:

1. They are highly motivated competitors and, therefore, more likely to overextend themselves.
2. They are sometimes required to wear heavy protective equipment (like baseball catchers), which adds resistance to heat dissipation.
3. The coach may deny them water during prolonged contests or practice sessions, which lowers their resistance to heat tolerance.

These factors, either singularly or combined, are as pertinent to environmental conditions that are usually considered "comfortable" as they are to hot environments. For example, rectal temperatures equal to or greater than 104 degrees are not uncommon, even in athletes who compete at environmental temperatures as low as 41 to 61 degrees.

I can personally attest to how the competitive spirit can sometimes run counter to common sense. I love running and during my first attempt at completing a marathon, I ran through the first two water stops during the first half of the race. I managed to finish the race, but predictably, I suffered from leg cramps in the latter stage of the race because I had failed to follow the basic rules of fluid replacement.

CLOTHING

Here is some practical advice to baseball players about clothing. The weight of the uniform is a factor in heat accumulation and fluid loss. The uniform can prevent the evaporation of sweat, greatly impairing body cooling. Concomitant with this are a greater loss of body water because of profuse sweating, and a significantly higher heart rate, or circulatory strain, both of which reduce tolerance to heat.

If heat illness occurs, always remove the uniform. Rectal temperature habitually stays high when the uniform is on and delays a return to normal body conditions.

Much needs to be said about certain traditional but dangerous customs in baseball attire. Pitchers who wear long-sleeve wool "sweatshirts" and catchers who wear protective equipment compound the buildup of body heat and inhibit the evaporation process, thereby causing severe fluid losses and high rectal temperatures. They should be encouraged to wear light loose-fitting undergarments beneath the mandatory uniform and equipment, and batterymen especially should drink copiously between every inning.

Baseball uniforms should be modified to meet climatic conditions. Lighter-weight, perforated-mesh uniform tops for high temperature conditions and mesh hats should be adopted for game use. As of this writing, they are only used in practices. Do not wear undershirts and heavy underwear in hot conditions. During cold conditions, warmer uniforms and undergarments should be worn to hold in body heat and prevent hypothermia.

Rubber suits should *never* be worn. It is a common daily sight in baseball to see coaches and players wearing rubber or nylon jackets under their uniform tops in practice in warm weather. They say that they want to "work up a sweat." They may experience signs of heat illness and disregard them. They may enter a game still not recovered from water deficit. Foolhardy behavior such as this hinders athletic performance and predisposes the athlete and coach to heat injury.

My final advice on clothing is that it should be solid enough to block the sun's rays and porous enough to allow evaporation. Porous nylon mesh shirts are the best. White is the best color for all clothing—caps, shirts, and pants—because it reflects the sun and doesn't absorb heat into the body.

I hope this treatment of the hydration, dehydration, and rehydration of the body has been instructive. I fervently wish that you never have to face the situation where there is "water, water everywhere and not a drop to drink." Constant replenishment of fluids, good nutrition, and comfortable clothing are cornerstones for athletic performance. An athlete should adopt the adage: "You are what you eat and drink and wear." With that in mind, we hope that you make the most of your God-given athletic skills.

CHAPTER SEVEN

The Maintenance Of Baseball Fitness: *Massage, Myotherapy, And Arm, Back, And Leg Conditioning*

By
Jeff Cooper, Head Trainer, Philadelphia Phillies
Tommy Craig, Head Trainer, Toronto Blue Jays
John Fierro, Head Trainer, Chicago Cubs
Gene Gieselmann, Head Trainer, St. Louis Cardinals
Rick Griffin, Head Trainer, Seattle Mariners
Dave Labossiere, Head Trainer, Houston Astros
Ron McClain, Head Trainer, Montreal Expos
Barry Weinberg, Head Trainer, Oakland Athletics

You have now learned how the pros practice fitness in key areas of flexibility, strength, nutrition, and hydration. But the game of baseball as played in the professional ranks is a wearing one, and there is rarely any time to back off from the stresses of the never-ending grind of the game on the major league level. The accommodations are first-class, and there is a glamour in having made "The Show," but the body can give out on you if it is not properly maintained throughout the season. In this chapter, a collection of PBATS trainers want to show you some of the techniques we use for maintaining the condition of our thoroughbred athletes.

MASSAGE

We start with a basic deep-friction massage, performed in these pages by Jeff Cooper, head trainer of the Philadelphia Phillies, on his assistant athletic trainer, Mark Andersen.

The shoulder massage is, of course, vital since so much of the game is determined by the pitching of the baseball. It has been well said that baseball is the only sport in which the defense—namely the pitcher—has the ball. Massaging and relaxing all the tissues and muscles in the arm and shoulder becomes a vital maintenance activity we trainers perform, usually before games but sometimes afterward as well.

Let's join Jeff as he works his way through the massage, photographed at the Phillies' spring training complex in Clearwater, Florida.

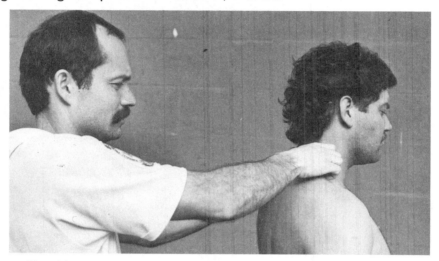

Shoulder massage, upper trapezius. Jeff Cooper, head trainer of the Philadelphia Phillies, works on Mark Andersen, assistant Phillies trainer. On location: Carpenter complex, spring training home of the Philadelphia Phillies, Clearwater, Florida, March 1987. (Tom DiPace)

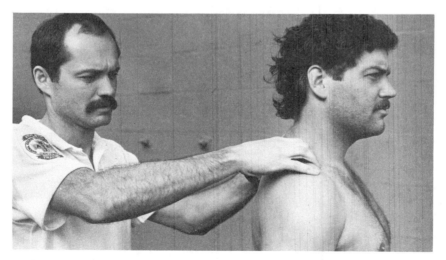

Shoulder massage, supraspinatus. Jeff Cooper and Mark Andersen. On location: Carpenter complex, March 1987. (Tom DiPace)

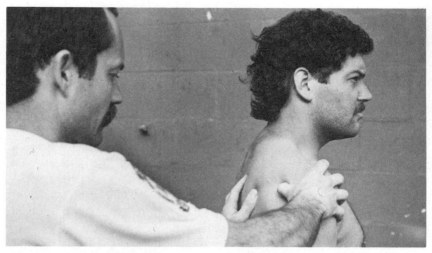

Shoulder massage, from supraspinatus to acromion. Jeff Cooper and Mark Andersen. On location: Carpenter complex, March 1987. (Tom DiPace)

Begin the shoulder massage with the upper trapezius (the large muscle of the upper back), tracing its course down to the spine of the scapula and its insertion at the acromion (the outer extremity of the scapula).

Lying under the upper portion of the trapezius is the supraspinatus, the most important muscle in the rotator cuff. Massage across the fibers of the muscle is an excellent technique in this area.

The supraspinatus is traced along its course until it dips under the acromion.

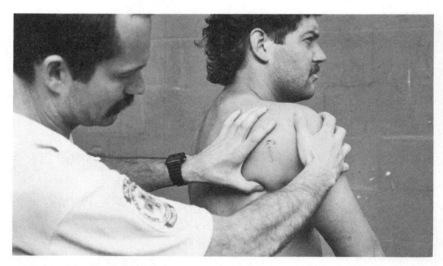

Shoulder massage, left hand at the teres muscles; right hand at anterior shoulder. Jeff Cooper and Mark Andersen. On location: Carpenter complex, March 1987. (Tom DiPace)

The right hand continues around to the anterior (front) portion of the shoulder and locates the following structures: the greater tuberosity, the long head biceps at the bicipital groove, and the lesser tuberosity. (*Tuberosity* is an anatomical term for the uneven projection, or elevation, on a bone—in this case the shoulder—to which muscles and ligaments are attached.) The left hand courses the lateral part of the scapula, picking up the teres major and the teres minor—the latter, one of the four rotator cuff muscles.

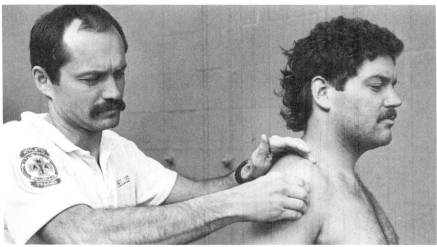

Shoulder massage, left hand on scapula at infraspinatus, right hand still at anterior shoulder. Jeff Cooper and Mark Andersen. On location: Carpenter complex, March 1987. (Tom DiPace)

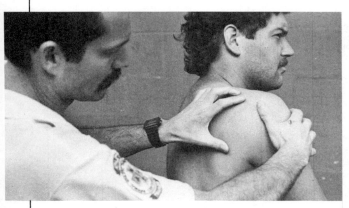

Shoulder massage, infraspinatus into tuberosity. Jeff Cooper and Mark Andersen. On location: Carpenter complex, March 1987. (Tom DiPace)

Shoulder massage, continuation of infraspinatus into tuberosity. Jeff Cooper and Mark Andersen. On location: Carpenter complex, March 1987. (Tom DiPace)

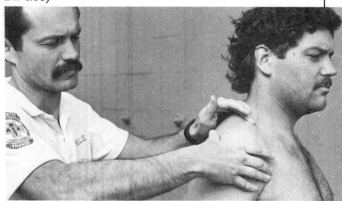

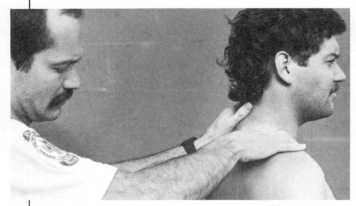 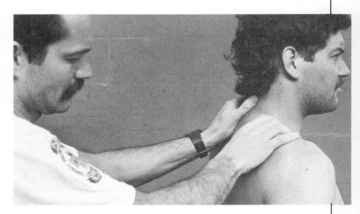

Shoulder massage, start of supraspinatus coursing toward spine. Jeff Cooper and Mark Andersen. On location: Carpenter complex, March 1987. (Tom DiPace)

Shoulder massage, continuation of supraspinatus coursing toward spine. Jeff Cooper and Mark Andersen. On location: Carpenter complex, March 1987. (Tom DiPace)

As the right hand continues to work the anterior portions of the shoulder, the left hand is moved into the fossa (the bone cavity) of the scapula. This is the site of origin of another rotator cuff muscle, the infraspinatus.

You change hands and course the infraspinatus to its insertion in the greater tuberosity.

The supraspinatus is then coursed back along its fossa (cavity) toward the spine.

The right hand descends along the spine to massage both the rhomboideus minor and major.

Continually distally (i.e., toward the farthest point removed from the shoulder) to the elbow, the insertion of the triceps brachia is massaged.

The muscle is massaged throughout its belly, coursing the long head from its scapular attachment.

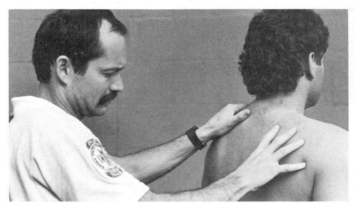

Shoulder massage, right hand begins descent into rhomboids. Jeff Cooper and Mark Andersen. On location: Carpenter complex, March 1987. (Tom DiPace)

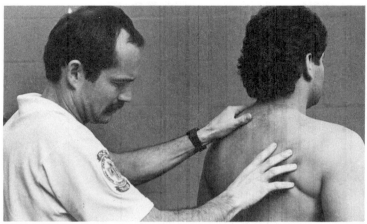

Shoulder massage, right hand continues descent into rhomboids. Jeff Cooper and Mark Andersen. On location: Carpenter complex, March 1987. (Tom DiPace)

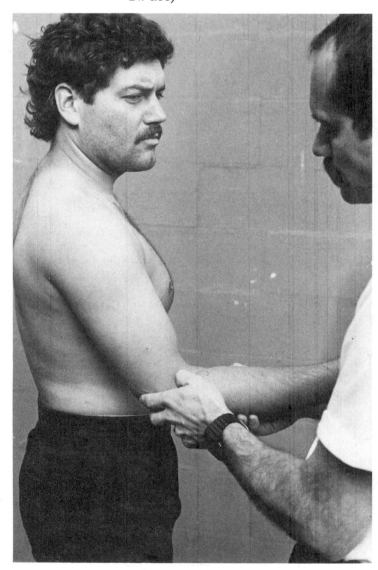

Arm massage, elbow at triceps insertion. Jeff Cooper and Mark Andersen. On location: Carpenter complex, March 1987. (Tom DiPace)

The lateral components of the elbow are then addressed at their origin on the distal portion of the humerus (the bone of the upper arm, extending from the shoulder to the elbow). The muscle bellies are coursed across the elbow joint.

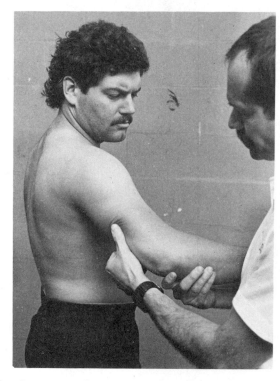

Arm massage, triceps muscle. Jeff Cooper and Mark Andersen. On location: Carpenter complex, March 1987. (Tom DiPace)

On the inner surface, the medial epicondyle of the humerus (the rounded surface at the end of the bone) is located, along with the common flexor tendon. The muscle bellies are coursed across the medial surface of the joint.

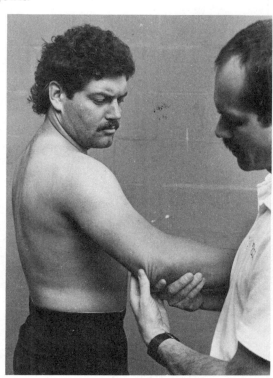

Arm massage, muscle belly at elbow joint. Jeff Cooper and Mark Andersen. On location: Carpenter complex, March 1987. (Tom DiPace)

The muscle bellies are addressed in a fashion working toward the midline of the forearm.

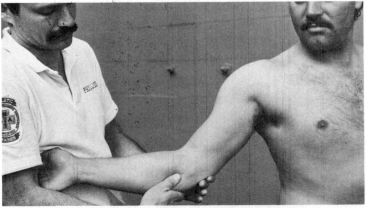

Arm massage, muscle belly of elbow joint near common flexor tendon and epicondyle of humerus. Jeff Cooper and Mark Andersen. On location: Carpenter complex, March 1987. (Tom DiPace)

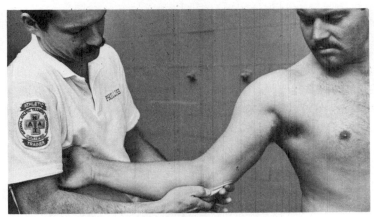

Elbow massage, toward midline of forearm. Jeff Cooper and Mark Andersen. On location: Carpenter complex, March 1987. (Tom DiPace)

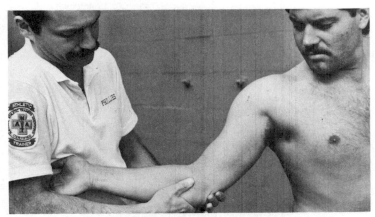

Elbow massage, continuation toward midline of forearm. Jeff Cooper and Mark Andersen. On location: Carpenter complex, March 1987. (Tom DiPace)

Jeff Cooper now explains a second massage, a lower limb massage.

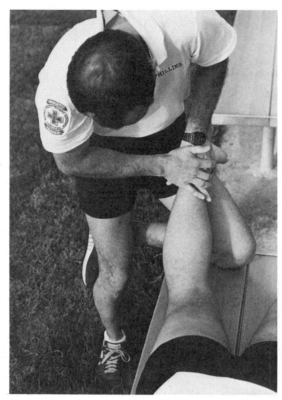

Lower limb massage, Achilles tendon. Jeff Cooper and Mark Andersen. On location: Carpenter complex, March 1987. (Tom DiPace)

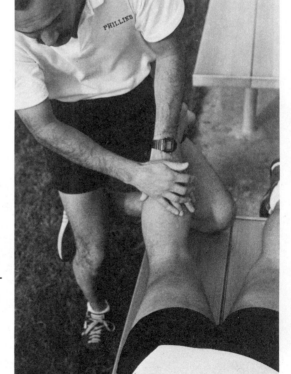

Lower limb massage, belly of gastrocnemius. Jeff Cooper and Mark Andersen. On location: Carpenter complex, March 1987. (Tom DiPace)

The lower limb massage is begun at the Achilles tendon using a hand-over-hand technique; i.e., the palm of one hand is applied to the back of the other.

The hands are moved proximally, stroking through the belly of the gastrocnemius muscle.

The hands continue through the popliteal space.

Then they go through mid-hamstring. Hand-over-hand stroking is continued, alternating on both the medial and lateral aspects of the leg. Following a general stroking procedure, more attention is paid to individual structures of the posterior leg.

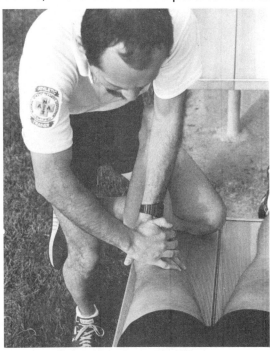

Lower limb massage, popliteal space (between popliteal tendon and lateral collateral ligament of knee). Jeff Cooper and Mark Andersen. On location: Carpenter complex, March 1987. (Tom DiPace)

Lower limb massage, mid hamstring. Jeff Cooper and Mark Andersen. On location: Carpenter complex, March 1987. (Tom DiPace)

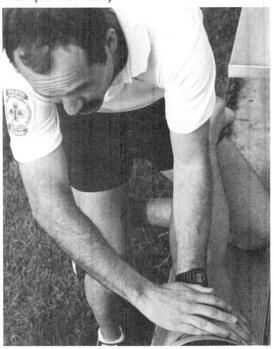

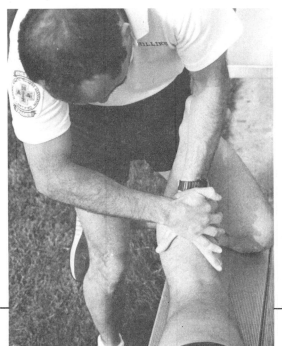

Lower limb massage, return to gastrocnemius at distal attachment to the heel. Jeff Cooper and Mark Andersen. On location: Carpenter complex, March 1987. (Tom DiPace)

Then we return to the gastrocnemius at its distal attachment at the heel and work its length to the popliteal space.

Particular attention is paid to both the medial components and the lateral components. While massaging the lower leg, the peroneals on the lateral aspect are addressed.

Continuing above the knee, we turn our attention to the medial hamstrings: the semimembranasus and the semitendinosus.

Laterally, the biceps femoris is addressed in its length.

After the leg has been worked in this specific distal to proximal fashion, return to the hand-over-hand stroking for completion of the massage.

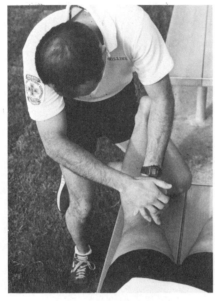

Lower limb massage, peroneals on lateral aspect. Jeff Cooper and Mark Andersen. On location: Carpenter complex, March 1987. (Tom DiPace)

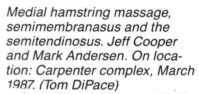

Medial hamstring massage, semimembranasus and the semitendinosus. Jeff Cooper and Mark Andersen. On location: Carpenter complex, March 1987. (Tom DiPace)

Completion of massage in upper thigh. Jeff Cooper and Mark Andersen. On location: Carpenter complex, March 1987. (Tom DiPace)

Gene Gieselmann, head trainer of the St. Louis Cardinals, continues our tips on massage with a series of traditional rubdowns, photographed at the Cardinals' spring headquarters in St. Petersburg, Florida. Our model is Cardinals pitcher Jeff Lahti, who was a highly effective relief pitcher until a series of upper- and lower-body injuries put him on the disabled list in 1986.

Gene performs a traditional pregame elbow and shoulder massage on Lahti, stretching his arm into the external and internal rotating positions he will use in the game.

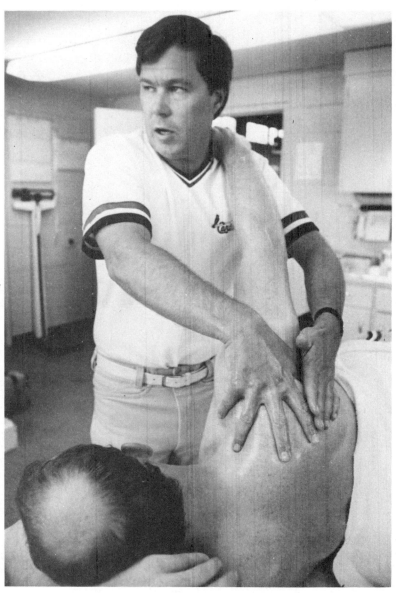

Rotator cuff massage, prior to shoulder stretch. Gene Gieselmann, head trainer of the St. Louis Cardinals, works on Jeff Lahti, St. Louis Cardinals pitcher. On location: Busch complex, spring training home of the St. Louis Cardinals, St. Petersburg, Florida, March 1987. (Tom DiPace)

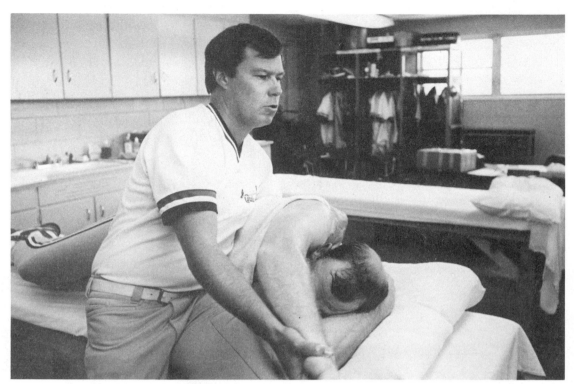

Shoulder stretch, starting position. Gene Gieselmann and Jeff Lahti. On location: Busch complex, March 1987. (Tom DiPace)

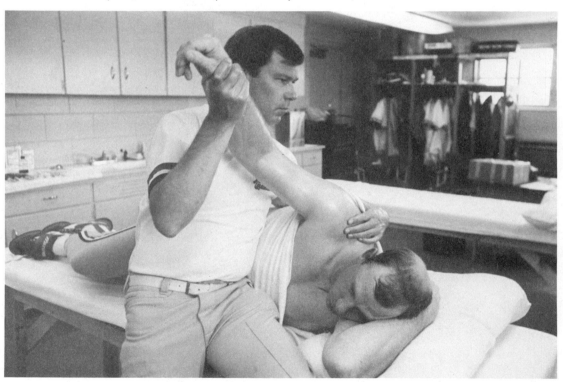

Shoulder stretch, first position. Gene Gieselmann and Jeff Lahti. On location: Busch complex, March 1987. (Tom DiPace)

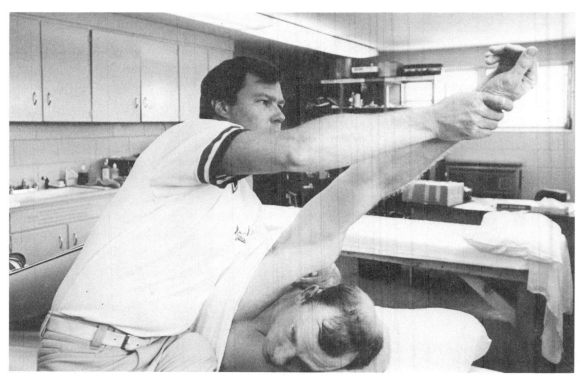

Shoulder stretch, second position. Gene Gieselmann and Jeff Lahti. On location: Busch complex, March 1987. (Tom DiPace)

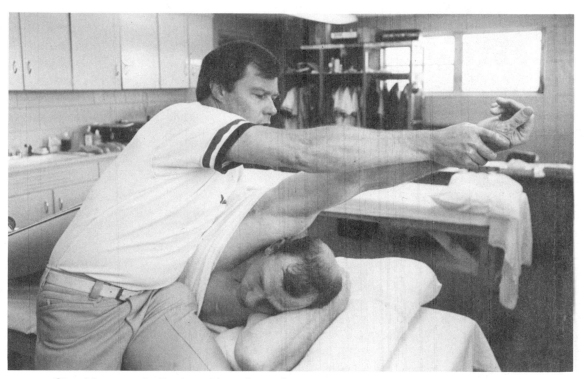

Shoulder stretch, final position. Gene Gieselmann and Jeff Lahti. On location: Busch complex, March 1987. (Tom DiPace)

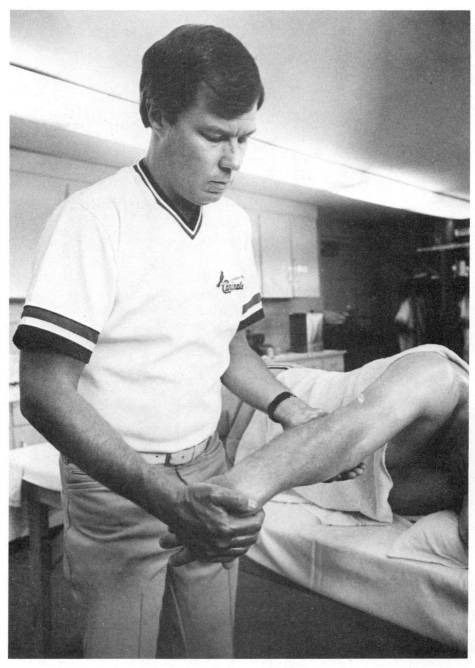

Elbow stretch (follows the shoulder stretch). Gene Gieselmann and Jeff Lahti. On location: Busch complex, March 1987. (Tom DiPace)

Gene also performs a thorough back massage on Lahti, starting with a basic lubricant selected from a variety of oils, balms, and powders on the market. Gene starts from the lower back muscles, the spinal erectors. He then works his way deep into the rhomboids and ends at the traps (trapezius) around the neck.

Massage serves a variety of ends. Physiologically it eliminates soreness by the skilled hands of a trainer and with the relaxed cooperation of the player. Psychologically, it provides great relief for the player, who feels both physically and mentally uplifted by the massage.

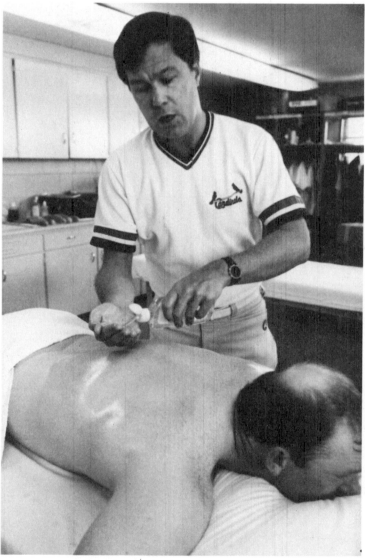

Pouring oil for back massage. Gene Gieselmann and Jeff Lahti. On location: Busch complex, March 1987. (Tom DiPace)

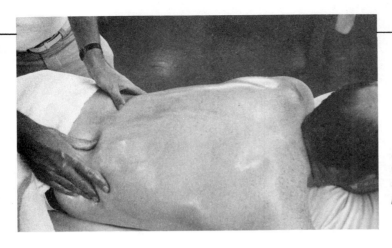

Massage of spinal erectors. Gene Gieselmann and Jeff Lahti. On location: Busch complex: March 1987. (Tom DiPace)

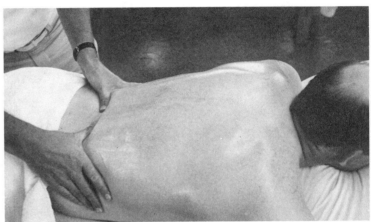

Spinal erector massage continued, working upward. Gene Gieselmann and Jeff Lahti. On location: Busch complex, March 1987. (Tom DiPace)

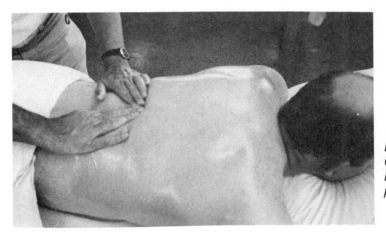
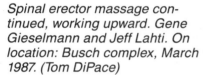

Lower rhomboid massage. Gene Gieselmann and Jeff Lahti. On location: Busch complex, March 1987. (Tom DiPace)

Mid-rhomboid massage. Gene Gieselmann and Jeff Lahti. On location: Busch complex, March 1987. (Tom DiPace)

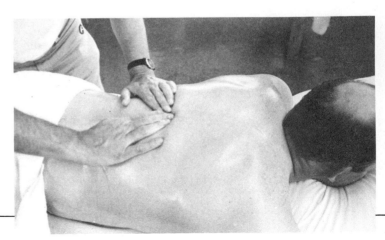

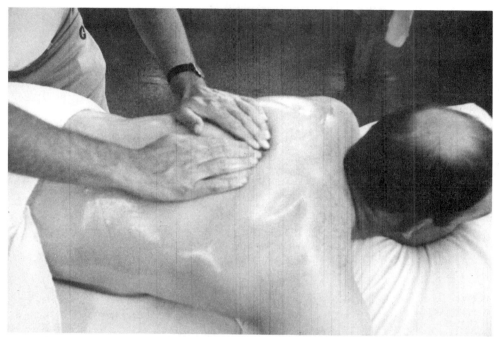

Upper rhomboid massage. Gene Gieselmann and Jeff Lahti. On location: Busch complex, March 1987. (Tom DiPace)

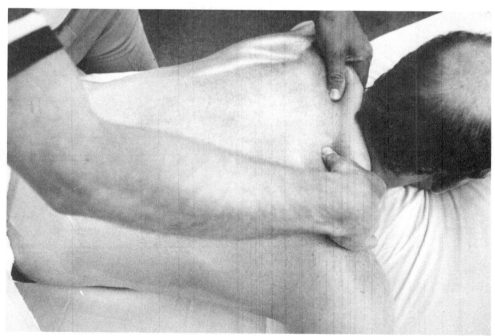

End of massage, at upper trapezius. Gene Gieselmann and Jeff Lahti. On location: Busch complex, March 1987. (Tom DiPace)

MYOTHERAPY

There is another maintenance technique, myotherapy, which many trainers use as a dry alternative to massage. Barry Weinberg, head trainer of the Oakland Athletics, is pictured performing it on his assistant athletic trainer, Larry Davis. Barry will explain some of its attributes.

Myotherapy is an easy and relatively painless way of providing relief to players through pressure point therapy. Myotherapy can be applied to any part of the body—back, neck, shoulders, feet, and legs. It is a dry method, requiring no oil or ointment like deep massage, and you do not need special equipment. It can be done anywhere—in the clubhouse, on a plane during a road trip, in the dugout during the course of a game—on any body part.

Myotherapy is a technique similar to accupressure. It is based on the knowledge that pressure points exist in key areas of the body. They are located along the beltline, the gluteals, the hamstrings, and in the rotator cuff area of the shoulder. Whether you are a player or just an ordinary citizen, there is remarkably little individual variance in where these points are located, and the trainer searches gently to find them. Shown are the four lower-back pressure points along the beltline of the player's uniform.

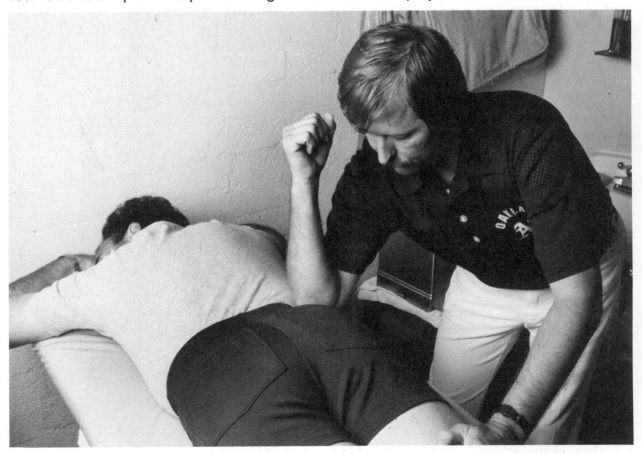

Belt-line myotherapy pressure-point treatment. Larry Davis, Oakland Athletics assistant trainer, applies elbow to Barry Weinberg, Oakland Athletics head trainer. On location: Phoenix Municipal Stadium, Phoenix, Arizona, March 1987. (V. J. Lovero)

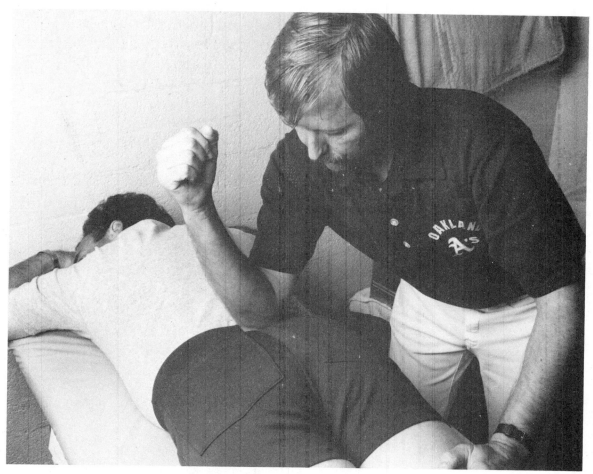

Belt-line myotherapy pressure-point treatment. Larry Davis and Barry Weinberg. On location: Phoenix Municipal Stadium, March 1987. (V. J. Lovero)

Once you find the point, you apply gentle pressure with the finger, thumb, or elbow for no more than seven seconds and then move on to the next spot. If there is pain at one of the points, you watch carefully and make sure that you hold no longer than seven seconds. You decrease the direct pressure applied because there is no desire to increase pain. It is wise in applying myotherapy techniques to be sensitive to the individual's discomfort and anticipate possible reflex actions that may be counterproductive.

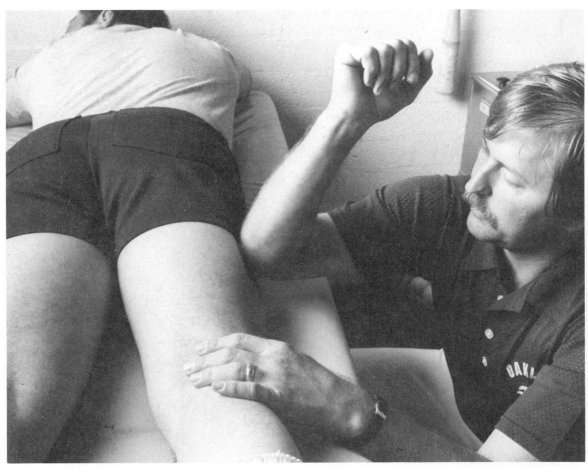

Hamstring myotherapy pressure-point treatment. Larry Davis and Barry Weinberg. On location: Phoenix Municipal Stadium, March 1987. (V. J. Lovero)

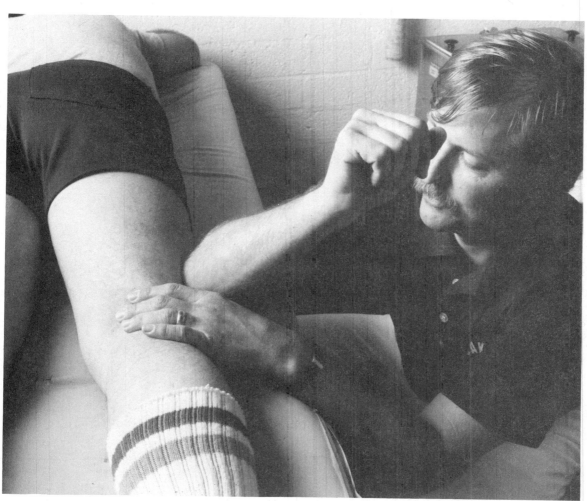

Hamstring myotherapy pressure-point treatment. Larry Davis and Barry Weinberg. On location: Phoenix Municipal Stadium, March 1987. (V. J. Lovero)

The four pressure points along the hamstrings are most easily found along the seam of the baseball uniform's pant leg. Similarly, there are five to six pressure points that can be found in the back pant pocket of the uniform in the gluteal region. If the player is not in uniform, the gluteal pressure points are most usually found around the gluteal dimple.

The best technique for myotherapy is for the trainer to lean into the spot with his elbow, thumb, or forefinger, applying direct pressure on the desired spot. It is unnecessary to apply pressure directly on a bone. The key is to work muscle regions to relieve pain and spasm. As in all the techniques practiced by the trainer, he learns from experience and develops a feel for the player's body geography.

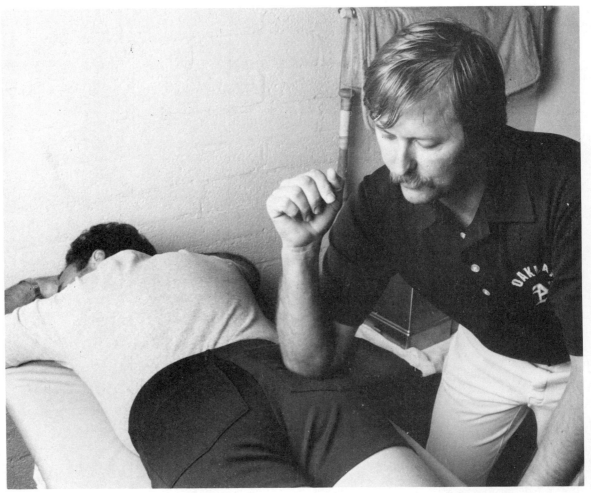

Gluteal myotherapy pressure-point treatment. Larry Davis and Barry Weinberg. On location: Phoenix Municipal Stadium, March 1987. (V. J. Lovero)

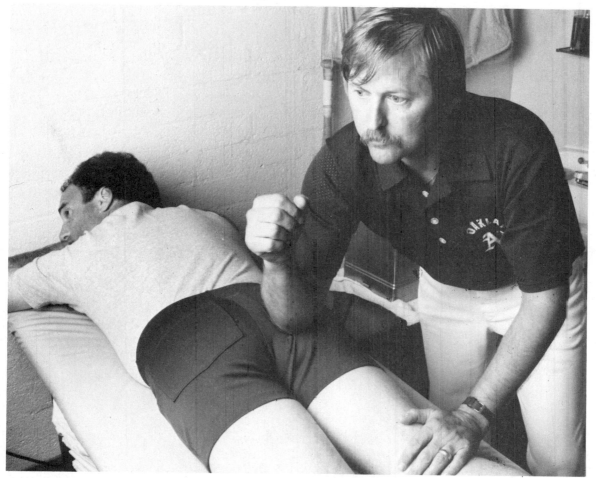

Gluteal myotherapy pressure-point treatment. Larry Davis and Barry Weinberg. On location: Phoenix Municipal Stadium, March 1987. (Tom DiPace)

Another advantage of myotherapy is that it often helps a player learn of muscular discomfort that he was unaware of in another part of his body. For instance, pressure on a lower back point may reveal a soreness in a calf muscle that needs attention.

Myotherapy can also be used as a diagnostic tool. Applying gentle finger pressure in the rotator cuff area may reveal a discomfort that, detected early, can be quickly addressed. Myotherapy also can be used as an adjunct to other modalities, like whirlpool and ultrasound treatment and ice.

A final plus for myotherapy is that it can be done quickly. For impatient players, a shoulder session can be done in 60 seconds. Of course, the traditional relaxation treatment of massage still has its place, but myotherapy is a relatively new wrinkle that has been of use to many players.

Having had our say on the general maintenance treatment for players in today's big leagues, let us look at some of the specialized treatments and exercises a player can engage in to keep all parts of his finely tuned athletic body maintained. Let us start with one of the most neglected parts of the athlete's body, the hand. Our guide will be John Fierro, head trainer of the Chicago Cubs.

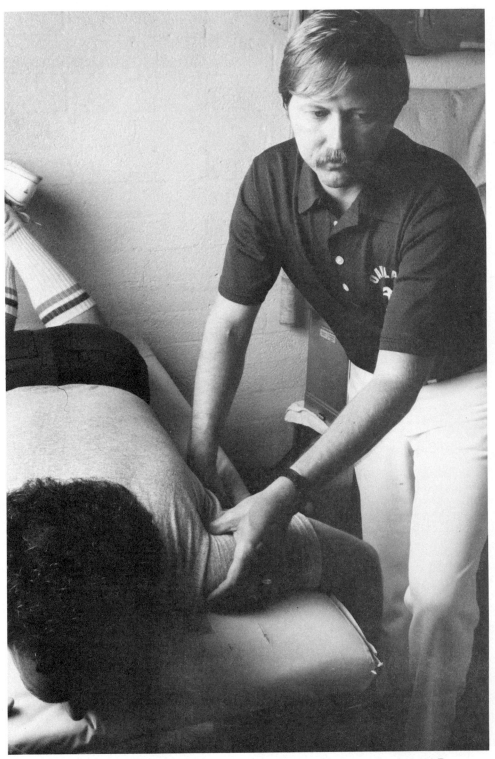

Rotator-cuff myotherapy pressure-point treatment. Larry Davis and Barry Weinberg. On location: Phoenix Municipal Stadium, March 1987. (V. J. Lovero)

MAINTAINING THE HAND AND ARM

The hand is too often taken for granted by athletes. Except for the foot, it is the most used part of the body in baseball, and it is subject to many injuries in all phases of the game. In baserunning, fingers get jammed or broken by diving back into bases or trying to steal them. Our star Cubs shortstop Shawon Dunston missed months of the 1987 season when he fractured the fourth finger of his right hand on a hand-first slide into second base.

In fielding, an improper tag can cause a hand injury if the gloved or bare hand hits a runner's body awkwardly. During my service in the minor leagues, I also saw a batter break his wrist on a checked swing. The torque (rotational force) of his bat was so great that when the player stopped his swing suddenly, the deflected force snapped his wrist.

Injuries of both the everyday and freak-occurrence varieties are inevitable in baseball, and nothing can really prevent them. But there are simple strengthening exercises which, if done regularly, can toughen your fingers, hands, and wrists and lessen the chance of injury or fracture due to weakness.

Putty Gripping The simple gripping of therapeutic putty many times a day is an excellent way to improve hand, arm, and elbow strength. Recent studies have shown that there is a high correlation between the strength of one's grip and the strength of one's entire body and shoulder girdle. Regular gripping of the putty strengthens the important muscle group, the forearm flexors, the extrinsic muscles of the hand. Putty gripping is very easily done. It can be gripped and manipulated several times a day: at home, before a game, and perhaps most ideally, during a game.

The wrist is often mentioned as the key body part for generating bat speed and power. "He has such quick wrists!" is the phrase that often describes great hitters. Actually, if you look closely at batters, a highly developed forearm is the source of much bat strength. Steve Garvey, the San Diego Padres' slugging first baseman and one of the most durable and successful of players until injury curtailed his 1987 season, is nicknamed "Popeye" because of the size and strength of his forearms.

There is a simple exercise to maintain forearm strength. It is demonstrated by Jesse Barfield, outfielder of the Toronto Blue Jays and the 1986 American League home run champion. The exercise, known as broomstick curls, is explained by Barfield's trainer, Tommy Craig.

Broomstick Curls Use a stick, a hammer, or a sawed-off bat with one to five pounds of weights attached, depending on your individual strength and comfort. As in all weighted exercises, find the right starting point for yourself. Do not overdo at the outset, but do not make it too easy either.

Grip the stick with your palms down and lower the weight slowly, winding the weight down by cranking the hand. You are working the forearm extensors. Then with the palms up, raise the weight, working the forearm flexors. You will find that this latter exercise, working the flexors, is much harder, so do not be disappointed if progress is slow in this area. Keep at it, as always exhibiting proper form and technique.

Broomstick curl, forearm exercise, weight down-working extensors. Tommy Craig, head trainer of the Toronto Blue Jays, observes Jesse Barfield, Toronto Blue Jays outfielder. On location: Cecil P. Englebert recreational complex, spring training home of the Toronto Blue Jays; Dunedin, Florida, March 1987. (Tom DiPace)

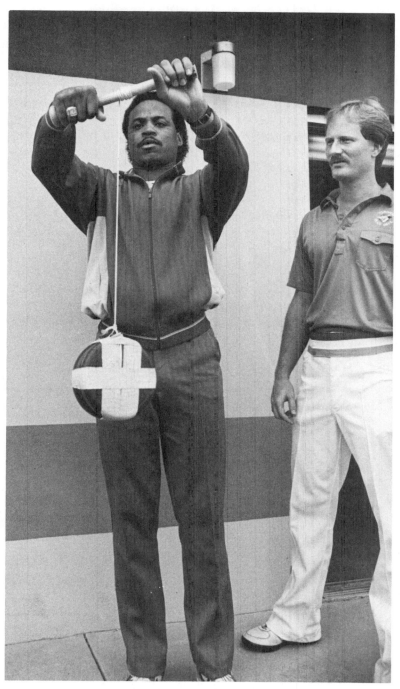

Broomstick curl, forearm exercise, weight up-working flexors. Tommy Craig and Jesse Barfield. On location: Englebert complex, March 1987. (Tom DiPace)

MAINTAINING THE SHOULDER

There is no area of the player's body more crucial and delicate than the shoulder, a complex of fifty muscles that enables the arm to perform the demanding and complicated motions of baseball. The key muscles in the shoulder for baseball are the four muscles in the rotator cuff, the supraspinatus, the infraspinatus, the teres minor, and the subscapularis. They are not power muscles like the adjoining deltoid, but they are thin reedy muscles that have the important assignment of holding the shoulder together after the arm has accelerated in throwing the ball.

Recent estimates indicate that a pitcher loses 5 to 10 percent of shoulder strength during the course of a season if he has thrown a starter's average of about 200 innings. The reliever has great wear and tear, too; he does not throw as many innings but warms up more often and almost always has to retire the toughest batters in the later stages of a game.

Shoulder weakness is an inevitable part of baseball, but it can be corrected by regular exercise with small weights. We have decided to devote a large section of the rehabilitation chapter to extensive shoulder exercises, but at this juncture we want to present two basic stretches that healthy pitchers perform before they pitch and again no later than a day after they have thrown.

The model is Jon Woodworth, who in 1987 completed his third year as athletic trainer for the Syracuse Chiefs, the triple-A farm club of the Toronto Blue Jays in the International League. He is assisted by the Blue Jays' head athletic trainer, Tommy Craig. These two important stretches can be done on a daily basis before exercise. The activity also includes a helpful mobilization of the shoulder joint. Other stretches, such as internal and external rotation, can be incorporated, but these two are done on a daily basis.

Shoulder Stretch #1: Supine Shoulder Flexion This is an important daily stretch because throwing shoulders become tight in the posterior region. Great emphasis should be placed on keeping the scapula from winging out—i.e., on keeping it close to the body. (Notice my right hand on Jon's shoulder blade.) Push the shoulder into flexion, being cautious not to push the shoulder past a comfortable range of motion. The stretch can be done in a "contract/relax" fashion. The player contracts and holds for five seconds, then relaxes for five seconds. Repeat three times.

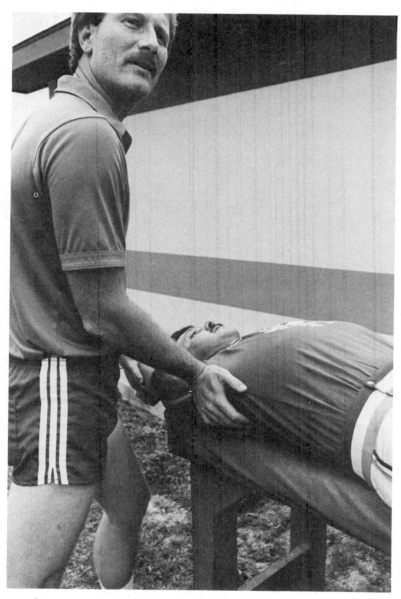

Shoulder flexion stretch, starting position: relax. Tommy Craig holds in place the scapula of Jon Woodworth, Toronto Blue Jays assistant trainer. On location: Englebert complex, March 1987. (Tom DiPace)

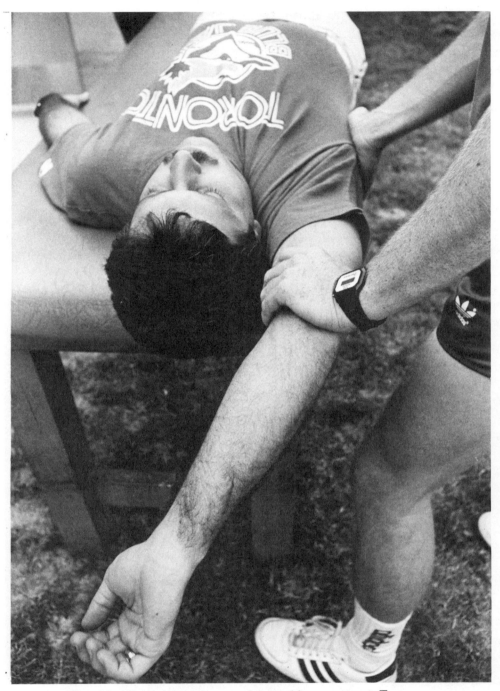

Shoulder flexion stretch, exercise position: contract. Tommy Craig and Jon Woodworth. On location: Englebert complex, March 1987. (Tom DiPace)

Shoulder Stretch #2: Supine Horizontal Adduction While lying on his back, the player reaches across his body as far as possible with his arm under his chin. The trainer pushes the arm into adduction (toward the midline of the body), while the player strives to keep his shoulder blade flat against the table. The "contract/relax" method is used in this stretch as in the first. Repeat three times. This stretch is particularly good for working the posterior rotator cuff muscles, the ones that decelerate the arm after throwing and in which most serious arm injuries occur.

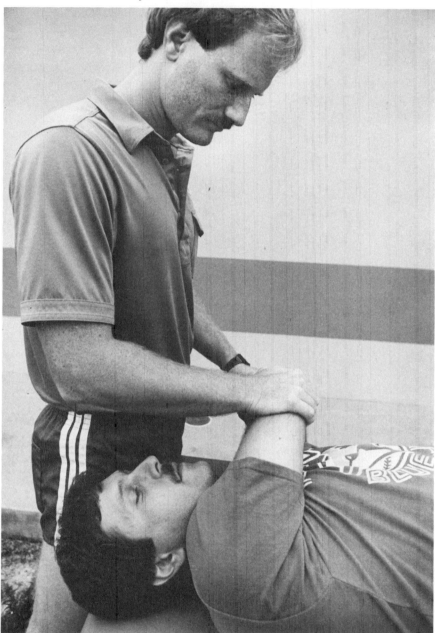

Supine horizontal adduction stretch, starting position: relax. Tommy Craig secures Jon Woodworth's elbow. On location: Englebert complex, March 1987. (Tom DiPace)

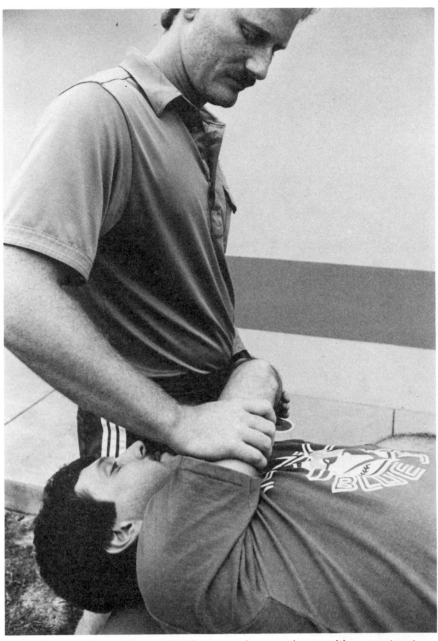

Supine horizontal adduction stretch, exercise position: contract. Tommy Craig and Jon Woodworth. On location: Englebert complex, March 1987. (Tom Di Pace)

MAINTAINING THE BACK

The back is an area of obvious importance for the professional baseball player. They say that 90 million Americans have experienced some kind of back pain. Many baseball players are certainly included among that number, but they are not likely to play with any consistency if the back pain lingers.

Dave Labossiere, head trainer of the Houston Astros, has a lot of experience working on back conditioning for baseball players. With the help of our model, Larry Starr, head trainer of the Cincinnati Reds, Dave explains the exercises, which are designed (1) to strengthen the "core," or center, of the body; (2) to educate the muscles of the pelvic area to control the motion available to them; and (3) to increase flexibility.

When developing a plan for conditioning and maintaining the condition of athletes, the back is a very important consideration. In almost all activities on the playing field, control of the "core," or center, of the body is probably the single most important element for proper execution. Developing strength and flexibility in the core enables optimum performance. In baseball, in activities like throwing and swinging, there is much trunk rotation, which develops tremendous torque (rotational force).

Just think of the stress that the game of baseball places on the back during the course of a game. If you are in the field, you are bent at the waist and must move quickly from that position to field the ball. If you are at the plate, there is stress on the back because of the strenuous rotation of the trunk. Astroturf also makes a great demand on the players' backs because the artificial surface is hard and does not give easily.

The following exercises are done every day as a warm-up in spring training, and we recommend that you try to get the players to keep up with them throughout the season—and certainly in the off-season, when the wear and tear of the daily grind is no longer a problem for conditioning. These exercises are designed to keep one of the most vital parts of the player's body, the back, as strong and as flexible as it can be.

Many of these exercises appear in the pamphlet *Trunk Stretching and Trunk Conditioning,* by Dr. Robert G. Watkins, orthopedic consultant to both the California Angels and the Los Angeles Dodgers. It is printed for PBATS by the Kerlan-Jobe Orthopedic Clinic in Inglewood, California, and all baseball trainers are indebted to Dr. Watkins and the Kerlan-Jobe Clinic for their work in developing these helpful back exercises. The exercises often have levels of difficulty (like the strength-training program discussed in chapter 4), but we present just the elementary level of exercise, which should suffice for starters.

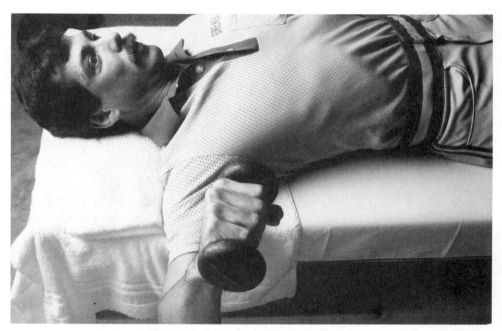

Internal rotation shoulder-strengthening exercise with small weight, starting position. John Adam, head trainer of the Milwaukee Brewers. On location: Compadre Stadium, Chandler, Arizona, March 1987. (V. J. Lovero)

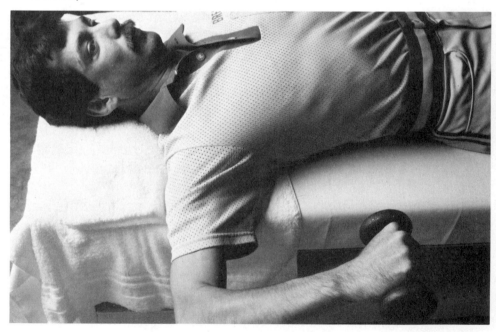

Internal rotation shoulder-strengthening exercise with small weight, exercise position. John Adam. On location: Compadre Stadium, March 1987. (V. J. Lovero)

BACK-STRENGTHENING EXERCISES   There is no cut-and-dried rule for how many repetitions and sets of these exercises you should do. Three sets of 8 to 10 repetitions is a good target. An important fact to consider, however, is that it is much better to do multiple low numbers of repetitions throughout the day than to do one high-repetition set. Especially when in a rehabilitative stage, you can irritate and inflame and possibly reinjure yourself with too many concentrated repetitions.

1. Sit-Ups Lie prone on the floor or mat with your hands folded across the chest, knees bent, and feet unhooked. Come partway up, shoulders and back lifted off the floor, and hold in midair for a count of four to eight. Do not come up more than 30 degrees because that does not add strength and may cause back strain. It is not the amount of motion that is important, but the isometric abdominal tone.

Watkins back-strengthening series: sit-up, starting position. Larry Starr, Cincinnati Reds head trainer. On location: Redlands complex, spring training home of the Cincinnati Reds, Tampa, Florida, March 1987. (Tom DiPace)

Sit-up, finishing position. Larry Starr. On location: Redlands complex, March 1987. (Tom DiPace)

2. Sit-Up Twists Lie prone, legs positioned approximately 12 inches apart, hands clasped behind the head, knees bent, and feet unhooked. Do a partial sit-up, rotating the right elbow toward the opposite left knee. This is held for a count of four to eight in the rotated position. Return to the starting position and repeat with a rotation to the opposite side.

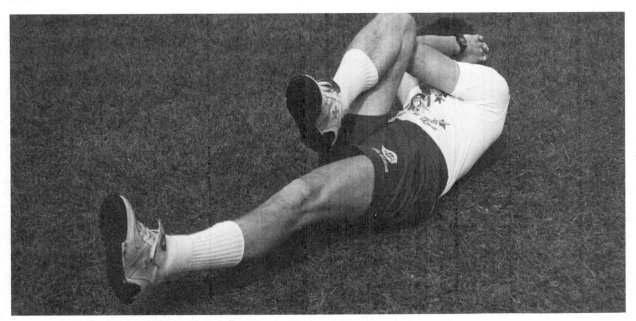

Sit-up twist, toward the right. Larry Starr. On location: Redlands complex, March 1987. (Tom DiPace)

Sit-up twist, toward the left. Larry Starr. On location: Redlands complex, March 1987. (Tom DiPace)

3. Back Extensions Lie facedown, hands clasped behind the waist. Bring the head and feet off the ground and hold for a count of four to eight. Remember, it is not the amount of motion but maintaining the trunk in a highly extended position that strengthens the abdominals in this exercise. You can injure yourself seriously if you overextend your back.

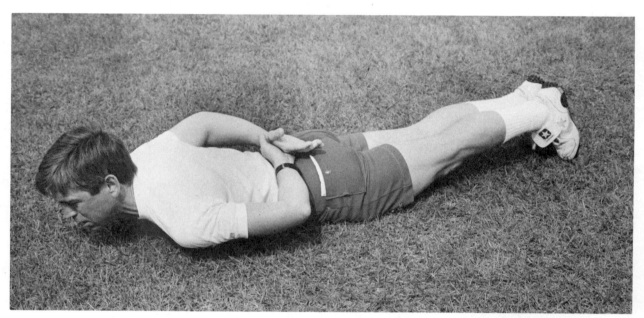

Back extension, starting position. Larry Starr. On location: Redlands complex, March 1987. (Tom DiPace)

Back extension, finishing position. Larry Starr. On location: Redlands complex, March 1987. (Tom DiPace)

4. Russian Twists Start in a sitting position on the ground or on a four-inch pad. The knees are bent and the feet may be hooked. Lean back to a position approximately six to eight inches off the floor. Arms are extended forward, palms together. The arms and trunk are then rotated a full 90 degrees to the left, then 90 degrees to the right. This motion is repeated for as many repetitions as possible—one full repetition being a turn to the left and the right and then a return to the upright sitting position. A rowing machine is often used in conjunction with this exercise.

Russian twist, starting position. Larry Starr. On location: Redlands complex, March 1987. (Tom DiPace)

Russian twist, toward the right. Larry Starr. On location: Redlands complex, March 1987. (Tom DiPace)

*Russian twist, toward the left. Larry Starr. On location:
Redlands complex, March 1987. (Tom DiPace)*

BACK-STRETCHING EXERCISES

5. Push-Ups, seven varieties   This basic exercise is designed to stretch and strengthen the back and to improve its basic curvature. Do 10 to 20 push-ups for each position of the hands.

Push-up, hands underneath (traditional). Larry Starr. On location: Redlands complex, March 1987. (Tom DiPace)

Push-up, clasped hands in front. Larry Starr. On location: Redlands complex, March 1987.
(Tom DiPace)

Push-up, hands facing out to the side. Larry Starr. On location:
Redlands complex, March 1987. (Tom DiPace)

Push-up, hands facing in toward the middle. Larry Starr. On location: Redlands complex, March 1987. (Tom DiPace)

V-stretch push-up, hands in front. Larry Starr. On location: Redlands complex, March 1987. (Tom DiPace)

V-stretch push-up, hands clasped in front. Larry Starr. On location: Redlands complex, March 1987. (Tom DiPace)

Partial upper-body push-up. Larry Starr. On location: Redlands complex, March 1987. (Tom DiPace)

6. Alternating Arm-Leg Stretch   Lying supine, inwardly rotate the right hip while stretching the right arm 90 degrees horizontally and extending the left leg forward. Hold for a count of eight. Then repeat to the opposite side.

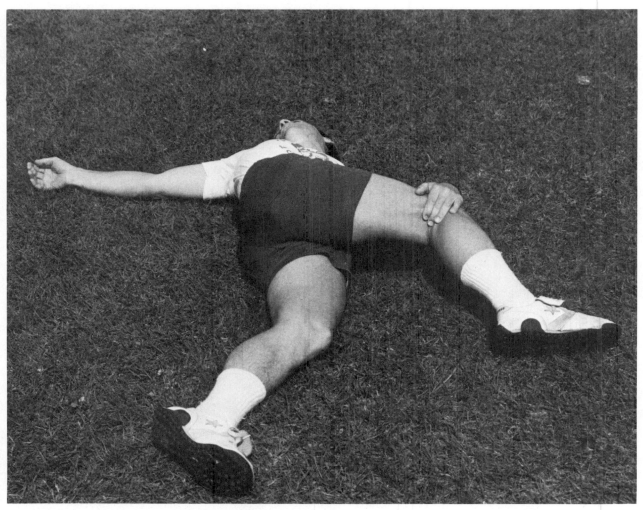

Alternating stretch (supine), left arm to right knee. Larry Starr. On location: Redlands complex, March 1987. (Tom DiPace)

7. Alternating Knee-to-Shoulder Stretch Lying supine, pull the right knee to the right shoulder. The knee is brought to the shoulder laterally—not in over the abdomen (a motion by which the thigh produces abdominal compression). Hold for a count of eight. The other leg is extended or flexed, whichever is more comfortable. Then bring the left knee to the left shoulder. Repeat.

Knee-to-shoulder stretch, left side. Larry Starr. On location: Redlands complex, March 1987. (Tom DiPace)

8. Bilateral Knee Stretch   Starting in a supine position, bring both knees to the chest and hold for 15 seconds.

9. Alternate Elbow-to-Knee Stretch   Starting in a sitting position with your hands by your side, bring your left elbow to the right knee and then the right elbow to the left knee.

Bilateral (double) knee stretch. Larry Starr. On location: Redlands complex, March 1987. (Tom DiPace)

Alternating stretch (seated), left elbow to right knee. Larry Starr. On location: Redlands complex. March 1987. (Tom DiPace)

10. Straight-Leg Twists Start with both feet upright in the air from a supine position. Twist the body to the right and then to the left, keeping the feet together.

Straight-leg twist, to the left. Larry Starr. On location: Redlands complex, March 1987. (Tom DiPace)

11. Lower Body Side-to-Side Twists Start supine in bent-knee position with head back on ground. Twist your lower body to the right and then to the left.

Straight-leg twist, to the right. Larry Starr. On location: Redlands complex, March 1987. (Tom DiPace)

Lower-body side-to-side twist, starting position. Larry Starr. On location: Redlands complex, March 1987. (Tom DiPace)

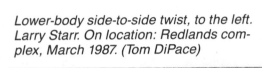

Lower-body side-to-side twist, to the left. Larry Starr. On location: Redlands complex, March 1987. (Tom DiPace)

Lower-body side-to-side twist, to the right. Larry Starr. On location: Redlands complex, March 1987. (Tom DiPace)

12. Scissors Kicks   Lying on your back, kick alternately straight up in the air and then kick toward the opposite side.

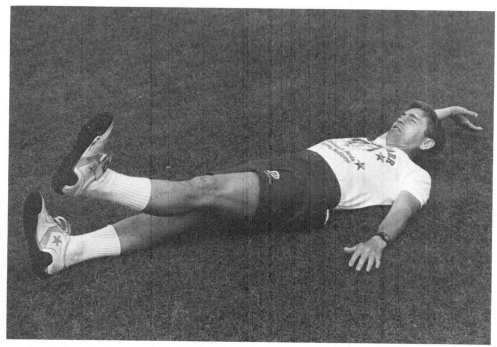

Straight scissors kick, left leg/right arm. Larry Starr. On location: Redlands complex, March 1987. (Tom DiPace)

Straight scissors kick, right leg/left arm. Larry Starr. On location: Redlands complex, March 1987. (Tom DiPace)

Scissors kick, right leg to left side. Larry Starr. On location: Redlands complex, March 1987. (Tom DiPace)

Scissors kick, left leg to right side. Larry Starr. On location: Redlands complex, March 1987. (Tom DiPace)

13. Swimmer's Kicks Lying prone, stretch out left arm with right leg in the air; then alternate right arm out with left leg in the air.

Swimmer's kick, right arm/left leg. Larry Starr. On location: Redlands complex, March 1987. (Tom DiPace)

These are just some of the back exercises that can be done to maintain a flexible trunk. If you are healthy, you may want to end the program with stretches for other parts of the lower body.

14. Double Thigh Stretch   In a kneeling position, stretch backward holding on to both ankles. Hold for about 10 seconds. This is a difficult exercise, not to be attempted by anyone with back pain.

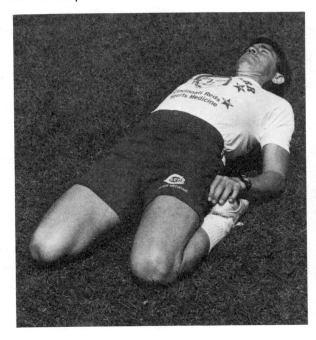

Double thigh stretch (also known as the camel). Larry Starr. On location: Redlands complex, March 1987. (Tom DiPace) Back-problem sufferers are cautioned against this exercise unless it is approved by your doctor.

15. Quadriceps Stretch   Lying supine with the base of the spine as close to a wall or fence as possible and one knee bent, hold the extended leg upright for 20 or 30 seconds and relax.

Ideally, you should build your body up to the point that a stretch can be held in most instances for one minute. Because most people lack the flexibility and attention span for that long a stretch, 20 to 30 seconds is a reasonable goal at the outset.

Hamstring stretch, leg resting against fence. Larry Starr. On location: Redlands complex, March 1987. (Tom DiPace)

MAINTAINING THE LEGS

The legs do not get the attention in baseball that the shoulders understandably receive, but there is a wise old saying: "It all goes when the legs go." Sports scientists estimate that leg movements comprise half of the pitching motion; so well-maintained legs are obviously important for hurlers. If you are a base stealer or fleet base runner, you certainly want your legs as finely conditioned and maintained as possible. In this section, Ron McClain, head trainer of the Montreal Expos, and Gene Gieselmann, head trainer of the St. Louis Cardinals, share some of their thoughts on leg conditioning. Ron has worked with such outstanding runners as Andre Dawson, Ron Leflore, and his current star, Tim Raines, and Gene has fine-tuned such speedsters as Hall of Famer Lou Brock and the current National League base-stealing king, Vince Coleman.

Daily stretching, which Herman Schneider illustrated in chapter 3 with his players Richard Dotson and Harold Baines, is an obvious starting point for any leg conditioning. All the paired and antagonistic leg muscles must be warmed up and stretched and then cooled down, a daily process which, as Herman Schneider so rightly says, "should become as habitual as brushing your teeth."

For the trainer whose team plays 81 home games on Astroturf as ours do, there are special concerns and preventive measures that can be taken. Astroturf can get as hot as 140 degrees in the summertime, so a lukewarm whirlpool (no hotter than 60 degrees) can bring relief to players if they stand knee-deep in the water for several minutes. The lukewarm water serves to bring down the player's body temperature, an important consideration as Dick Martin showed so graphically in chapter 6. The whirlpool can also ease the microtears in the muscle fibers that inevitably occur on Astroturf. But whirlpool use should be measured carefully.

GENE GEISELMANN: Vince Coleman used to sit in a whirlpool for a half hour before a game. He thought the treatment loosened him up and stimulated him for the upcoming game in the St. Louis heat. I ultimately convinced him that too much of a good thing is damaging and that sitting too long in a whirlpool can enervate you, not prepare you for game action. Whirlpool is an excellent modality in rehabilitation, but for maintaining good condition, I recommend massage and gentle stretching.

RON McCLAIN: We have the opposite problem in Montreal regarding temperature. Canada is very cold early and late in the season, and there is an ever-present danger of pulled muscles in frigid environments. To keep our players warm and primed for game action, the Expo's organization has installed a stationary bicycle in the area behind our dugout. Regular players ride it between innings, and bench players can use it at any time to keep their legs warm and their aerobic readiness high for a possible pinch-hitting or other game appearance. We also provide a netted area 50 yards beyond the dugout underneath the stands. Players can sprint distances up to 20 yards to stay loose and well prepared for game situations. Our dugouts are also heated, and an exercise physiologist is on call at all Montreal home games.

When Maury Wills stole 104 bases for the Los Angeles Dodgers in 1962, breaking Ty Cobb's 57-year-old record, the art of the stolen base returned to baseball. In 1974, the St. Louis Cardinals left fielder Lou Brock broke Wills' record with 118 steals for the season. By the time Brock retired, he also held the career stolen base record of 938.

As noted above, both Gene Gieselmann and Ron McClain have served as trainers for a number of base-stealing masters. Here they offer some thoughts on the art of base stealing and its accompanying skill, sliding.

GENE GIESELMANN: Base stealers tend to be devilish personalities who possess ample confidence and the skill to back up their daring. Neither Brock nor Coleman are ever afraid of failing, because unless you are willing to risk something, you will never succeed. Even if they are occasionally thrown out, disrupting the opposition is always a positive result in the cat-and-mouse aspect of baseball. Good baseball stealers always make life tough on the defensive team.

Technically, I like to see runners use the foot-first slide. Lou Brock almost always stole bases that way. Injury to the hand is far less likely in foot-first sliding as the Cardinals' slugging first baseman Jack Clark found out early in the 1986 season. Trying to stretch a double into a triple, Clark tore ligaments and fractured a bone in his right thumb with a hand-first slide. He missed most of the 1986 season but healed thoroughly and had an outstanding 1987.

But Vince Coleman has been very successful sliding hand-first into bases (as has Ricky Henderson of the New York Yankees, who holds the current single-season record of 130 stolen bases). We have noted throughout this book that every individual has his unique quirks. So if the player consistently steals bases and remains injury free doing things his way, who is to make a judgment on form alone?

RON McCLAIN: I have seen injuries occur on poorly executed foot-first slides. I once saw a player tear up his vital anterior cruciate knee ligament because his left foot hit the ground so awkwardly on his slide that the impact drove the right knee backward, tearing the ligament. But in general, I believe that a properly executed foot-first slide is the safest. If you wear sliding pads on your legs and slide on your hip, you can avoid what the players called "strawberries," the skin abrasions that occur when you hit the ground haphazardly. Tim Raines has become almost exclusively a foot-first slider, except in situations where the play may be so close that he wants to use his quick hands to dive into a base and avoid a tag.

Raines is certainly an advertisement for what all-year conditioning can do for a professional athlete. It was no surprise to me at all that Tim Raines could step into the Montreal lineup in May 1987 and get four hits, including a grand-slam home run, without having had a day of spring training. He then proceeded to have a banner year. Raines had never gotten out of playing shape despite having no job offers as an unsigned free agent after the 1986 season.

I think a good way of closing our leg conditioning segment is to show you some of the interval running program that Tim Raines and our other speedsters practice to stay in optimal shape throughout the calendar year. After the 1979 season the Montreal Expos were the first baseball organization to institute an off-season conditioning program. The cold weather in Quebec was a dictating factor, but so was an understanding that the rare qualities of speed and quickness must not be left idle but should be constantly maintained.

I knew all about the virtues of quickness because I had been a trainer on the national championship Indiana University basketball team of 1972. Under coach Bobby Knight's constant goading, those teams ran and ran, and I saw first-hand the speed and skills of such players as Quinn Buckner, Scott May, and Bobby Wilkerson. As a trainer in the Cincinnati organization during the heyday of "The Big Red Machine," I witnessed the great speed of such players as Joe Morgan, Ken Griffey, and Cesar Geronimo.

Since coming to Montreal in 1980, I've worked with such fleet talent as Rodney Scott, Miguel Dilone, Ron LeFlore, and—among players still active—Andre Dawson (now with the Chicago Cubs), Herman Winningham, and the remarkable Tim Raines.

So here is the interval-distance running program that Raines and other speedsters use to build up their maximum speed and strength. The principle of the program is based on specificity of exercise. If you want to be a sprinter, you must sprint. If you want to steal bases, you must work on your explosiveness.

Studies of world-class sprinters have shown that the key to explosiveness is in the first 10 steps out of the blocks—and even more specifically, in the first 6 to 8 of these 10 steps. So the interval running program is designed to work on both the horizontal and vertical lift in those crucial first steps out of the blocks. Long-distance running during the off-season is a fine way to build your overall cardiovascular aerobic fitness, but if you want to excel at the short bursts of speed common in running the bases, you must work on the smaller distances:

First, run 30 to 40 yards at three-quarter speed. Ten repetitions.

Second, run the same 30 to 40 yards *backward* at *half* speed. Ten repetitions.

Third, run forward at full speed for 20 yards. Ten or more repetitions.

Of course, this speed work is not done to the neglect of weight and flexibility work. By now, you should know the key to baseball fitness is balance: balance of muscles, balance of strength and flexibility, and an overall balance of your training program.

You gradually establish this running routine during spring training and then repeat it daily during the season, usually before a game after infield and batting practice are completed. I am proud that in my seven years in Montreal as head trainer, we have kept our swift base runners virtually free of disabling injury. It proves that with carefully thought-out preparation and regular conditioning, the baseball player can keep his legs primed and ready to go for a full season.

FITNESS FOR THE FOOT

Before concluding this chapter on maintaining baseball shape, we need to examine an often neglected subject, the foot and the proper footwear for a baseball player. Rick Griffin, head trainer of the Seattle Mariners and a former minor league trainer in the Cincinnati organization, has researched and written scientific studies about athletic gait and the proper kind of shoes. Here Rick offers some advice on fitness for the foot.

Everything in baseball begins with the feet, especially for middle infielders; yet there is very little discussion about the care and maintenance of the player's foot or about the shoes that he wears to cover and protect them.

I want to close our maintenance chapter with a look at the right kind of baseball shoe for comfort and prevention of injury. There are so many athletic shoes of all kinds on the market today that a young player may feel overwhelmed at making a choice. There is always advertising hoopla, and a youngster might be tempted to buy the shoe endorsed by his favorite player. *Don't do it that way.*

Sturdy heel counter demonstrated in left shoe, compared to right shoe. Demonstrated by Rick Griffin, head trainer of the Seattle Mariners. On location: Diablo Stadium, spring training home of the Seattle Mariners, Tempe, Arizona, March 1987. (V. J. Lovero)

Remember that every infielder is different when it comes to size, shape, skill, pain tolerance, and sensitivity. Try on as many shoes as necessary until you find one that is snug and will give you the proper support. It should feel comfortable when you first try it on. If not, don't buy it.

It should have a sturdy heel counter. If you can push it down upon pressing, it is not going to last.

There should be a cardboard last within the shoe and traversing its entire length. The absence of this supportive last will cause an instability in the shoe and can increase the chance of injury.

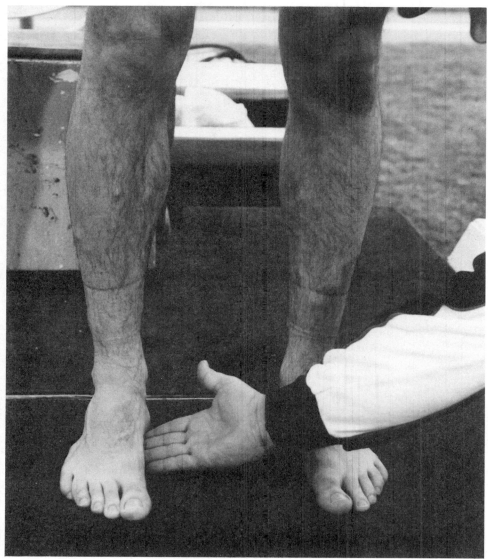

Flat feet (fallen arches), indicated by the absence of space between the foot and the ground. Demonstrated by Rick Griffin. On location: Diablo Stadium, March 1987. (V. J. Lovero)

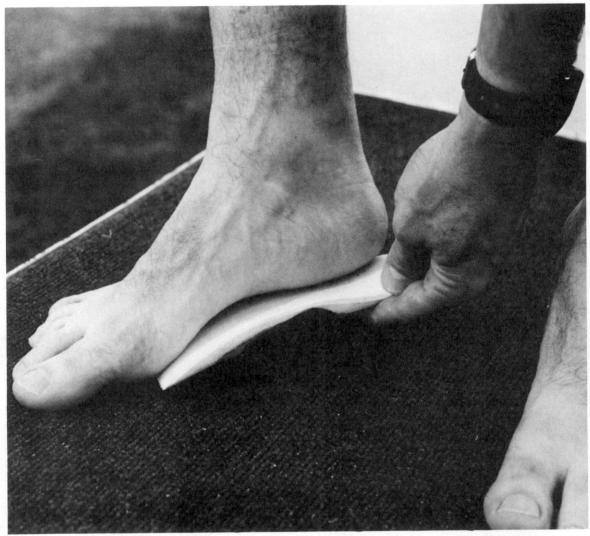

Orthotic device that alleviates the problem of flat feet. Demonstrated by Rick Griffin. On location: Diablo Stadium, March 1987. (V. J. Lovero)

Three athletic shoes that have worn differently: the one on the right with full last and added orthotic is the best. On location: Diablo Stadium, March 1987. (V. J. Lovero)

Orthotics are increasingly common additions to players' shoes in today's baseball. I would estimate that well over a quarter of today's players wear some kind of soft orthotic devices in their playing shoes. An orthotic corrects a variety of problems that occur when the foot is improperly shaped, a malady sometimes called "flat feet." What happens is that instead of the foot absorbing the major stress of running, the burden is taken by the muscles of the lower leg. The orthotic assures that the stresses of running are properly distributed in the foot and leg muscles.

Good orthotics can eliminate a very common foot ailment, plantar fascitis, which is the tearing on the fascia (fibrous connective tissue) of the bottom of the foot. The pain is felt usually under the heel bone, and inadequate arch supports and poorly fitting shoes are a major cause.

The many shoes of the modern player. Mark Langston, Seattle Mariners pitcher. On location: Diablo Stadium, March 1987. (V. J. Lovero)

Recent medical studies have indicated that well-chosen shoes can reduce the occurrence of shin splint injuries by 70 percent. These injuries usually occur in endurance training when the fascia, tendinous connective tissue, pulls away from the bone.

So the foot is a vital part of the athletic body, and it must be properly maintained and cared for. The days of the old leather athletic shoe—or kangaroo skin shoe that was bought a size or two too small and was stretched out—are over. The modern player uses dozens of pairs of shoes in the course of a season of practice and game play. A look at the spring training locker of the Mariners' star southpaw Mark Langston attests to that.

CHAPTER EIGHT

Bouncing Back: *Rehabilitation In Today's Baseball*

By
John Adam, Head Trainer, Milwaukee Brewers
Bill Buhler, Head Trainer, Los Angeles Dodgers
Tommy Craig, Head Trainer, Toronto Blue Jays
Gene Gieselmann, Head Trainer, St. Louis Cardinals
Rick Griffin, Head Trainer, Seattle Mariners

Testing, flexibility, strength, nutrition, psychology—all of these aspects all vital to a player's health and durability. But the time does come, inevitably, when all the preventive knowledge cannot avert injury. Although not as injury-ridden as football, baseball does have its violent encounters between body and body, and ball and man.

Great strides have been made in rehabilitating players carefully yet quickly. Bill Buhler, head trainer of the Los Angeles Dodgers, has witnessed the rapid growth in this field and provides a knowledgeable introduction.

INTRODUCTION TO REHABILITATION

I have worked as a trainer in the major leagues since I joined the Dodgers in 1957, their last year in Brooklyn. I followed them out to the West Coast, where in 1987 I completed my 31st season in the majors, which makes me the dean of active big league trainers.

I have been around many great teams and superior athletes, but the most significant change that I have witnessed in my career is the emergence of the field of sports medicine, a specialty almost unheard of even 15 years ago. In the old days there were only 16 major league clubs and hundreds and hundreds of clubs in the minor leagues. There was a fierce survival of the fittest, and even if a player wasn't that fit, he usually played because his job might not be there if he sat down.

A trainer did whatever he could to ease a player's pain, improvising as he went along. I recall a strong but wild hurler the Dodgers had in the minors in the fifties. One night, he threw over 200 pitches in five innings of work and came back to the clubhouse with a severely swollen elbow. I thought that ice might help this pitcher. Applied to the elbow, it could reduce the swelling and capillary bleeding and cut down the amount of oxygen that his swollen muscles needed. "Can you stand a high concentration of ice?" I asked our youngster, because this method had not been tried before. "I'll try anything," he replied, and within four days, he was back taking his turn in the starting rotation.

I kept this treatment in mind when I arrived in Brooklyn, but I did not force it on anyone. We had some excellent pitchers—Carl Erskine, Sal Maglie, and Don Newcombe—who were set in their ways and not interested in changing their regimens. But we also had a southpaw "bonus baby" on the team, a promising but wild pitcher who had to stay on the roster because the baseball rules at the time required any player who had received a sufficiently large bonus to remain on the major league squad. The few times this left-hander pitched, his elbow swelled up considerably. I asked him if he could tolerate ice, and he nodded. The struggling left-hander's name was Sandy Koufax.

Sandy went on to great success in Los Angeles and ultimately entered the Hall of Fame, and so ice treatment has become very popular. It obviously cannot make you a better pitcher, but it clearly can provide relief for the aching elbow and shoulder. Of course, every individual is different. Charlie Moss recalls that when Ferguson Jenkins pitched for the Boston Red Sox, that great right-hander never used ice or anything after a game; he just showered and went home.

Sandy Koufax, on the other hand, not only tolerated a lot of ice on his elbow but could withstand a considerable amount of heat, too. Using heat as a pregame loosening modality can be traced to Koufax also. Sandy retired after the 1966 World Series because of the pain from traumatic arthritis in his elbow. It is only speculation, but his career might well have been extended if only the great advances of sports medicine had been available in the sixties.

For instance, arthroscopic surgery has been very common in the last decade. The arthroscope is a compact instrument equipped with both a minicamera and needles. Arthroscopy serves both to diagnose and correct through surgery, with remarkably quick recovery time. It is possible that an arthroscope could have removed from Sandy Koufax's elbow the bone spurs that arthritis had caused, and thus enabled him to continue his outstanding career.

In 1974 I was fortunate to be a participant in another great advance in sports medicine, the historic tendon transplant operation on Tommy John's left elbow. I remember vividly that day of the 1974 season when Tommy hesitated before throwing a pitch and then, one pitch later, walked off the mound disconsolately, knowing he had incurred a severe injury. Dr. Frank Jobe, team physician of the Los Angeles Dodgers, then performed an operation that took a tendon from Tommy's right forearm and placed it in his left (pitching) elbow. The operation had been done on nonathletes before, but never had a highly ranked professional athlete had such surgery on such a vital part of his anatomy.

We were operating in uncharted waters and therefore proceeded slowly with rehabilitation. Sixteen weeks after the surgery, Tommy John first tried to throw a baseball. His left hand was so weak that his fingers were taped together just so he could hold the baseball. His first throws were so meager that his wife, Sally, could catch him without a glove.

Then, as his strength grew slowly back, he encountered a setback that may, in hindsight, have been a blessing in disguise. Calcium had built up where the tendon had been inserted in the left elbow, and began to impinge on the ulnar nerve. Tommy underwent a second operation to reposition the nerve and to aid the process by which the tendon was being transformed into a functioning ligament in the elbow. After another seven months of inactivity, Tommy resumed his rehabilitation under the guidance of myself and my colleague Jack Homel. Never had I had a harder-working or more determined patient than Tommy John. Barely eighteen months after the surgery, he was ready to resume his career, which has seen him remain a consistent winner in the big leagues at the age of 44. I cannot think of a better example than Tommy John's recovery to show you what sports medicine and hard work can do together.

Many players have now had the "Tommy John operation" and come back. Having had his excellent career with the Houston Astros curtailed by elbow problems, Joe Sambito underwent the transplant operation and has worked his way back into the bullpen corps of the Boston Red Sox. Rehabilitation is now much faster since we know where we are going. Brian Holton, a pitcher with the Los Angeles Dodgers, had the operation and was throwing from a mound within six months. In the elbow rehabilitation exercises that follow shortly in this chapter, Paul Molitor of the Milwaukee Brewers will be one of our models. Paul is the first position player so far who has worked his way back to proficiency in the major leagues after the transplant operation. Paul electrified the baseball world in 1987 with one of the longest consecutive-game hitting streaks in history, 39 games.

What wonders then have I seen in sports medicine! I have seen tendons transplanted into ligaments. I have seen dyes injected into joints (arthrograms), which enables tissue damage to be assessed through leakage detected in X-ray photography. And I have seen the emergence of arthroscopy, the procedure that can both diagnose and surgically eliminate muscle damage. With arthroscopic knee operations, for instance, a player can be home without hospitalization and without the need for crutches! Often, only a Band-Aid indicates that you even had an operation.

It is an amazing world of progress in today's sports medicine, but I think that every doctor and trainer would agree that the optimal situation for any player is to never need surgery at all. A continuing theme of this book should be repeated here: *If you learn proper form and mechanics in your general and sport-specific athletic skills, you may never need surgery and rehabilitation.* If you follow faithfully the strength and flexibility exercises in this book and maintain your skills in hitting and throwing, you may never need to undergo the tedious process of rehabilitation.

But injuries are inevitable in any sport. Even though baseball is not as consistently violent as football or basketball, there are times when immovable objects and irresistible forces collide. Injury results, and most doctors and trainers will tell you that players, like other human beings, do not immediately accept their fate. There is a sequence of emotions from denial to anger to depression. Ultimately, the athlete comes to the final and most realistic stage, acceptance, and then he is ready to face the consequences: enforced rest or surgery, and then rehabilitation and strengthening.

In the rehabilitation exercises and explanations that follow, we spend a lot of time on the shoulder and the elbow, because the repetitive act of throwing is the greatest source of wear and tear and of injury in baseball. Pitchers suffer the greatest stress because of the number of pitches they must throw and the added complication of throwing off an elevated pitching mound. In the infrequent times that an outfielder throws a ball during a game, he can wind up without the hindrance of a mound and can even somersault forward after he releases the ball. A pitcher has no such luxury.

So let us find about how the pros "bounce back," using their resources of grit and determination to hasten their return to the field of action. You will find the rehabilitation exercises are very similar to the ones we have shown you in earlier chapters on flexibility, strength training, and maintenance. *The one difference is that they must be repeated over and over again to build up the strength in the recovering area as well as in all the adjoining muscle groups.* Having said my piece as the most veteran baseball trainer, I hand you over to the youngest head trainer in the American League, Tommy Craig of the Toronto Blue Jays, who will be your first guide into the world of rehabilitation in today's baseball.

Throughout this book, we have tried to show you the many components of fitness for baseball—from flexibility and strength work to proper nutrition. Baseball's demands on the body are enormous. It is almost impossible to go through a season without some aches and pains or some injury, hopefully a minor one. The key to keeping your problems to a minimum is a high level of conditioning.

In this chapter, I and my colleagues John Adam, head trainer of the Milwaukee Brewers, and Rick Griffin, head trainer of the Seattle Mariners, are going to demonstrate exercises to keep you fit and sharp in four key joints of the baseball player's body: the shoulder, the elbow, the knee, and the ankle. In most cases, these exercises will be the same whether you are trying to maintain muscle strength or are coming back from an injury or surgery. *The only variations will be in the number of repetitions and number of sets of these exercises that you will do in a given day.* This will depend on whether you are idle, on a throwing program, or are still pitching actively.

If you are a recuperating player, your physician will advise you when to begin a guarded exercise program to restrengthen the muscles before you return to throwing. *The worst thing that can happen to an impatient athlete eager to return to the playing field is to go too fast in his rehabilitation and thereby have a recurrence of injury and reduce his recovery chances.* On the other hand, one of the major changes in rehabilitation in recent years has been the quickness in returning a player to exercise and then a supervised interval throwing program. With a reduced period of inactivity, your muscle groups will have less chance to atrophy. So once the pain and soreness are gone after surgery, it is in your interest to begin rehabilitation quickly.

Another general principle in rehabilitation is to make sure to work all the muscles around the particular joint or the site of surgery. For instance, a surgically repaired elbow joint often comes back more stable than it was before surgery, but all the muscle groups surrounding the elbow must be restrengthened to offer more stability to the repaired ligament, which cannot be restrengthened. Similarly, hamstrings and quadriceps may be weak after a knee is surgically repaired. *The principle of maintaining muscle balance is vital to both injury prevention and rehabilitation.*

Here is an example of the difference in exercise between a recuperating player and a normally conditioned player. On an off-day a healthy pitcher might perform one or two sets of 10 to 15 repetitions of shoulder exercises with small weights (two to five pounds) twice a day. A reliever might do the same exercises after the game on a day that he did not pitch. A pitcher working his way back from arm surgery might do the same exercises three times a day—morning, noon, and night—starting with 3 sets of 10, and progressing up to 8 to 10 sets, according to his strength, the time available, and his fatigue point.

There is no doubt that rehabilitation from an injury can be a drawn-out and boring process. The exercises may be tedious, but if you want to return to the field quickly and soundly, *they must be done*. And if you want to remain injury free, they must be done consistently for the remainder of your career.

THE SHOULDER

The ultimate goal for a healthy shoulder is to be able to perform, on a regular basis, exercises with small weights. But before you are ready for weight work, you must have regained your full range of motion. A good way to accomplish this is to perform a series of six range-of-motion stretches. These stretches are designed for the postsurgical patient and are commonly performed by the player who, weak after an operation, is having trouble simply lifting his arm over his head. A small, weighted bat can help the recovering player regain some motion at first. Then he should start the following stretches without assistance.

Faithfully doing these exercises should enable the player to regain his normal range of motion within 7 to 10 days. He should then be ready, with his doctor's approval, to go on to some strengthening exercises and the weight work pictured in this chapter. *But let pain be your guide.* Do not force your way through any of these stretches because you may suffer a relapse and find your return to action delayed.

RANGE-OF-MOTION STRETCHES

1. Circumduction   Lean over with your involved arm hanging straight down and your other arm on the table. *Be relaxed.* Moving your body, let your arm swing in clockwise and counterclockwise ovals, forward and backward, and side to side. Do at least one minute every hour you are awake.

2. Supine Flexions   Lie on your back. Grip a small hammer or sawed-off baseball bat fragment (one to three pounds) in both hands with elbows straight. Bring both arms over your head as far as possible and hold for a five count. Return to starting position. Ten repetitions three times per day.

3. Supine External Rotation   Lie on your back on the table with the involved arm out to the side at 90 degrees and the elbow at 90 degrees to the table. Use the hammer (or bat) to push the arm straight back into external rotation. Hold for a five count. Relax and repeat. Ten repetitions three times a day. Repeat this at a 135-degree abduction and at full abduction.

4. Supine Internal Rotations   Lie on your back on the table with the involved arm out to the side at 90 degrees and the elbow at 90 degrees to the table. Use the hammer (or bat) to push the arm straight into internal rotation. (Abduction beyond 90 degrees to 135 degrees is not possible in internal rotation.) Hold for a five count. Relax and repeat. Ten repetitions three times a day.

5. Supine Abductions   Lie on your back on the floor with your involved arm out to the side as far as possible and externally rotated as far as possible. With a hammer or sawed-off bat held in the right (or injured) hand, slide that arm along the floor as close to the ear as possible. Use the left (or well) hand to help pull the injured arm or hammer. Hold for a five count. Relax and repeat. Ten repetitions three times a day.

6. Rope and Pulley   The rope and pulley should be in a doorway with the hook in one corner of the door jamb. Sit in a chair with your back against the door jamb under the pulley. Clasp the handles of the pulley.

a. With elbow straight, raise your arm out to the front using your muscles. When you have it as high as possible, then assist by pulling on the rope. Take your arm as high as possible, hold for a five count, then lower the arm using as much muscle power as possible. Repeat with three sets of 10 repetitions.

b. With elbow straight and *arm out to the side* and palm facing upward, repeat with three sets of 10 repetitions.

To reiterate the important point about rehabilitation, stengthening, and any fitness exercise, it is best to start with a few correctly performed sets and repetitions and then move upward to more sets and repetitions, especially for the rehabilitating player.

Once your range of motion has been restored, you should be cleared by your doctor to begin weight work. One of our models for shoulder exercises is Mark Eichhorn, an outstanding relief pitcher for the Toronto Blue Jays, who spent over a year recovering from arm trouble in the minor leagues. Although Mark never needed surgery, he had pain in the shoulder when throwing overhand and developed a weakness and imbalance of strength in the front and back musculature. First, he had to restrengthen his complete shoulder girdle, both front and back, including his rotator cuff muscles. Once he was strong, he corrected and adjusted his throwing mechanics, changing from an "over-the-top" style to a side-arm and occasionally "submarine" delivery. He has established himself as an outstanding major league pitcher.

He repeats these exercises one or two times a day during the regular season and often three times every other day during the off-season. (The off-day is important; it allows normal recuperation from the exercises.) These exercises take only 15 to 20 minutes for the entire program—it is time well spent. The weights are light—at most five pounds, with three pounds acceptable, and one pound or even less as a start for a recuperating player.

Remember! As in all the exercises we have discussed in this book, proper form and technique is more important than quantity of weight. We use light weights with two to five sets of 10 to 15 repetitions two or thee times daily—which, especially for the shoulder, is a good imitation of the demanding work of pitching. Emphasis should be placed on low weight and high repetition in doing these programs, because this is equal to a 5¼-ounce baseball being thrown many, many times in a game, not to mention in an entire baseball season.

I call the following exercises "The Essential Six," because they are the basic movements that every rehabilitating and healthy player must perform to maintain optimum throwing condition. There are well over a dozen positions from which to exercise the shoulder, but if you are faithful with these six, you will maximize your physical condition and minimize your chance for injury. Our models are Mark Eichhorn, under my supervision, and Robin Yount, center fielder of the Milwaukee Brewers, who has recovered from two operations on his throwing shoulder to reassert his star status. Robin is under the supervision of John Adam, head trainer of the Milwaukee Brewers. Neither Eichhorn nor Yount need be reminded about performing these exercises day in and day out. But even before you get hurt, or to avoid getting injured, learn these exercises now.

"THE ESSENTIAL SIX" SHOULDER EXERCISES

1. Shoulder Abductions with Internal Rotation   This exercise is sometimes called the "empty can" exercise because the motion of the small weight (from zero to five pounds, depending on the player's condition) is like the motion of pouring out water from a can. Standing, start with the weight at your side, thumb down. Move your arm inward about 30 degrees (or about 2 inches away from the seam of your uniform pant leg.) Lift the weight to eye level; then lower slowly down to the side. This exercise isolates the supraspinatus, the most important of the rotator cuff muscles. Pitchers and everyday players both do these vital exercises.

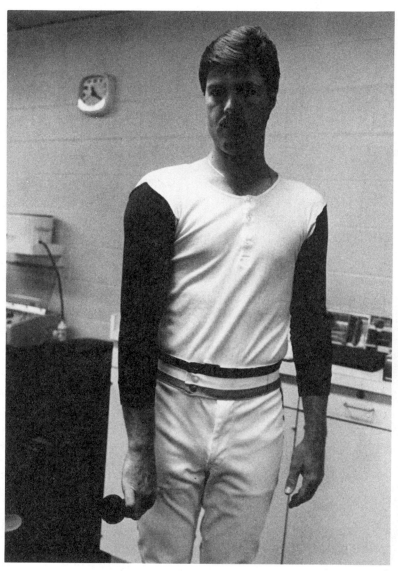

"The Essential Six" shoulder exercises, no. 1: shoulder abduction with internal rotation; starting position, thumb down and weight at pant seam. Mark Eichhorn. On location: Exhibition Stadium, Toronto, Canada, June 1987. (Fred Thornhill)

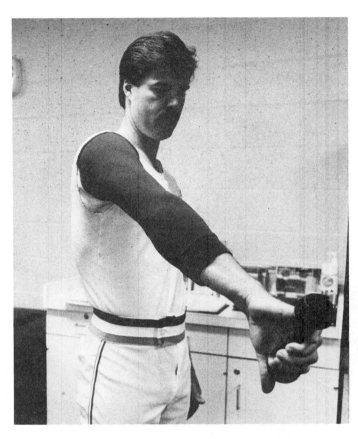

Shoulder abduction with internal rotation, arm moving away from the side to the front of the body, 15 to 30 degrees, with arm internally rotated. Mark Eichhorn. On location: Exhibition Stadium, June 1987. (Fred Thornhill)

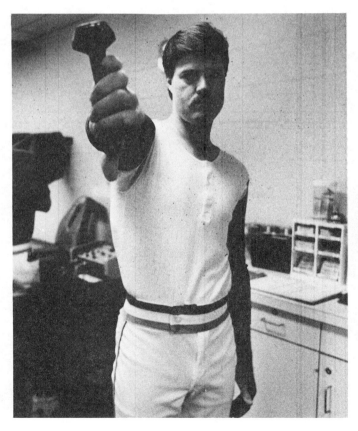

Shoulder abduction with internal rotation; peak position, arm up near shoulder height, internally rotated about 15 degrees. Mark Eichhorn. On location: Exhibition Stadium, June 1987. (Fred Thornhill) This exercise is the most important of the essential six because it works the major rotator-cuff muscle, the supraspinatus.

2. Shoulder Abductions   Standing, start with the weight at your side, thumb down. Raise the arm out to the side of the body to shoulder level, rotating the arm externally as you raise it overhead. Hold for a three to five count; then lower slowly, with a controlled movement, rolling into the thumb-down position. Do two or three sets of 10 to 15 repetitions, two or three times a day; add reps/sets according to how often you are playing and how strong you feel.

"The Essential Six" shoulder exercises, no. 2: shoulder abduction; starting position, thumb down and weight at pant seam. Mark Eichhorn. On location: Exhibition Stadium, June 1987. (Fred Thornhill)

Shoulder abduction, arm moving up and out to side of body. Mark Eichhorn. On location: Exhibition Stadium, June 1987. (Fred Thornhill)

Shoulder abduction, arm rotated externally up to shoulder level. Mark Eichhorn. On location: Exhibition Stadium, June 1987. (Fred Thornhill)

Shoulder abduction, thumb turned up in preparation for final movement. Mark Eichhorn. On location: Exhibition Stadium, June 1987. (Fred Thornhill)

Shoulder abduction, final position, arm extended overhead. Mark Eichhorn. On location: Exhibition Stadium, June 1987. (Fred Thornhill)

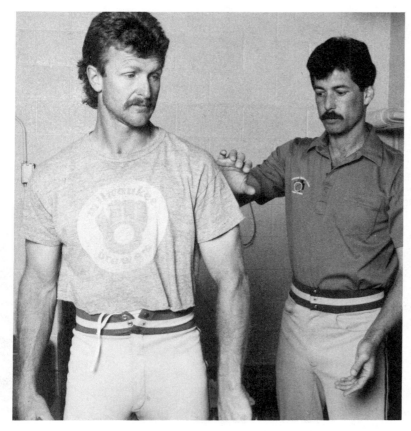

Shoulder abduction (alternate sequence), starting position. Robin Yount, Milwaukee Brewers centerfielder, with weight in nonthrowing hand; supervised by John Adam, Milwaukee Brewers head trainer. On location: Compadre Stadium, spring training home of the Milwaukee Brewers, Chandler, Arizona, March 1987. (V. J. Lovero)

Shoulder abduction, arm brought out about 15 to 30 degrees from the side, with trainer isolating shoulder to make sure it is being exercised. Robin Yount and John Adam. On location: Compadre Stadium, March 1987. (V. J. Lovero)

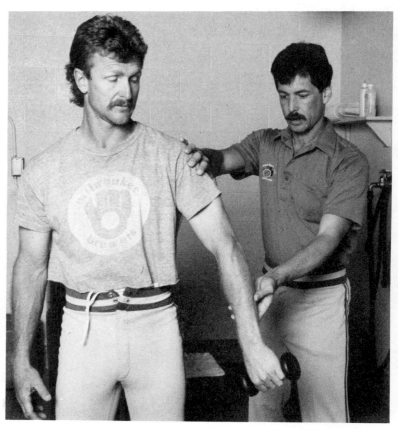

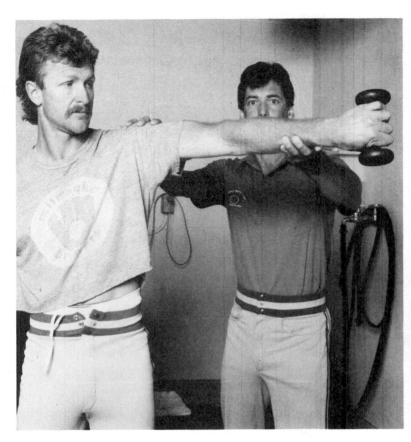

Shoulder abduction, arm rotated internally to shoulder level, with trainer checking on proper form. Robin Yount and John Adam. On location: Compadre Stadium, March 1987. (V. J. Lovero)

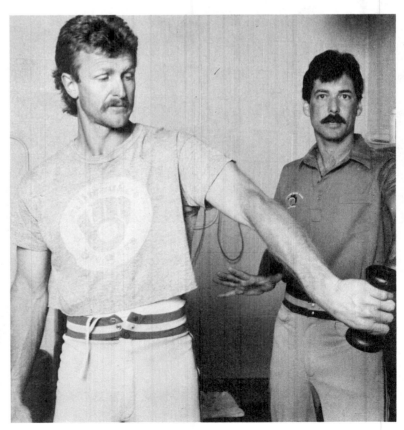

Shoulder abduction, return toward starting position, thumb down and arm brought about 30 degrees from the side. Robin Yount and John Adam. On location: Compadre Stadium, March 1987. (V. J. Lovero)

3. External Rotations and Abductions (Prone) Lying facedown on the table, hang your throwing arm down over the edge of the table with the weight held thumb up. Raise the arm 30 degrees into abduction with the thumb up, pointing toward and passing the ear. Lower slowly to the starting point with the arm hanging down to the floor. This exercise works another key rotator cuff muscle, the infraspinatus.

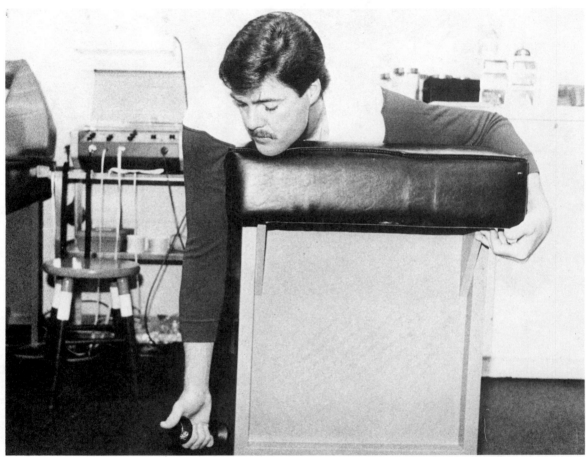

"The Essential Six" shoulder exercises, no. 3: external rotation and abduction (prone); starting position, lying on stomach, arm with weight hanging down off side of table, thumb up. Mark Eichhorn. On location: Exhibition Stadium, Toronto, Canada, June 1987. (Fred Thornhill)

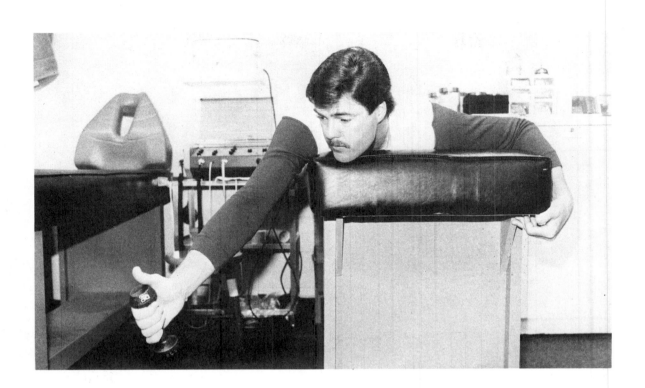

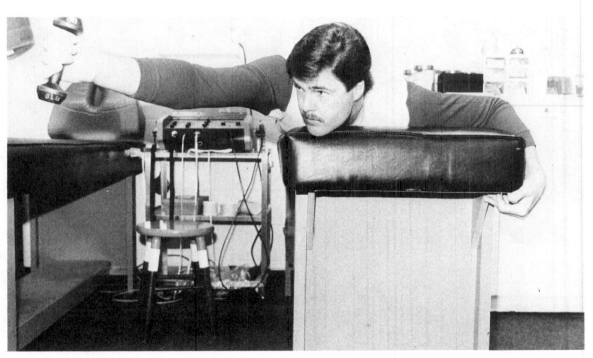

External rotation and abduction (prone), arm brought into 100-degree abduction, passing ear. Mark Eichhorn. On location: Exhibition Stadium, June 1987. (Fred Thornhill)

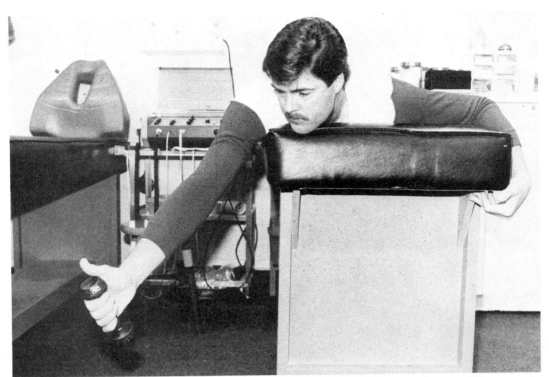

External rotation and abduction (prone), return route to starting position, at about 30 degrees abduction. Mark Eichhorn. On location: Exhibition Stadium, June 1987. (Fred Thornhill)

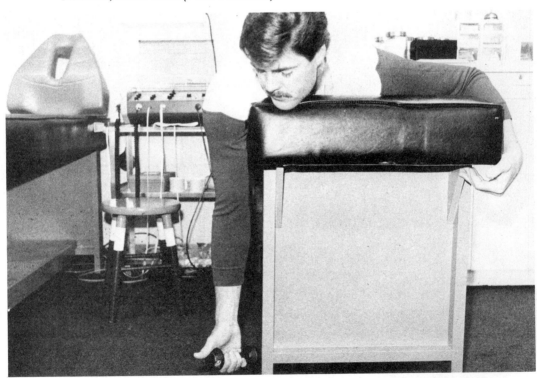

External rotation and abduction (prone), return to starting position. Mark Eichhorn. On location: Exhibition Stadium, June 1987. (Fred Thornhill)

4. External Rotations—Cocking of Arm while Prone   Lie prone on the table. With the forearm extended over the edge of the table at a 90-degree angle and the elbow flush on the edge for maximum support, lift the weight into external rotation. Slowly return to the starting position. External rotation is the most difficult exercise for baseball players, and it is usually saved for last in a series of exercises. It can also be done on the side, as Robin Yount demonstrates.

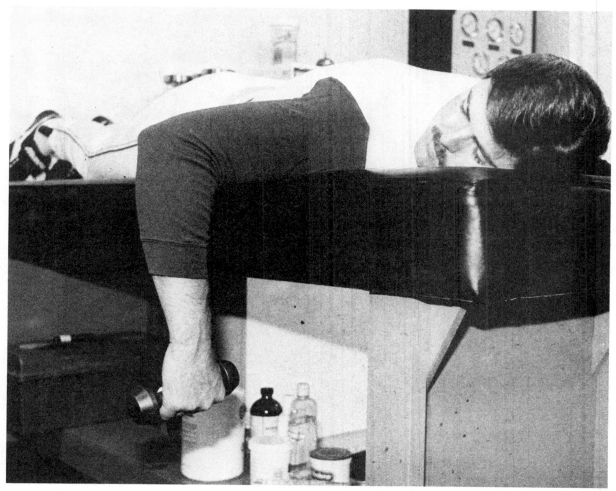

"The Essential Six" shoulder exercises, no. 4: external rotation (cocking of arm, prone); starting position, lying on stomach, arm with weight hanging down while supported at the elbow on the edge of the table. Mark Eichhorn. On location: Exhibition Stadium, June 1987. (Fred Thornhill)

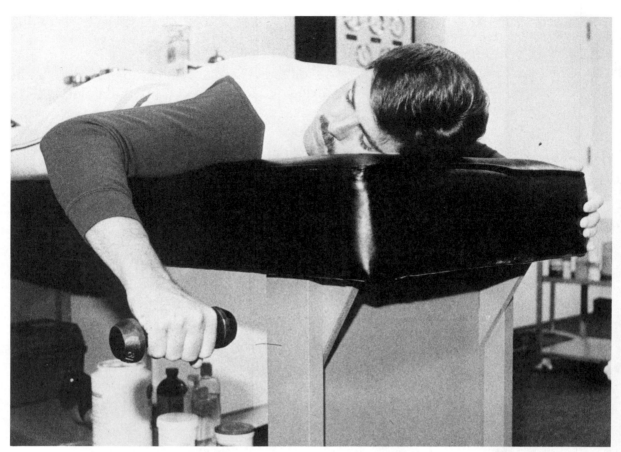

External rotation (cocking of arm, prone), slow movement into external rotation. Mark Eichhorn. On location: Exhibition Stadium, June 1987. (Fred Thornhill)

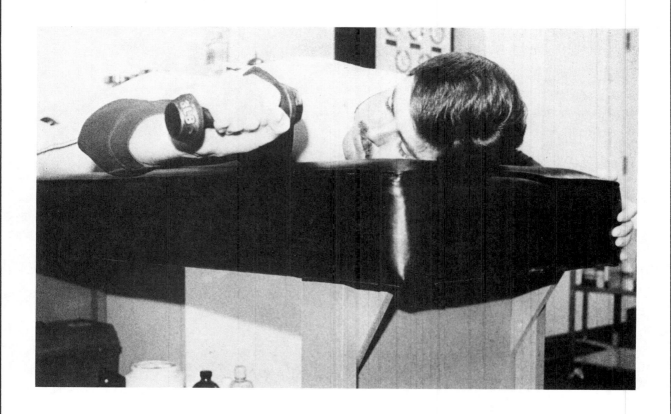

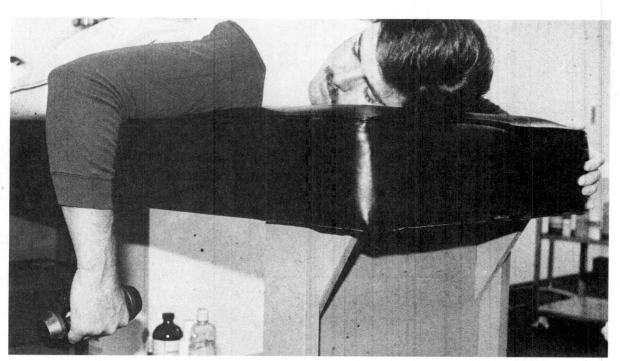

External rotation (cocking of arm, prone), back at starting position. On location: Exhibition Stadium, June 1987. (Fred Thornhill)

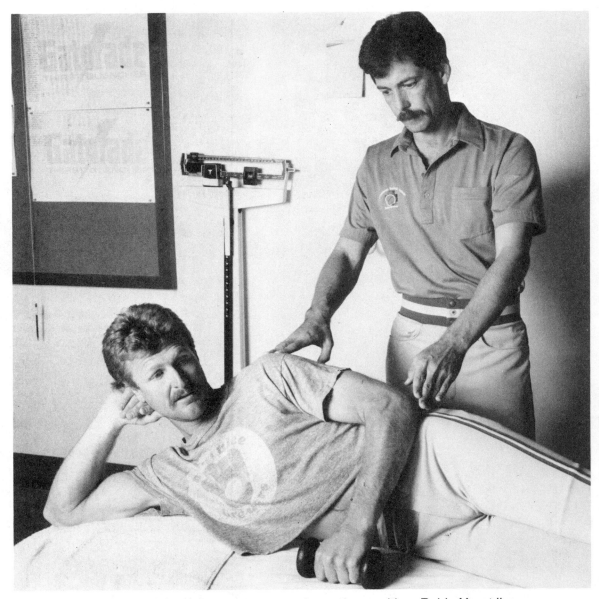

External rotation (alternate sequence), starting position. Robin Yount lies on his side on the table, his elbow supported on his hip, with weighted hand on table as John Adam supervises. On location: Compadre Stadium, Chandler, Arizona, March 1987. (V. J. Lovero)

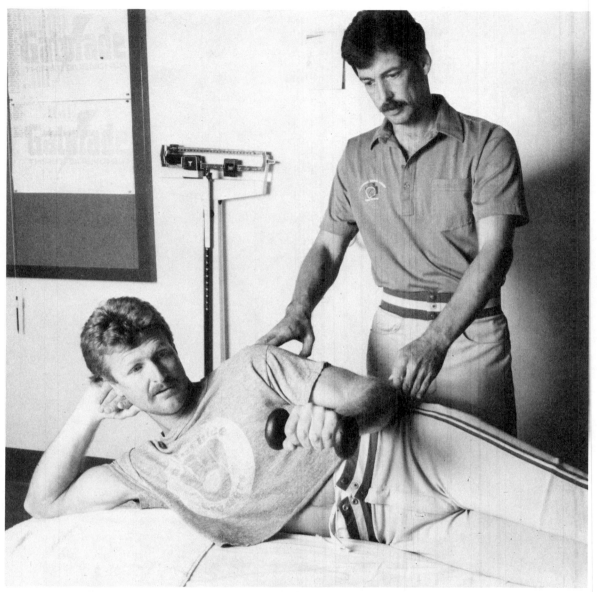

External rotation, weight brought parallel to table. Robin Yount and John Adam. On location: Compadre Stadium, March 1987. (V. J. Lovero)

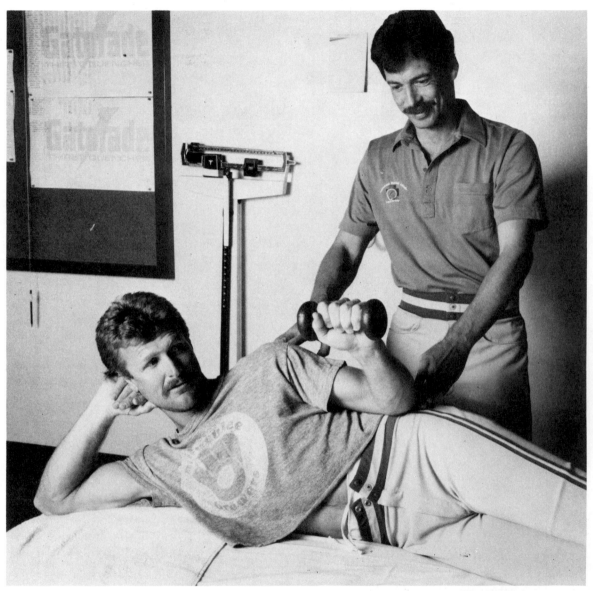

External rotation, peak position, weight not quite 90 degrees to table. Robin Yount and John Adam. On location: Compadre Stadium, March 1987. (V. J. Lovero) This is a humbling exercise, and the weight is usually under five pounds. It works the external rotator-cuff muscles, especially the teres minor.

5. Prone Horizontal Abductions   Lying prone on the table with the involved arm hanging straight to the floor, raise the arm out to the side, thumb up to eye level. Hold for a good three count; then lower and relax. This exercise works all the rotator cuff muscles to some extent.

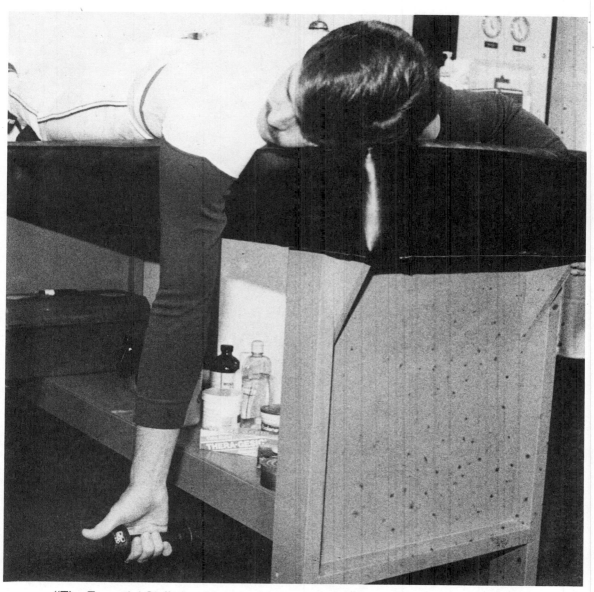

"The Essential Six" shoulder exercises, no. 5: prone horizontal abduction; starting position, lying on stomach with the involved arm hanging straight to the floor, thumb facing out. Mark Eichhorn. On location: Exhibition Stadium, Toronto, Canada, June 1987. (Fred Thornhill)

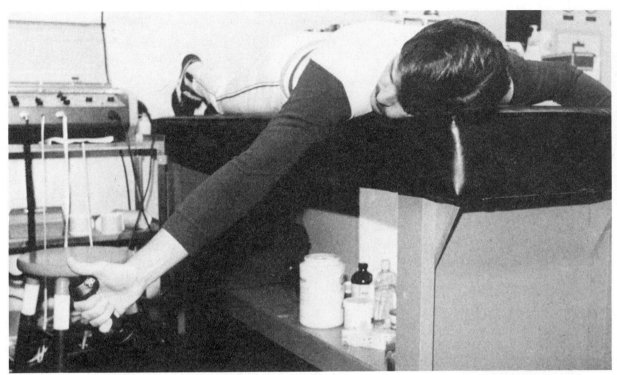

Prone horizontal abduction, weight brought out to side and up. Mark Eichhorn. On location: Exhibition Stadium, June 1987. (Fred Thornhill)

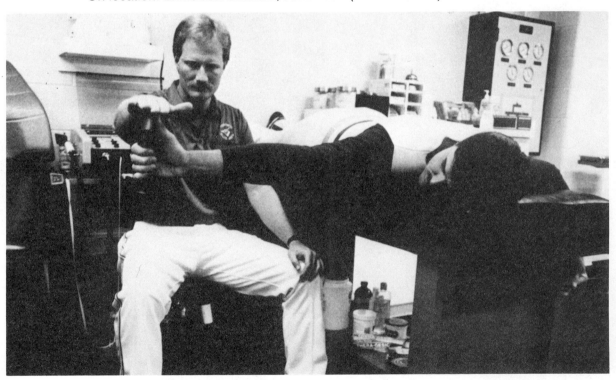

Prone horizontal abduction, final position, weight brought up about 90 degrees. Mark Eichhorn and Tommy Craig, Toronto Blue Jays head trainer, make sure that the weight does not come too high, which would cause the arm to lose stability. On location: Exhibition Stadium, June 1987. (Fred Thornhill)

6. External Rotations with Extension   Lying prone on the table, raise the involved arm to the ceiling, toward the back (posteriorly). Hold for a good three count; then lower to the starting point. This exercise works primarily the teres minor muscle.

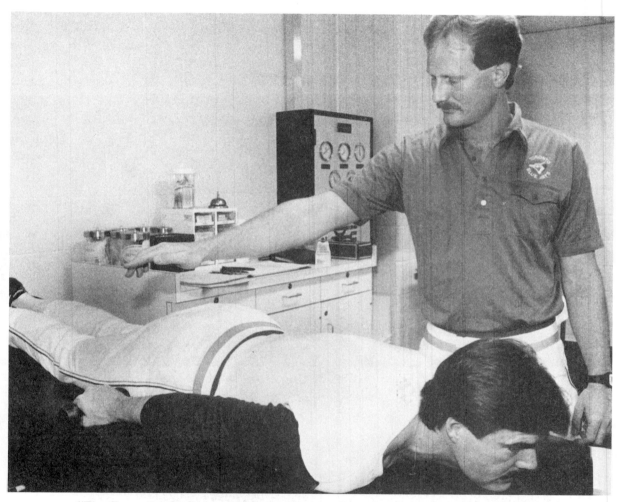

"The Essential Six" shoulder exercises, no. 6: external rotation with extension; starting position, lying prone with arm on table, weight at pant seam. Mark Eichhorn and Tommy Craig. On location: Exhibition Stadium, June 1987. (Fred Thornhill)

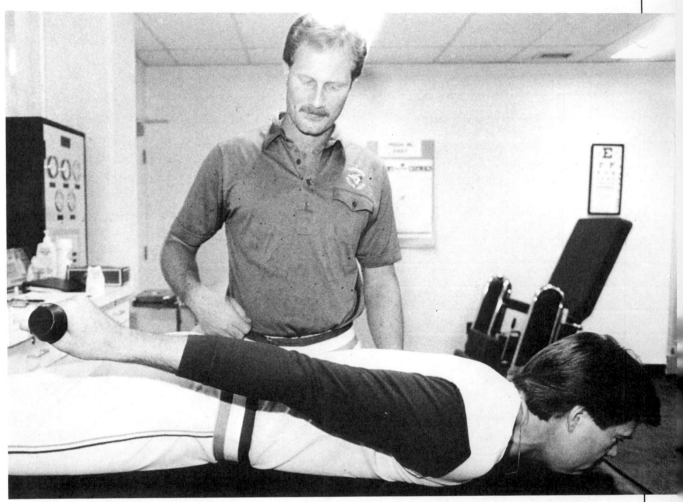

External rotation with extension, arm beginning posterior rise toward ceiling.
Mark Eichhorn and Tommy Craig. On location: Exhibition Stadium, June 1987.
(Fred Thornhill)

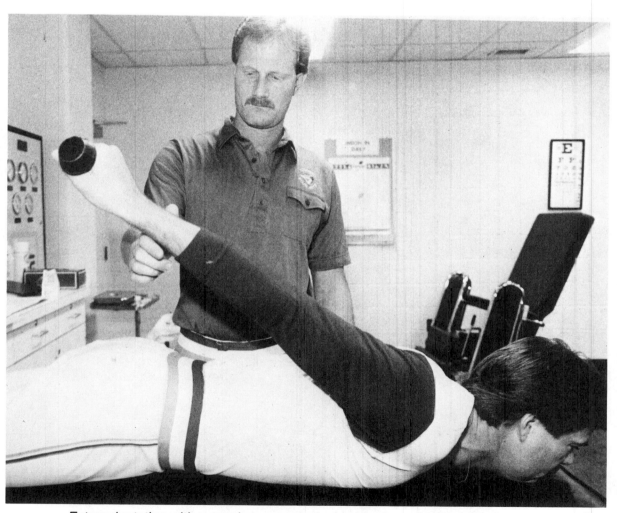

External rotation with extension, arm continuing rise toward ceiling. Mark Eichhorn and Tommy Craig. On location: Exhibition Stadium, June 1987. (Fred Thornhill)

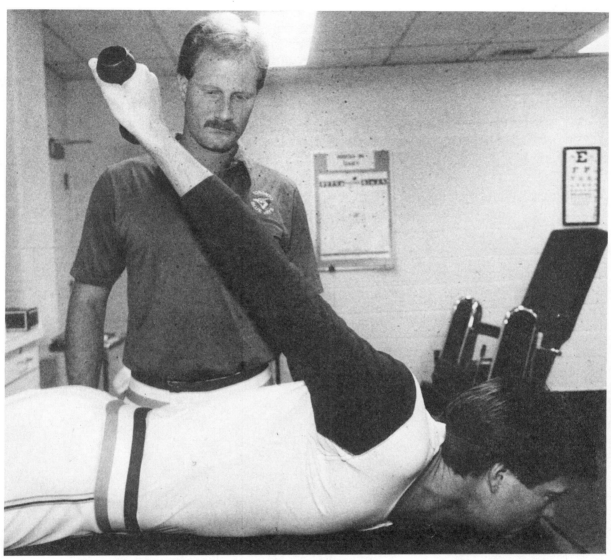

External rotation with extension, final position, arm about 45 degrees up. Mark Eichhorn and Tommy Craig. On location: Exhibition Stadium, June 1987. (Fred Thornhill) The arm should be lowered slowly and carefully in all these prone exercises.

If you run into pain or complications, alter the program by resting more often, doing the program every other day and/or reducing the number of sets until the arm feels good again. Allow more recovery time between workouts if necessary.

When doing "The Essential Six" as a maintenance program, frequency and amount depend strictly on the player's regular work schedule and the amount of exercise he wants to do in addition to that. A starting pitcher knows when he will pitch in most cases, but a reliever does not. Two or three sets of 10 with three to five pounds twice daily for starters is ideal; once a day is sufficient.

For the reliever, one set of 10 to 15 with three to five pounds is recommended before the game, and possibly a second set of 10 to 15 of each exercise after the game, if he did not pitch that day.

Once "The Essential Six" shoulder exercises have been performed, there are additional strengthening exercises which can be performed—without weights at first and then with weights added.

1. Shoulder Shrugs   Stand with your arms by your side. Lift your shoulders straight up to your ears, hold for a two count, then pull your shoulders back and pinch shoulder blades for a two count. Relax the shoulders. Do 5 to 10 repetitions three times a day. Start with no weight in your hands and gradually work up to five pounds.

2. Shoulder Flexions   Stand and raise your arm out to the front of your body as high as possible. Hold for a two count and then lower the arm. Do 5 to 10 repetitions three times a day, starting with no weight and working up to five pounds.

3. Shoulder Abductions   Stand and raise your arm out to the side of the body as high as possible while rotating the arm externally. Hold for a two count, and then lower the arm. As before, do 5 to 10 repetitions three times a day, starting with no weight and working up to five pounds.

4. Prone Horizontal Abductions   Lie on the table on your stomach, with the involved arm hanging straight to the floor. Raise your arm out to the side. Hold for a two count, lower the arm, and relax. Do 5 to 10 repetitions three times a day, starting with no weight and progressing up to five pounds.

5. Internal Rotations   These exercises should not be neglected, even though the internal rotators are the strongest shoulder muscles because of their constant use in the act of throwing. John Adam, head trainer of the Milwaukee Brewers, demonstrates a basic internal rotation exercise using a weight under five pounds. As in the other exercises, this can be done at first without weight.

All these shoulder exercises can be supplemented by work with Theraband, a flexible rubber substitute the easy pliability of which is demonstrated by Mark Eichhorn. Rubber bands of double strength can also be used, as well as rubber tubing of varying strength, which, when equipped with handles, can be attached on one end to a stationary object like a doorknob and held on the other end. All the motions of internal and external rotation exercise can be performed by these devices. They have many advantages: They are inexpensive, easy to handle, and can be used without a trainer—at home, during travel, or at leisure moments at work.

Theraband exercises especially strengthen the posterior muscles of the shoulder, muscles which need special attention because they decelerate the arm once the ball has been released. These muscles are very much like the parachute on the back of a dragster; therefore, the stress of throwing is greater in this area, and any exercise to strengthen this region is especially valuable.

THE ELBOW

The principle of elbow rehabilitation and maintenance of elbow strength is the same as for the shoulder and the other key joints in the body. If you are recovering from surgery, you must do more repetitions of the exercises throughout the day. If you are seeking to keep your strength, you can cut down on the number of series that you perform, but as always, you must show proper form and technique in these exercises. It is a cliché that if you practice poorly, you will play poorly. It is equally true for exercise. If you get into bad habits with rehabilitative or strengthening exercises, you will find that good technique will fail you on the diamond. And the elbow is an extremely important and active part of throwing the baseball. It must be kept up over the shoulder level in the cocking and acceleration stages of throwing, and then it comes down sharply in the deceleration stage.

Here is a 10-exercise program for maintaining the elbow. You will recognize a couple of the exercises from the maintenance chapter of this book, but as I have stressed, there is a fine line between maintenance and rehabilitation work. The more familiar you become with these exercises, the better conditioned an athlete you will be, and the more able to perform your great skills with consistency and longevity.

1. Deep Friction Massage   Deep transverse friction massage across the area of elbow that is sore. Five minutes three times a day. (See the Jeff Cooper massage in chapter 7.)

2. Grip   Grip therapeutic putty, which we have found is better than a rubber ball or other hand- and arm-strengthening devices. Use as continuously as possible all day long. The motion works the hand through a full gripping procedure, making for stronger extrinsic muscles in the hands as well as in the forearm muscle groups. We need not belabor how important a strong grip is to someone who makes a living swinging a baseball bat. (See John Fierro's explanation in chapter 7.)

3. Extensor Stretch   This stretch of the arm is performed by flexing the wrist. Straighten the elbow completely. With the palm facing down, grasp the back the hand and push the wrist down and back as far as possible. Hold for a 10 count. Release. Do 25 repetitions three times daily.

Wrist extensor stretch, working forearm flexors. Tommy Craig. On location: Englebert complex, March 1987. (Tom DiPace)

4. Flexor Stretch   This stretch of the arm is performed by extending the wrist. Straighten the elbow completely. With the palm facing up, grasp the middle of the hand and thumb and push the wrist down and back as far as possible. Hold for a 10 count. Release. Do 25 repetitions three times daily.

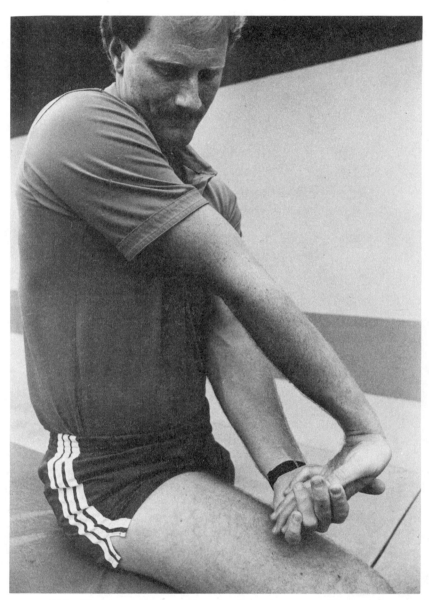

Wrist flexor stretch, working forearm extensors. Tommy Craig. On location: Englebert complex, Dunedin, Florida, March 1987. (Tom DiPace)

5. Wrist Curls   The forearm should be supported, palm facing upward. Using a one- to five-pound weight or hammer, lower the hand as far as possible and then raise it up as high as possible. The advantage of a hammer is that its weight is at the end and thus builds up the inner elbow, the area where most injuries occur. Do three sets of 10 to 15 repetitions two or three times daily. Increase the weight according to progress in strengthening and the purpose of the exercise. To repeat, if maintenance is the goal, increase the weight and decrease the repetitions. If rehabilitation is the goal, lower the weight or keep it steady and increase the sets and reps.

Forearm-extensor strengthening exercise, pronation (palm downward), starting position. Paul Molitor, Milwaukee Brewers infielder and designated hitter, with three-pound weight. On location: Compadre Stadium, Chandler, Arizona, March 1987. (V. J. Lovero)

6. Wrist Reverse Curls   The forearm should be supported, palm facing downward. Using a one- to five-pound hammer, lower the hand as far as possible. Hold for a two count. Do three sets of 10 to 15 repetitions two or three times daily, add weight depending on progress and purpose.

Note that Paul Molitor is sitting down in these exercises, a maneuver John Adam applauds. "He isolates the wrist better in the seated position and also builds up his biceps," John notes. "If you stand up, you unnecessarily involve other muscles, and your hips can rock and the isolation effect on the wrist is lost."

Wrist curl, forearm flexor strengthening exercise, supination (palm upward), with weight supported on thigh. Paul Molitor. On location: Compadre Stadium, March 1987. (V. J. Lovero)

7. Neutral Wrist Curls   The forearm should be supported with the wrist in neutral position. With a hammer (or sawed-off bat) held in normal hammering position, the lower wrist is brought into ulnar deviation as far as possible. Hold for a two count. Do three sets of 10 to 15 repetitions two or three times daily.

Wrist curl, forearm strengthening exercise with bar and three-pound weight, neutral position. Paul Molitor. On location: Compadre Stadium, March 1987. (V. J. Lovero)

8. Pronations   The forearm should be supported with the wrist in neutral position. Hold the hammer in normal hammering position. Roll the wrist and bring the hammer to the center line of the body as far as possible. Hold for a two count. Raise back to starting position. Do three sets of 10 to 15 repetitions two or three times daily.

Forearm pronation with weighted bar. Paul Molitor. On location: Compadre Stadium, March 1987. (V. J. Lovero)

9. Supination The forearm should be supported with the wrist in neutral position. Hold the hammer in normal hammering position. Roll the wrist, causing the hammer to go away from the midline as far as the wrist will turn. Hold for a two count. Raise back to starting position. Do three sets of 10 to 15 repetitions two or three times daily.

Forearm supination with weighted bar. Paul Molitor. On location: Compadre Stadium, March 1987. (V. J. Lovero)

10. Broomstick Curls Demonstrated in chapter 7 by power hitter Jesse Barfield of the Toronto Blue Jays.

As you can see in these elbow exercises, a lot of attention is devoted to building up the arms. This follows from the basic principle that we cannot stress enough: *You must have muscles balanced on every side of a joint.* The stronger the arm and wrist, the stronger will be the elbow. (Shortly, we will show you that a strengthened quadriceps muscle is vital for a durable and flexible knee.)

Before we turn to the lower body, there is one last program I want to share with you, an interval throwing program which, once completed, will be a sign of your readiness to return to action on a throwing mound. As I am sure you realize, the act of throwing from a pitching mound is just another complication that only a healthy hurler can manage to cope with.

The interval throwing program will help get you ready. It involves alternate-day throwing with your weight work done on the day off. This is a graduated throwing program that is designed to minimize chance of injury. As in every exercise and program in this book, follow the instructions; do not overdo the work, but on the other hand, do not cut corners with it either. And as always, *listen to your body—it will tell you when to slow down.* A dull aching at the elbow tendon is normal, but if there is either swelling or sharp pain at one of the elbow joints, stop and back off.

THE INTERVAL THROWING PROGRAM

Warm up from 45 feet with easy lob tosses. Throw 25 or 30 tosses. Rest between 5 to 15 minutes. Then throw another 25 to 30 and call it a day. The objective of this program is to throw the allotted number of pitches without pain.

After a few days of throwing without pain at this distance, you can step up to 60 feet with the same sequence: 25 to 30 throws, rest, another 25 to 30 throws. The next step is moving back to 90 feet with the same sequence; 120 feet; and 150 feet. Always, it is not hard throwing but tossing in long arcs, stretching the arm and elbow muscles out. You might start the longer tosses in center field and throw the ball to second base: first on a few bounces, then on one bounce as you get stronger, and finally you are ready for 180-foot throwing.

At 180 feet, the interval throwing program calls for 100 throws in the same sequence of 25/rest/25/rest/25/rest/25. At this stage, perhaps as quickly as three weeks after you begin the program, you should have both full strength and confidence back in your arm. You can now return to throwing from a mound and worrying again about getting hitters out instead of wondering where your next pain may be coming from.

REHABILITATING THE KNEE

Knee injuries in baseball are certainly not as common as elbow and shoulder problems, but the maintenance of this crucial joint is still a vital part of baseball conditioning. The knee is a more complicated area than many people think because it is more than a simple hinge. It also glides, slides, and rotates, and it is thus not the most stable of joints. It depends for its normal function on a lot of soft tissue structures: ligaments, tendons, cartilage, and the special cartilage-like structure within the knee called the meniscus.

Much knee rehabilitation work centers on strengthening the quadriceps muscle, the largest muscle in the entire body. Located at the front of the thigh and connecting the trunk and the leg, it is responsible for the straightening out (extension) of the knee and leg. It is called the quadriceps because it is a four-part muscle.

1. Quad Sets   The simplest of exercises, you tighten and then relax the front part of your thigh, the quadriceps, in each leg, separately. You perform these quad sets as much as 200 to 300 times a day as part of the rehabilitation. For the rehabilitating knee to regain its stability, it is vital to strengthen those muscles adjacent to it.

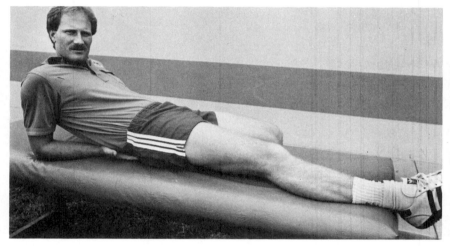

Right quadriceps set, the first exercise on the route to knee rehabilitation, right leg extended and tightened. Tommy Craig, Toronto Blue Jays head trainer. On location: Englebert complex, Dunedin, Florida, March 1987. (Tom DiPace)

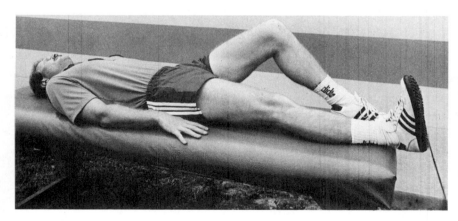

Right quadriceps set and straight-leg raise, starting position, bent left knee. Tommy Craig. On location: Englebert complex, March 1987. (Tom DiPace)

2. Hamstring Stretch   This is best done on a table with the uninvolved leg on the floor at the side of the table. With your involved leg stretched out straight slightly over the edge of the table, bring your head toward your knee and hold for several seconds. Relax and repeat. Do 10 repetitions per set, always resting briefly between repetitions. Hamstring stretches can be done periodically throughout the day in the same sequence of sets and repetitions. After surgery to a knee, the toughest movement to regain is extension; so these are important stretches. You will recognize this stretch as one frequently performed by hurdlers.

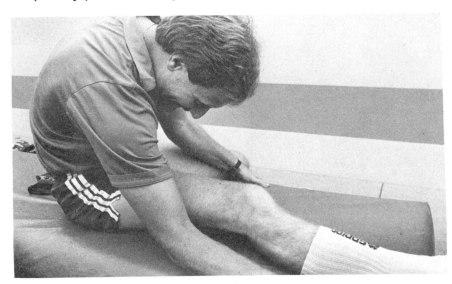

Hamstring stretch on table, head brought to knee and held for 10 to 15 seconds. Tommy Craig. On location: Englebert complex, Dunedin, Florida, March 1987. (Tom DiPace)

Quadriceps exercise (seated) with cuff weight, starting position. Tommy Craig. On location: Englebert complex, March 1987. (Tom DiPace)

Quadriceps exercise (seated) with cuff weight, peak position, leg extended straight out. Tommy Craig. On location: Englebert complex, March 1987. (Tom DiPace)

3. Hamstring Curls   Stand up against a wall with your uninvolved leg up at a right angle to the wall. Place your hands on the wall, slightly below waist level, for support. Lift your involved leg up at a right angle to the floor. Hold for 10 to 15 seconds, relax, and repeat. Perform three sets of 10 repetitions.

Hamstring curl with weight, hands held against wall for 10 to 15 seconds. On location: Englebert complex, March 1987. (Tom DiPace)

4. Straight-Leg Raises   Lying on a table (or the floor) with your head back and your uninvolved leg bent at the knee, lift your involved leg straight into the air at no more that a 45-degree angle. Keep your head back and down, and never force the leg beyond the straining zone. Relax and repeat. Do three sets of 10 leg raises with a brief rest between. Do as many sets during the day as you feel capable of performing.

Straight-leg raise, exercise position. Tommy Craig. On location: Englebert complex, March 1987. (Tom DiPace)

Straight-leg raise with ankle weight, starting position, weighted foot off end of table. Tommy Craig. On location: Englebert complex, March 1987. (Tom DiPace)

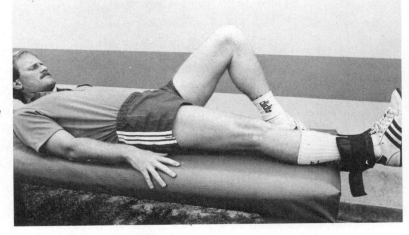

Straight-leg raise with ankle weight, peak position. Tommy Craig. On location: Englebert complex, March 1987. (Tom DiPace) This is an important exercise because leg extension is the most difficult movement to regain after knee surgery.

5. Hip Abductions   Standing, lift the involved leg slowly out to the side at approximately 45-degree abduction, and then slowly put it back down. Do three sets of 10 repetitions.

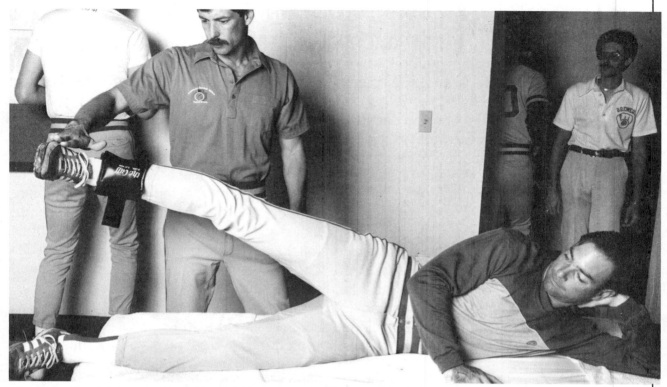

Hip abduction (pictured with cuff weight but started without weight in basic rehabilitation), peak position. Paul Molitor, Milwaukee Brewers infielder and designated hitter, under supervision of John Adam, Milwaukee Brewers head trainer. On location: Compadre Stadium, Chandler, Arizona, March 1987. (V. J. Lovero)

After 7 to 10 days of doing these four basic exercises, you should be ready to strengthen yourself further by adding cuff weights to your ankle. But never put on weights without clearance from your doctor. Once you have been given the OK, you can add weights in increments to your ankles—ranging from 2 pounds up to as much as 20 pounds. Pictured is the straight-leg raise with cuff weights. Regaining the flexion/extension movement in the leg is a crucial part of rehabilitation; so once again, do as many sets and repetitions as your strength allows.

All these exercises can be preceded by a warm-up of cardiovascular work on the exercise bicycle. You may not feel strong enough yet to do much jogging as a warm-up, but a 5- to 15-minute session on the exercise bicycle is an excellent means of getting the blood flow going in the lower body before you exercise it.

For our last rehabilitating joint, the ankle, I turn you over to John Adam of the Milwaukee Brewers. Along with Rick Griffin of the Seattle Mariners, John will show you the methods for treating acute ankle sprains and then rehabilitating them.

REHABILITATING THE ANKLE

Probably the most common lower body injury in baseball is the sprained ankle. A sprain is a disruption of the ankle ligaments; the more ligaments disturbed, the more severe the sprain.

There are so many ways in baseball to turn and sprain an ankle. You can step into a hole or on some foreign object in the outfield. You can twist it when accidentally running into a teammate or opponent. Perhaps most commonly, you can sprain your ankle landing incorrectly on a base as you attempt to beat out a hit. It is estimated that 90 percent of baseball's plays occur at first base, so it is not surprising that injuries can occur there. Many of you probably saw a national-TV "Game of the Week" in June 1987 when Ryne Sandberg, All-Star second baseman of the Chicago Cubs, severely sprained his ankle as he sprinted down the line to beat out an infield hit. Trying to avoid a collision with St. Louis first baseman Jack Clark, Sandberg landed awkwardly on the inside of first base. He spent almost a month on the disabled list before he was ready to play again.

Quick treatment of a sprained ankle can be the difference between days and weeks of playing time lost. Most of you have heard of the first aid acronym RICE— *rest*, *ice*, *compression*, and *elevation*. It applies very importantly to treating sprained ankles.

Rest. Once a player has been injured and carefully removed from the playing field, he must rest. If he has to move around at all, he must do so on crutches.

Ice. The player must place ice on the injured area four or five times a day for 15-minute periods. The ice can be easily applied with an ice pack and will reduce the swelling and the soreness—but *do not overdo it.* I have seen impatient athletes, eager to get back to action, proudly tell me that they have iced their ankle for over a half hour. Such extensive icing may actually be detrimental to healing because it can lead to frostbite. To repeat, icing four or five times a day is fine, but only for 15-minute periods.

Compression. Fasten the ice pack directly onto the swollen area to hasten the healing. In the periods when the ice is not on the ankle, compression is aided by wrapping the ankle with an old-fashioned, 3-inch-wide elastic bandage. If you do not have access to a trainer or someone knowledgeable in first aid, you can apply the bandage yourself, but it is not easy. Start with the leg outstretched; begin with the bandage at the top of your foot and work it inside, underneath the foot, back up on the outside, then across in front of the ankle and around behind it—forming a figure eight. (If the sprain is not bad, you can get by with a 1½-inch tape instead of the thicker wrap.)

Elevation. You always rest the ankle with the foot up on a chair, or some other secure resting spot. By keeping the ankle above the heart, you insure that the blood flow circulates away from the injured area.

Immediate RICE treatment on a simple ankle sprain can reduce swelling within 48 hours. You can then begin the following range-of-motion and strengthening exercises. But as in all injuries, let the pain of the player determine the progress. Ankles and feet are so important to an athlete's playing condition that it is better to be safe than sorry.

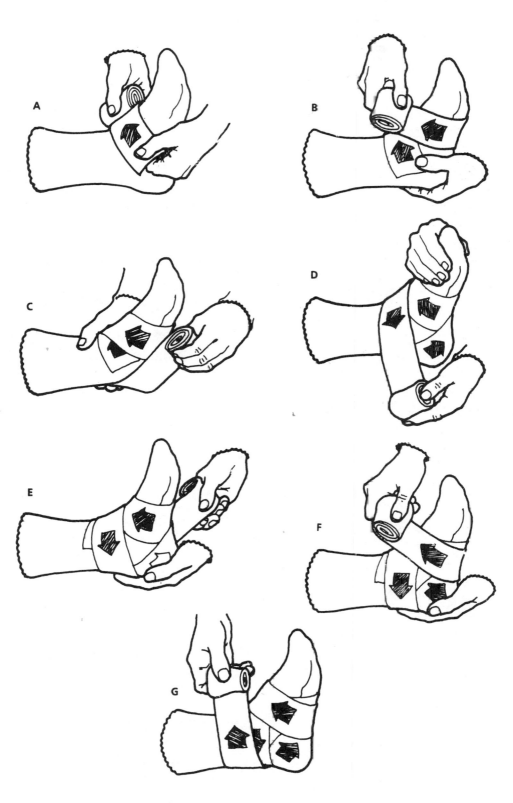

Drawing: figure-eight method of wrapping an ankle.

Alphabet Exercises   The player is seated on a chair above a whirlpool bath set at 102 degrees. He dangles his injured ankle into the water at the point where the whirlpool jet enters. In so doing, he gets both the massage effect of the jet and the circulatory effect of the warm water.

He then performs a series of exercises in which his foot "writes" the letters of the alphabet from A to Z. He repeats the alphabet several times because ankle rehabilitation is like the rehabilitation of any injured part of the body. The more repetitions and sets that you perform, the stronger you get, the sooner you are back on the playing field.

Heel Cord/Achilles Tendon Stretch   Having successfully shown full range of motion with the alphabet, you now start to strengthen the calf muscles above the ankle. This follows a basic principle that the successful rehabilitation of a joint is only possible by strengthening the adjacent muscles.

Paul Molitor demonstrates the basic heel cord stretch position. He stands against a wall with both hands placed about at shoulder height. One leg is angled back with the heel on the ground, and his front leg is bent at the knee. He holds for 15 to 20 seconds and then repeats on the alternate leg. Six repetitions with both legs, or until you feel loose.

Ankle strengthening can also be aided by wrapping a towel—or the rubber substitute, Theraband—under the foot with the leg outstretched. Hold for 10 to 15 seconds. Ten repetitions at least.

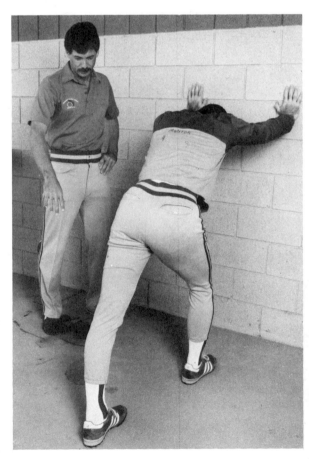

Heel cord/Achilles tendon stretch. Paul Molitor stretches out left leg with heel on ground under John Adam's watchful eye. Molitor will hold for 15 to 20 seconds and then stretch right leg. On location: Compadre Stadium, Chandler, Arizona, March 1987. (V. J. Lovero)

Once progress is evident in these preliminary strengthening exercises, it is time to move on to the manually assisted exercises (illustrated by Gene Gieselmann of the St. Louis Cardinals) and other exercises that can be done with rubber tubing (illustrated by Rick Griffin of the Seattle Mariners). Rick Griffin has studied and written about the foot of the athlete in many sports. He will now be your guide through the various manually assisted exercises that can bring an injured ankle back to normal, strengthened for the everyday grind of baseball.

The important thing about any exercise in rehabilitation is for the player to realize that the object is to strengthen the injured body part—in this case, the ankle—slowly It is *not* a competition between the trainer and the player. The goal is to increase the range of motion in the player, and the resistance offered by the trainer in these exercises is the means to that end. If the player has pain, he must admit it and back off until the pain subsides. There is no area more crucial to the athlete than his feet; so he must be honest with himself and with you. You do not want a pain to linger on indefinitely in such a vital area.

The goal in all these exercises is to work up to 20 repetitions in each set. But at first, be satisfied with 6 to 8 reps. Remember always the dictum about proper form and proper technique. Once three sets of 20 repetitions have been achieved, the player can extend the number of repetitions as part of his endurance training.

Resistive Ankle Exercises The full range of motion in the ankle must be returned before the player can be cleared for action. So, as you see, Gene places the resistance of his hand in the proper angles of movement of the ankle. The most difficult movement for the recuperating player is the dorsiflexion because the upper leg muscles atrophy quickly. The movements up and down in these resistive exercises are extremely important because that motion imitates the activity of running.

Once the player has succeeded in gaining back his full range of motion in the assisted stretches, he can move on to work with surgical tubing. The good thing about tubing is that it is flexible enough that the resistance can be increased if the player is getting stronger, or decreased if he is still not strong enough. The exercises with inexpensive tubing can be done by the player at home without any assistance. They key thing to remember in doing these exercises is to concentrate on good form and work on firing the muscles quickly. This will aid in building up the explosive power necessary to run and play baseball.

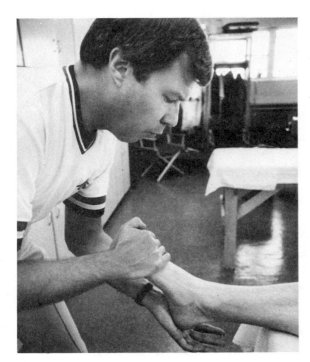

Ankle dorsiflexion, starting position. Gene Gieselmann, St. Louis Cardinals head trainer, secures heel of player and prepares resistance on top of foot. On location: Busch complex, St. Petersburg, Florida, March 1987. (Tom DiPace)

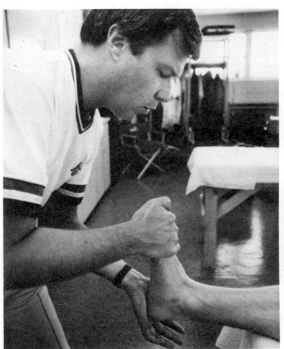

Ankle dorsiflexion, exercise position, player bringing foot upward against resistance. Gene Gieselmann. On location: Busch complex, March 1987. (Tom DiPace)

 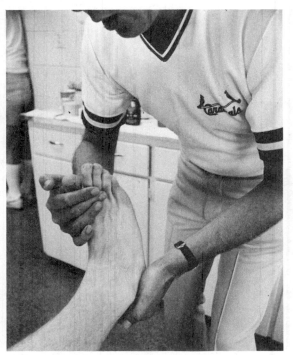

Ankle eversion, player pushing outward against resistance. Gene Gieselmann. On location: Busch complex, March 1987. (Tom DiPace) The ankle can move outward only about 10 degrees in this position, but it is important movement because ankles often get turned moving in this direction.

Ankle inversion, player pushing inward against resistance. Gene Gieselmann. On location: Busch complex, March 1987. (Tom DiPace)

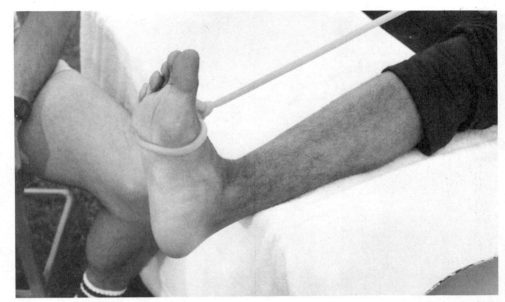

Ankle plantarflexion with surgical tubing, starting position. Rick Griffin, Seattle Mariners head trainer, supervises. On location: Diablo Stadium, Tempe, Arizona, March 1987. (V. J. Lovero)

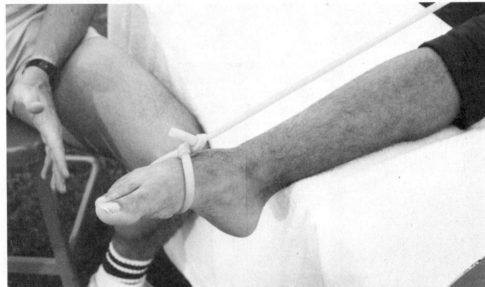

Ankle plantarflexion with surgical tubing, exercise position as player pushes downward against tubing's resistance. On location: Diablo Stadium, March 1987. (V. J. Lovero)

Ankle dorsiflexion with a towel. Paul Molitor. On location: Compadre Stadium, Chandler, Arizona, March 1987. (V. J. Lovero)

CHAPTER NINE

Fitness For Little Leaguers

By
Ned Bergert,
Assistant Athletic Trainer, California Angels

In *The Professional Baseball Trainers' Fitness Book,* we have taken you for quite a journey through the varied aspects of baseball fitness: flexibility, strength, nutrition, psychology, and rehabilitation. But before we close up shop and shout, "Play ball, but first, be fit!" we want to make one last stop: a chapter on fitness for Little Leaguers.

Long before a player becomes a minor league prospect, he is a Little League enthusiast—and he may someday want to emulate his heroes. Although the dream of making it in the big time is a one-in-a-million shot, to dream is to be alive and hopeful, and all applaud it. But we want to make sure that Little Leaguers are not rushing themselves and doing things that could hurt their chances at remaining happily active later on life. So here is Ned Bergert, assistant athletic trainer of the California Angels, to offer PBATS' modification of its big league exercises, our guide to Little League fitness for both boys and girls.

By the best estimate of Little League, Inc., 2.5 million children worldwide—including 1.8 million children in the United States—play Little League baseball. According to the Little League office, less than 2 percent of these children have injuries that require medical attention. The number of unreported or undetected injuries is unknown, but it certainly must be considerable. In this chapter we will discuss several long-held beliefs about injuries involving Little League players and ways to prevent them or lessen their severity.

Many children today are playing organized baseball as early as the age of six, beginning with "tee" baseball, a game in which there is no pitcher, the ball being batted off a tee. Studies of young children indicate that by the age of six, 84 percent have attained a mature enough level of motor development to be able to engage in the physical act of throwing.

The mature throwing pattern differs from the earlier pattern; it utilizes a greater base of support and thus provides opposition of movement between legs and arms so that greater power can be obtained from the throw. In mature throwing, the weight is transferred to the right foot during the preparatory phase. The left foot moves forward and receives the weight during the delivery phase of the throw. (The action is reversed for left-handers.) Such action enables a marked trunk rotation to occur. Coupled with the arm's horizontal adduction (drawing toward the center of the body) during the forward swing, this rotation enables the child to achieve the maximal use of body leverage for attaining speed at the most distal segment (that part farthest away)—namely, the hand.

The skill of throwing effectively—i.e., the ability to project an object accurately and with sufficient force through space—requires coordination of many distinct mechanisms. Years of experimentation may be needed before an effective throwing pattern is mastered. In teaching a child to throw and in evaluating techniques, parents and coaches should keep in mind the difficulty of mastering the process. Be patient with the child, because the goal of Little League should be establishing solid and effective basic skills, and most importantly, to enable the child to enjoy the game.

Once a child has learned the basic rudiments of throwing, it is inevitable that he will at some time wish to pitch or be asked to pitch. As a Little Leaguer begins to explore the art of pitching, he should seek to perfect one good type of pitch, usually a fastball. To develop good velocity (speed) should be the first goal of any young pitcher. Then move on to developing control by learning consistent mechanics. Additional pitches can then be worked on by experimenting with different grips on the seam, and trying to master speed changes with the change-up. Only when all the first three areas have been mastered should you work on breaking pitches. Notice that trying out curveballs comes last because it is simply anatomically impossible for a youngster of Little League age to really throw a curveball correctly. His hand and fingers are too small to grip the ball firmly with two fingers, and his shoulder drops instead of coming back, thus placing dangerous stress on the elbow. Also, his hips do not rotate correctly but twist, and that can lead to a lower-torso injury. All he can do is make an "effect" on the ball, but at risk to his health. In other words, do not throw curveballs until you are skeletally mature.

How much and how often should a Little Leaguer pitch? Little League, Inc., is very concerned about "overuse syndrome," injuries occuring from too much repetition of throwing. A technical medical definition of overuse syndrome is "a chronic inflammatory condition caused by repeated microtrauma from a repetitive activity."[1] Little League, Inc., accordingly recommends that no youngster pitch more than the equivalent of six innings a week, or the equivalent of 100 pitches.

That limit includes all serious throwing during a week. In addition to game pitching, one must also look at how much throwing is done from other positions of the ball field, during practice (both for the team and at home), and in general play. All these factors have to be accounted for when one talks about how much throwing a child is doing.

Generally, a child who is throwing in excess is being pushed by an adult. When children play by themselves, they will stop the activity if it is painful. Overuse injury occurs when an adult is pushing or pressuring a child. Pain is nature's way of telling a

[1] From: Bill Kozar and Russell Lord, "Overuse Injury in the Young Athlete: Reasons for Concern," *The Physician and Sportsmedicine,* vol. 11, no. 7, July 1983, p. 118.

child and a parent that something is wrong. When it speaks, you should heed its voice. *Too often, these injuries may occur because some parents and coaches believe that the game is more important than the child.*

OVERUSE INJURIES IN LITTLE LEAGUERS

Among the injuries which Little Leaguers contract are injuries commonly referred to as Little League elbow and Little League shoulder; stress fractures of the metatarsals of the foot; and stress reaction in the lower back. I want to discuss here the first two injuries, which are the most common.

Little League elbow is caused by the downward motion of the wrist and fingers when releasing the ball. The force of the throw radiates up the arm to the weakest portion, the inner knob of the elbow (the medial epicondyle). With repetitive use of the throwing muscles, tremendous stress eventually produces a small rip or tear in the muscle origin at the attachment to the bone. In growing children, the muscle origin is attached to a growth center, or prebone, which is not as strong as the bone itself. Thus, Little League elbow is the product of stress to the growth center, tending to pull the growth center away from the main trunk of the bone.

Little League elbow rarely is detected on one pitch. It starts instead as a gradual buildup of pain over a two- or three-day period. Whenever a pain or injury persists, it is wise to stop throwing and have the condition diagnosed by a doctor. Treatment will depend on the severity of the injury and the age of the Little Leaguer. All throwing must be stopped if Little Leaguers report this pain. It may require a hiatus of six to nine weeks. The player should also be discouraged from throwing curveballs and encouraged to keep his long-term interest in baseball in perspective. To be a star at 10 and unable to pick up a ball at 15 is something that must be stopped.

Once all pain has disappeared, a program of "long toss" and a strengthening program should be started prior to a return to full-velocity throwing. Of course, all treatment should be monitored by a physician who is familiar with both pediatric and sports medicine. The "long toss" program is very similar to the interval throwing program which Tommy Craig discussed in the previous chapter on rehabilitation. The distances will be somewhat shorter, of course, starting with about 25 to 30 feet and then gradually moving up to a maximum of about 120 feet. Make certain that the youngster is thoroughly warmed up by jogging, cycling, etc., before he begins this "long toss" program.

Little League shoulder is another injury caused by excessive throwing. Like the elbow, the shoulder has growth centers, or plates, which are subject to a great deal of stress when repetitive throwing is done without ample recovery time. A resulting instability appears in the shoulder capsule. Throwing should cease when Little League shoulder is detected, but an exercise program can strengthen and tighten the posterior shoulder. Healing is also aided by normal growth, time, and physical maturity.

In the prepubescent athlete, the strengthening and flexibility is very modest. It is based on internally imposed overloads instead of an externally determined resistance or goal. Excellent internally imposed overloads include chin-ups, push-ups, rope climbs, wheelbarrow walks, and tandem stretching-strengthening exercises.

Once a child has reached a postpubertal stage of development, working with light weights will be of benefit for general strengthening purposes. Postpuberty usually begins around 16 in boys; earlier in girls, at around age 13. Of course, there is always individual variation, which can be detected in boys by varying degrees of facial hair. In prepubertal boys and girls, weight training does not significantly improve strength or increase muscle mass because the strengthening hormones naturally produced by the body, androgens, are insufficiently circulating.

When used in measured amounts (less than the maximum called for in adult programs), weight training for adolescents can be beneficial to athletes in all sports. Weight training lowers the potential for injury because a strong muscle has more resistance and will not weaken as much as an untrained muscle. When the program is understood and followed, weight training is a safe technique as well.

In his book, *Joy and Sadness in Children's Sports,* sports scholar Rainer Martins offers sage advice for parents trying to develop and maintain their children's sports interest. Martins writes:

> For the 6- to 10-year-old, the emphasis should be on awakening interest in many sports, having fun, and learning basic athletic skills.

> For the 11- to 14-year-old, the need is for versatility, in many sports while maintaining proper techniques, and tolerance for increased training.

> For the 15- to 18-year-old, the time is ripe for an increased training load, specialized work such as specific weight training, and extensive competition.[2]

Little Leaguers can profit on a smaller scale from all the exercises in this book—especially the stretches and warm-ups, which were well documented in chapters 3 and 7. Little Leaguers can also profit from small-weight work, as they grow into mature athletes, using both small dumbbells and Velcro-strapped wrist weights. In the eleven exercises with which we close this chapter, notice how the small weights and Velcro-strapped weights are used and can be used interchangeably. You can find these exercises and additional stretches and warm-ups in the excellent pamphlet *Play Ball! The Official Little League Fitness Guide* by Dr. Frank Jobe and Diane Moynes (Inglewood California, Champion Press, 1986).

1. Shoulder Abductions Start with your arms at your sides, holding small one- or two-pound barbells or with small weights strapped to your wrists. Bring the weights all the way up to shoulder height with arms outstretched and then slowly lower. Repeat 10 times.

Little League sequence, exercise 1: shoulder abduction; starting position, arms at side. On location: Anaheim Stadium, Anaheim, California, July 1987. (V. J. Lovero)

Shoulder abduction, peak position, arms outstretched. On location: Anaheim Stadium, July 1987. (V. J. Lovero)

2. Shoulder Flexions or Front Deltoid Raise   Start with your arms at your sides, holding small weights or Velcro-strapped weights. Bring the weights slowly up until they reach shoulder height. Pause and return to starting position. Repeat 10 times.

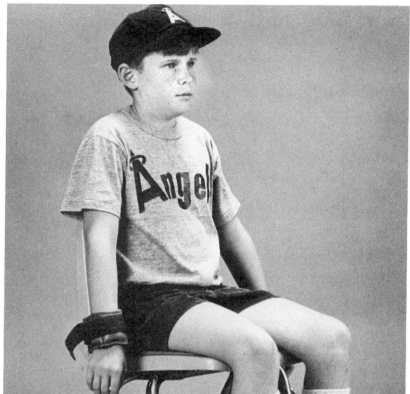

Exercise 2: shoulder flexion (front deltoid raise); starting position, seated (or standing), arms at side. On location: Anaheim Stadium, July 1987. (V. J. Lovero)

Shoulder flexion, peak position, arms in front at shoulder height. On location: Anaheim Stadium, July 1987. (V. J. Lovero)

3. Diagonal Shoulder Lifts (or the "empty pop can" exercise.)   While standing or sitting, put your arms at your sides with your thumbs pointed downward to the floor. Move your arms forward about 30 degrees (at about your hip bone) and slowly raise arms upward. Make sure your thumbs remain pointed to the floor and your arms are 30 degrees from the sides. Keep elbows straight. Raise arms until even with the shoulder. Pause and return to starting position. Repeat 10 times with each arm or with both arms together.

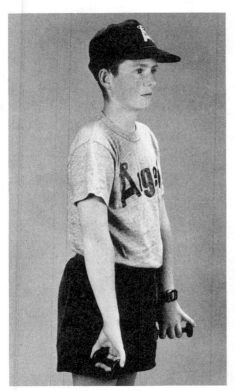

Exercise 3: diagonal shoulder lift, or "empty pop can" exercise; starting position, weights at side, thumbs down. On location: Anaheim Stadium, July 1987. (V. J. Lovero)

Diagonal shoulder lift, "empty pop can" position, weights at 30 degrees from body, thumbs down. On location: Anaheim Stadium, July 1987. (V. J. Lovero)

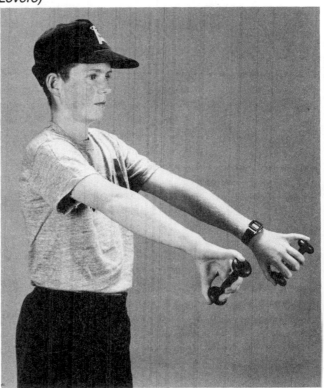

4. External Shoulder Rotations Lie on your side on a table with your involved elbow in contact with your body. Slowly raise your hand, holding the weight up until it is pointed toward the ceiling. Pause and then slowly lower the weight to the starting position. Repeat 10 times with each arm.

Exercise 4: external shoulder rotation; starting position, lying on side on the table with elbow supported at hip. On location: Anaheim Stadium, July 1987. (V. J. Lovero)

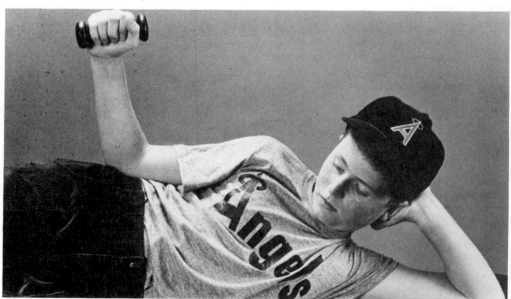

External shoulder rotation, peak position, arm at less than 90 degrees to table. On location: Anaheim Stadium, July 1987. (V. J. Lovero)

5. Internal Shoulder Rotations Lie on your back on a table or the floor, again keeping your elbow in contact with your body. Raise the weight until it is pointed straight up. Pause and return to starting position by lowering the weight slowly. Repeat 10 times on each arm.

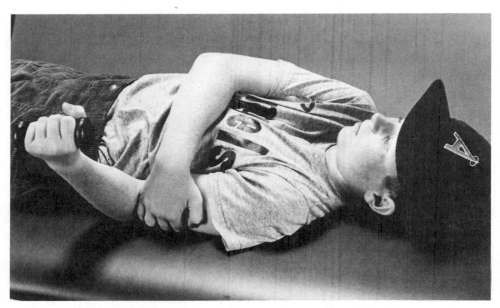

Exercise 5: internal shoulder rotation; starting position, lying faceup on the table, elbow supported by off-hand. On location: Anaheim Stadium, July 1987. (V. J. Lovero)

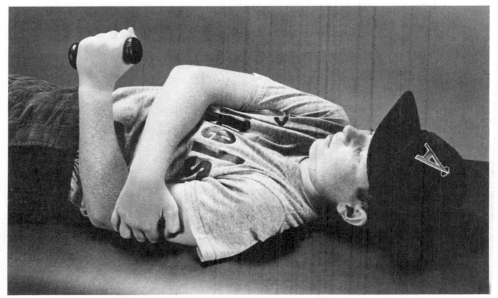

Internal shoulder rotation, peak position, arm brought slightly beyond a right angle toward the midline of body. On location: Anaheim Stadium, July 1987. (V. J. Lovero)

6. Prone Horizontal Abductions Lie on your stomach on a table, with your arms hanging straight down. Slowly raise the weight out to the side to the height of the table. Pause and return to starting position. Repeat 10 times on each arm.

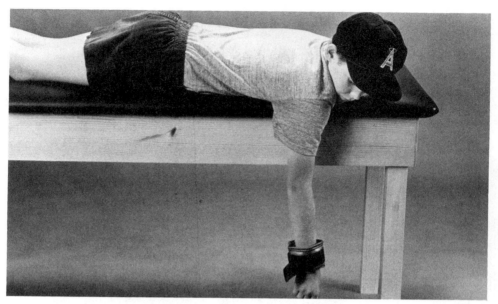

Exercise 6: prone horizontal abduction; starting position, lying on stomach, arm straight down to the floor. On location: Anaheim Stadium, July 1987. (V. J. Lovero)

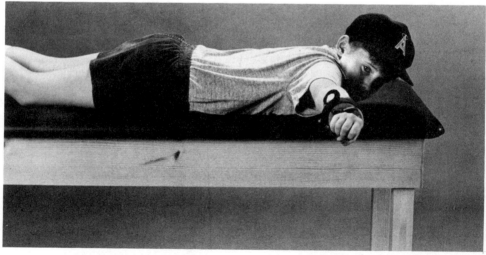

Prone horizontal abduction, peak position, arm brought out parallel to table. On location: Anaheim Stadium, July 1987. (V. J. Lovero)

7. Prone Extensions with External Rotations   Lie on your stomach on a table, with your arms hanging straight down. Slowly bring the weight back and out to the side at about 30 degrees. Pause and slowly return to starting position. Repeat 10 times on each arm.

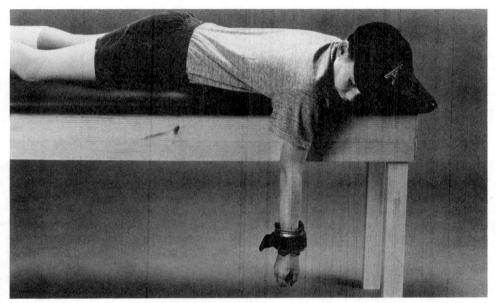

Exercise 7: prone extension with external rotation; starting position, lying on stomach with arm hanging straight down. On location: Anaheim Stadium, July 1987. (V. J. Lovero)

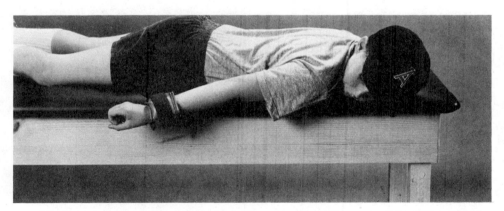

Prone extension with external rotation, peak position, arm brought out and back like the wing of a bird. On location: Anaheim Stadium, July 1987. (V. J. Lovero)

---

[2] *From:* Rainer Martins, *Joy and Sadness in Children's Sports* (Champaign, Illinois: Human Kinetics Publiishers, 1978), p. xx.

8. Biceps Curls (or Arm Curls)   Starting with a wrist weight, sit or stand with your arms at your side. Slowly bend your elbow and lift the weight as high as it will go; then return slowly to the starting position. Repeat 10 times on each side.

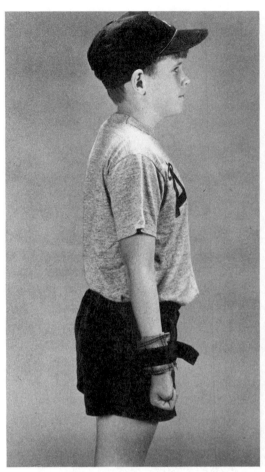

Exercise 8: biceps curl; starting position, arm on side with fist clenched. On location: Anaheim Stadium, July 1987. (V. J. Lovero)

Biceps curl, exercise position, arm brought up and flexed. On location: Anaheim Stadium, July 1987. (V. J. Lovero)

9. Lying Triceps Extensions (or Elbow Extensions)   Lie on your back on the floor or on a table, your elbow pointing straight up and your hand behind your head, palm down, holding a small dumbbell or Velcro weight. Support the back of the arm with your other hand. Raise your forearm until it is pointed at the ceiling. From this starting position repeat 10 slow flexions and extensions of the elbow. Repeat with the other arm. This exercise strengthens the triceps. Notice how the stabilization and isolation of the elbow that in grown-ups must be done by a trainer can be done by yourself if you know the basic rules of exercise and fitness.

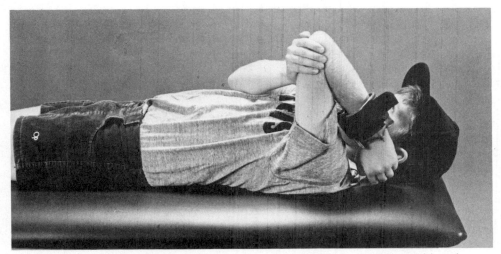

Exercise 9: elbow extension (lying triceps extension); starting position, lying faceup on table, arm flexed and elbow held by off-hand. On location: Anaheim Stadium, July 1987. (V J. Lovero)

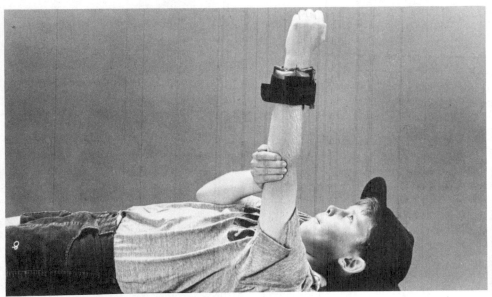

Elbow extension, finishing position, arm straight up in air, hand still on elbow. On location: Anaheim Stadium, July 1987. (V. J. Lovero)

10. Wall Push-Ups   Stand on the balls of your feet at a 45-degree angle to the wall, placing your hands on the wall at shoulder height, your arms bent. Slowly push your body away from the wall until your arms are straight. Notice that as you push off, your feet come flat to the floor. As you get stronger, this exercise can be done on the floor as a regular push-up. It builds up your chest, triceps, and shoulders.

Exercise 10: wall push-up; starting position, hands extended against wall (or table) with heels flat on ground. On location: Anaheim Stadium, July 1987. (V. J. Lovero)

Wall push-up, finishing position, chest forward, arms bent, and weight on toes. On location: Anaheim Stadium, July 1987. (V. J. Lovero)

11. Assisted Bent-Knee Sit-Ups Lying on your back with your knees bent, cross your arms over the opposite shoulder as your partner secures your legs. Come up slowly toward your knees, with your feet remaining flat on the ground. Raise your head and trunk up until your hands reach your knees, and then slowly return to the starting position. Repeat 10 times.

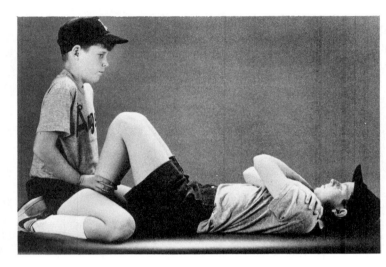

Exercise 11: assisted bent-knee sit-up, starting position, knees bent, arms folded across chest, with partner securing your legs. On location: Anaheim Stadium, July 1987. (V. J. Lovero)

Assisted bent-knee sit-up, finishing position, arms still crossed, head up and legs still secured. On location: Anaheim Stadium, July 1987. (V. J. Lovero)

Remember that the weights used are quite small, between one and two pounds maximum, because Little Leaguers should not be doing heavy weight lifting while their growth centers are still not mature. But there is nothing wrong with adding small weights to your exercises (indeed it is highly recommended)—and when maturity comes, your muscles will have learned some of the basic methods of strengthening.

It is time to leave you now, but I hope our guide to fitness will be consulted by all kinds of athletes of all ages. Kids who correctly practice our exercises in this chapter will undoubtedly find that they feel better and stronger, and they should play longer at their best. Look at the number of major leaguers who continue to play the game of baseball at the highest level at extraordinary ages—the over-40 brigade, to name just a few, includes pitchers Don Sutton and Tommy John, infielders Darrell Evans and Graig Nettles, and catchers Bob Boone and, almost 40, Carlton Fisk. It is a commitment to continuing fitness that is common to all of them. Even if you have no hope of going on to a larger athletic stage, we hope these chapters have provided some ideas and some wisdom to last you permanently. Remember: It is wonderful to play ball, but first, stay fit!

APPENDIX A

The Off-Season Conditioning Calendar

By Larry Starr,
Head Trainer, Cincinnati Reds

In this guide to fitness we have talked constantly about the importance of staying in shape all year round. Before we close, we thought it might help if you saw how major leaguers and promising prospects keep fit during the months when they are away from the ballpark. You can be certain that the veterans playing major league baseball well into their forties—an unheard of number compared to a few years ago—are not idle after the World Series.

Individuals will vary in how much they exercise between seasons and what kinds of activities they will do, but we all agree that the basic areas of fitness must be maintained: (1) aerobic, (2) flexibility, (3) strength, and (4) nutrition. The off-season conditioning calendar will not mention much about nutrition—except to say that diet should be far easier to maintain in the off-season because your job as a baseball player does not force you away from home constantly. The joy of the off-season for most players is to have a happy and stable family life.

OFF-SEASON AEROBIC CONDITIONING

The midfall and winter months are the time for the baseball player to build his endurance and his good cardiovascular foundation. Running several days a week is highly recommended.

You can start slowly if you do not have a particular preference for running. If you love running, you can do as much as you can in the off-season but not to the neglect of interval (sprint) work as the regular season draws closer.

Serious off-season work should usually begin on or around November first. It is reasonable to allow players, especially those who have competed in the postseason, to take off whatever remaining days are left in October; nowadays, however, there are precious few!

Dr. Fritz Hagerman, physiologist and consultant to the Cincinnati Reds, designed this off-season program as one organized method for attaining year-round cardiovascular fitness.

The goals of the running program are to improve endurance and sprint power and to reduce leg muscle injuries. The program is designed as follows:

WEEK	MONDAY/WEDNESDAY/FRIDAY DISTANCE RUNNING	TUESDAY/THURSDAY SPRINTS/JOGS
11/5–9	15 minutes each day	4 x 200-yard runs with 200-yard jog (Tu)
		5 x 40-yard runs with 40-yard jog (Th)
		5 x 100-yard runs with 100-yard jog (Th)
11/12–16	15 minutes each day	same as above
11/19–23	20 minutes each day	same as above
11/26–30	20 minutes each day	same as above
12/3–7	25 minutes each day	6 x 200-yard runs with 200-yard jog (Tu)
		6 x 100-yard runs with 100-yard jog (Th)
		10 x 40-yard runs with 40-yard jog (Th)
12/10–14	25 minutes each day	same as above
12/17–21	25 minutes each day	same as above
12/24–28	25 minutes each day	same as above

12/31–1/4	30 minutes each day	8 x 200-yard run with 200-yard jog (Tu)
		7 x 100-yard run with 100-yard jog (Th)
		15 x 40-yard run with 40-yard jog
1/7–11	30 minutes each day	8 x 200-yard runs with 200-yard jog (Tu)
		7 x 100-yard runs with 100-yard jog (Th)
		15 x 40-yard runs with 40-yard jog (Th)
1/14–18	30 minutes each day	same as above
1/21–25	30 minutes each day	same as above
1/28–2/1	30 minutes each day	same as above
2/4–8	30 minutes each day	10 x 200-yard runs with 200-yard jog (Tu)
		8 x 100-yard runs with 100-yard jog (Th)
		20 x 40-yard runs with 40-yard jog (Th)
2/11–15	30 minutes each day	same as above
2/18–22	30 minutes each day	same as above
2/25–29	30 minutes each day	same as above

By the end of February, spring training will have started and you are in the preseason already. Having done the interval work, stressing speed and endurance, you will be ready to pick up where you left off last year—or even better, improve on your performance. It is certainly true that the best players are the ones who are never standing still but constantly improving.

The main purpose in running, beyond general conditioning purposes, is to work out at nearly 75 percent of your maximum heart rate. To determine what heart rate you should be shooting for, find your maximum heart rate by subtracting your age from 220. If you are 20 years old, for example, your maximum heart rate will be 200 heartbeats per second. The target for you to shoot for is 60 to 75 percent of that maximum heart rate, or 120 to 150 heartbeats per minute. If you are not reaching that level, you are not working hard enough.

By the time the preseason of spring training has arrived, the endurance aspect of aerobic conditioning tapers off to one or two days a week. Sprints are increased to 10 to 15 sprints at 40 to 60 yards four or five times a week. As Opening Day nears, the number of sprints at the same distance go up to 15 to 20. Running activities specific to baseball are then made part of the program. For instance, to simulate base running, sprints are replaced by running a single and then jogging home, running a double and then jogging home, etc. We also do a drill using traffic cones or some other type of object that emphasizes cutting, sprinting, and stop-and-go activities so prevalent in baseball.

OFF-SEASON FLEXIBILITY CALENDAR

The kinds of stretches and exercises done before games and throughout spring training are ideal to continue in the off-season. As baseball players will tell you, it is fun to be conditioned and exercise when the grind of the season does not interfere with your improving endurance, flexibility, and muscle tone. My fervent advice to budding and established athletes is: *Stretch every day of the year to improve or maintain flexibility in the entire body; to enhance the stretching exercises, always try to relax and breathe normally.* So keep chapter 3 of this book handy and follow those stretches and exercise commandments faithfully.

ANAEROBIC OFF-SEASON CONDITIONING

What applies to stretching in the off-season also applies to strength training. (If, however, you are a pitcher or a player coming off some kind of injury, you must be cautious about the amount of weight that you utilize in the off-season.)

If you are healthy and want to keep the kind of muscle fitness and muscle tone that served you well during the season, go for the program that Barry Weinberg and Dave McKay illustrated in chapter 4. Heed their commandments and strictures, too. In strength training, you must take your days off to allow the minor irritations and soreness to fade and to let the natural growth process of your improving muscle occur.

SPORT-SPECIFIC SKILL CONDITIONING

Last but not least in your off-season program, do not forget about honing your baseball skills (or if you are an athlete in other sports, do not let your sport-specific talents lie idle). Keep throwing in the off-season, starting with the easy long-arc toss and then bringing your arm close to Opening Day readiness by the time spring training opens. That way, time spent in Florida or Arizona is polishing not rebuilding time. The same goes for keeping hitting skills sharp. Visit a batting cage and work in graduated increments before it is time to face live, hungry, and ambitious pitching in the preseason games.

APPENDIX B

A Trainer's Guide To Medical Terms

By Bill Buhler,
Head Trainer, Los Angeles Dodgers

abduction   movement of an extremity away from the body, or parts away from the midline of the body; the act of drawing away from the midline.

abductor   any muscle that moves a part away from the median axis of the body.

abrasion   any injury that rubs off the surface of the skin.

A-C joint   acromio-clavicular joint (the point or summit of the shoulder); pertaining to the acromion process (of the scapula) and the clavicle.

Achilles tendon   the large tendon located in the back of the ankle and made up by the blending of three muscles.

acroarthritis   arthritis of the extremities.

acromion   process found at the top of the scapula which articulates with the lateral end of the clavicle to form the acromio-clavicular joint.

acute   having a sudden beginning, a short course, and severe symptoms.

adduction   movement of an extremity toward the body, or parts toward the midline of the body; the act of moving toward the midline.

adductor   any muscle that moves a part toward the median axis of the body.

adhesion   abnormal union of two parts, often after an inflammation.

aerobic   relating to continuous exercise at three-quarter speed and below, raising heart rate to improve heart and lung function and muscle for greater stamina.

afferent   toward, or to convey toward; the center.

anaerobic pace   muscle exercise without oxygen, lasting only a short time, with high pulse rate.

anterior   in front of; the front surface of.

anti-inflammatory   any agent that prevents inflammation.

arteriogram   film demonstrating arteries after the injection of an opaque medium.

arthrogram   X-ray technique for joints using air and/or dye injected into an affected joint (to show torn cartilage).

arthroscope   instrument used for visualization of the interior of a joint cavity.

aspiration   withdrawal of fluids from a body cavity by means of a suction or siphonage device.

asymptomatic   without symptoms.

atrophy   to shrivel or shrink (as in muscular *atrophy*).

avulsion   forcible tearing away of a part or structure.

axilla   armpit.

baker's cyst   cyst caused by excessive joint-fluid buildup that indicates trouble within the knee joint; inflammation of the gastrocnemius bursa.

Bankhart's operation   procedure for prevention of recurrent dislocation of shoulder joint.

basal metabolism   amount of energy needed to sustain life in a resting state.

biceps   bulging muscle on front of upper arm.

biceps femoris   one of three hamstring muscles located on the lateral posterior side of the thigh. Its actions are extension of the thigh at the hip and flexion of the leg at the knee.

bruise   discoloration of the skin caused by an extravasation of blood into underlying tissues.

bursa   fibrous sac lined with synovial membrane and containing a small quantity of synovial fluid.

bursitis   inflammation of a bursa.

calcaneus   heel bone.

capsule   ligaments that surround a joint.

capsulitis   inflammation of the capsule.

cartilage   smooth, slippery substance that prevents bone ends from rubbing, and thus grating, against each other.

charley horse   contusion to the arm or thigh.

chondromalacia   roughening of slippery cartilage surface (best known is roughening of underside of kneecap).

clavicle   collarbone.

cortisone   an anti-inflammatory preparation.

concentric contractions   muscle shortening.

condyle   a rounded or knuckle-like prominence found at the end of a bone which usually articulates with another bone.

congenital   existing from birth or before.

contusion   injury to muscles and tissues caused by a blow from a blunt object.

Cybex   a computer-equipped orthotron; device for testing isokinetic strength; device that can give a detailed profile of the condition of various muscle groups in the human body, including the measurement of maximum dynamic strength throughout the range of motion of a particular joint.

cyst   abnormal sac containing liquid or semisolid matter.

deltoids   muscles at the top of the arm, just below the shoulder.

dislocation   a displacement of organs or articular surfaces so that all apposition between them is lost.

distal   away from.

eccentric contraction   muscle lengthening.

ecchymosis   black and blue spot in the skin caused by a contusion.

edema   accumulation of fluid in the organs and tissues of the body.

efferent   away from; pushing out from the center.

effusion   accumulation of fluid, or the fluid itself, in various spaces in the body; e.g., joints.

elbow   joint of arm and forearm (humerus, radius, and olecranon ulna).

EMG   electromyogram test to check nerve function.

epicondyle   (medial and lateral(bony knob surface locted at the end of the humerus bone which serves for attachment of forearm muscles. Located on the inside and outside edge of the elbow.

erector spinae   (sacrospinalis) group of back muscles with its largest mass located in the lower part of the back. Its primary action is extension of the spine.

everted   turned out.

extension   straightening out after flexion.

external rotation   angled to the outside.

extrinsic   from without.

fascia   connective tissue sheath, consisting of fibrous tissue and fat, which unites the skin to the underlying tissues.

femur   thighbone.

fiber   threadlike structure.

fibula   the smaller of the two bones in the lower leg (located to the outside).

flexion   bending, as in flexing an arm or leg.

flexor   muscle which on contraction flexes or bends a part.

fossa   cavity or depression found in bone.

fracture   breach in the continuity of a bone (varieties: simple, compound, comminuted, impacted, and incomplete, or greenstick).

ganglion   cystlike swelling found in the region of a joint or the sheath of a tendon.

gastocenemius   large superficial calf muscle. Primarilly used for plantar flexing the foot at the ankle joint as well as flexion at the knee.

glenoid   cavity on the scapula into which the head of the humerus fits to form the shoulder joint.

glenohumeral   pertaining to the glenoid cavity of the scapula and humerus.

gluteus   (maximus, medius, minimus) group of three buttock muscles with the largest and most superficial being the gluteus maximus. Its functions are extension of the thigh at the hip and outward rotation of the thigh.

groin   depression between the thigh and abdomen.

hallux   big toe.

hamate   one of the eight bones of the wrist.

hamstring   tendon running from the buttocks to the back of the knee (often injured through lack of proper preexercise stretching).

hematoma   tumorlike mass produced by an accumulation of coagulated blood in a cavity.

humerus   bone of the upper arm.

hypothermia   a decrease in body's core temperature.

hypohydration   loss of fluids.

impingement   banging together of two surfaces not normally in contact.

inferior   lower; beneath; toward the bottom.

infraspinatus   one of four rotator cuff muscles located on the posterior surface of the scapula. It works in harmony with the teres minor to prevent dislocation of the shoulder joint.

interosseus membrane   uniting membrane between the tibia and the fibula formed of collagenous fibrous tissues. It has two functions: it serves as origin for many of the muscles of the lower leg, and it transmits stress from the shinbone (tibia) to the calf bone (fibula).

intrinsic   inherent or inside.

isokinetic exercise   exercise based on constant speed and constant resistance.

isometric exercise   exercise based on the principle that two equal forces working against each other produce no movement (useful in early rehabilitation).

isotonic exercise   exercise based on shortening and lengthening muscles with the same weight.

joint   area where two bones meet.

joint mice   loose bodies within the knee joint.

knee   the point of juncture of the femur and tibia. .

kneecap   patella.

lateral   relating to the outer side of the body.

lattisimus dorsi(lats) broad muscle which is located over the lower and middle portions of the back. Primarily used for pulling activities.

lesion   wound; injury; tumor.

ligament   a band of fibrous tissue that connects bone to bone or cartilage to bone, supporting and strengthening a joint.

malleolus   an extension of bone having the shape of a hammerhead on either side of the ankle.

medial   pertaining to or near the middle.

meniscus   crescent-shaped piece of gristle usually found in the knee joint; semilunar cartilage.

metacarpals   five bones of the hand, just before the fingers.

metatarsals   five bones of the foot, just before the toes.

myositis   inflammation of a muscle.

necrotic   relating to the death of a portion of tissue.

neuritis   inflammation of a nerve.

orthotic   any device applied to or around the body in the care of physical impairment or disability.

osteochondritis dissecans   lesion caused by the loosening of a piece of bone or cartilage from its attachment to the femur.

osteomyelitis   inflammatory disease of bone usually caused by infection with streptococcus or staphylococcus.

otic   pertaining to the ear.

overweight   exceeding desirable weight by more than 10 percent.

patella   kneecap.

pectorals   chest muscles beneath the breast leading up to the shoulder.

peroneals   (peroneus brevis, longus, tertius) group of three muscles located on the lateral side of the lower leg. The peroneus brevis and longus plantar flexes and everts the foot. The peroneus tertius dorsi flexes the foot.

phlebitis   inflammation of a vein.

pitcher's elbow (olecranon fossa)   damage to the olecranon and triceps caused by repeatedly snapping the elbow straight (e.g., by throwing).

plantar   pertaining to the sole of the foot.

plantar fascia   tight band of muscle beneath the arch of the foot.

plantar fascitis   tearing of the arch ligament located on the bottom of the foot.

plantar wart   painful wart occuring on the bottom of the foot.

pleura   thin tissue covering the lungs and lining the interior walls of the chest cavity.

pleurisy   inflammation of the pleura.

PNF (proprioceptive neuromuscular facilitation)   an approach to therapeutic exercise based on the principles of functional human anatomy and neurophysiology.

popliteal space   *Could not find this term.* However the popliteus muscle attaches the outer condyle of the femur bone to the medial surface of the tibia bone. The popliteal space might be the space that exists between the two points.

posterior   at the back part, or rear, of the body.

proprioceptive neuromuscular facilitation   the transmission of information from the (sensory receptors in the skeltal muscles, tendons and joints which are sensitive to stretch, tension and pressure) to the central nervous system. This provides information for appropriate motor behavior during physical activity. ie: contraction or relaxation of a muscle.

proximal   near the source; nearest any point being described.

quadriceps (quads)   powerful muscle in the front of the thigh that inserts into the superior (or upper) pole (or margin) of the patella and which has four parts. (The portions most susceptible to strains lie in the central area; they are called the vastus intermedius and the rectus femoris sections and lie directly over the front of the femur.)

radiography   taking of X rays.

radius   forearm bone on the thumb side.

referred pain   pain felt in an undamaged area of the body away from the actual injury.

rehabilitation   planned program in which the convalescent or disabled person progresses toward, or maintains, the maximum degree of physical and psychological independence of which he or she is capable.

rhomboids   (major and minor)muscle group located betwen the scapula and spine. In coordination with the trapezius muscles helps maintain good shoulder posture.

root canal   pulp cavity of tooth root.

rotator cuff   set of four shoulder muscles, all of which originate on the scapula and insert on the humerus. The muscles are the supraspinatus, infraspinatus, teres minor, and subscapularis. The cuff consists of both muscle and tendon fibers and keeps the shoulder joint strong and stable.

runner's knee   overuse syndrome caused by microtrauma to the sleeve of the knee joint.

sacroiliac   relating to the juncture of the hipbone and lower part of the spine.

scan   injection of radioactive fluid (equal in radioactivity to approximately one X ray) which is then displayed on a computer monitor or film.

scapula   shoulder blade.

sciatic nerve   largest nerve in the body, located in the back of the leg.

semimembranasus   together with the semitendinosis form the middle of the hamstring group situated on the back of the thigh. Their primary function is extension of the thigh at the hip and flexion of the leg at the knee. Also inward rotation of the thigh.

semitendinosis   see semimembranasus-location and function are the same.

sesamoid bone   small mass of bone or cartilage that lies within and adds strength to tendons as they cover a bony point. (The best known is the kneecap.)

shin   front part of the lower leg.

shinsplint   catchall syndrome describing pain either in the front of the leg or on the inner aspect of the leg.

shoulder   joint between the arm and the body, formed by the humerus and the glenoid cavity of the scapula.

skull   bones of the head (22 in all).

spondylitis   inflammation of one or more of the vertebrae.

spondylolisthesis   forward displacement of a lumbar vertebra.

sprain   violent twisting, straining, or pulling of a ligament.

strain   pulling or twisting of a muscle or tendon.

stress fracture   break in a bone caused by continual repetition of movement.

stress X ray   X ray taken when a portion of the body is stressed to its maximum, used to determine whether the ligaments are intact.

subluxation   incomplete dislocation of a joint. It usually implies that the joint can return to normal position without formal reduction.

subcapularis   one of four rotator cuff muscles located on the anterior part of the sub-scapula. Helps keep the head of the humerus bone in the glenoid fossa to prevent shoulder dislocation.

superficial   near the surface.

superior   in anatomy, the upper of two parts; toward the top, or above.

supre-iliac crest   top crest of the pelvic bone. Point of attachment for various abdominal muscles.

supraspinatus   one of four rotator cuff muscles located on the supraspinous fossa of the scapula. Helps hold the head of the humerus bone in the glenoid fossa.

synovial fluid   lubricating fluid for joints and tendons, produced in the synovium, or inner lining, of a joint.

synovitis   damage to the synovium.

talus   ankle.

tarsus   arch of the foot.

tendinitis   inflammation of the tendon and/or tendon sheath, often caused by chronic overuse and/or sudden injury.

tendon   fibrous tissue that connects muscle to other tissues.

tennis elbow   pain and tenderness on the outside of the elbow.

teres minor   one of four rotator cuff muscles located on the posterior surface of the scapula. Works together with infraspinatue to prevent dislocation of the shoulder joint.

teres major   muscle located on the posterior surface of the scapula. It works with the lattissimus dorsi muscle in downward and backward movements of the humerus.

tibia   larger of two bones in the lower leg; shinbone.

tobaccosis   tobacco poisoning.

trachea   windpipe.

trapezius   large muscle group which runs from the base of the skull to the thoracic verterbrae and between the scapula and vertebral column. Its primary purpose is fixation of the scapula while shoulder movement is occuring.

triceps   muscle in the upper arm that extends the elbow.

tuberosity   a large round prominence on a bone which serves as an attachment for muscles and ligaments.

ulna   one of two bones in the forearm, running from the point of the elbow and lying on the outer (little finger) side.

ulnar   relating to the ulna.

valgus   outward rolling.

varus   inward rolling.

vola   the sole of the foot or the palm of the hand.

vola manus   palm of the hand.

vola pedis   sole of the foot.

volar   relating to the palm or the sole.

wrist   junction between the two forearm bones (radius and ulna) and the eight wrist bones (trapezium, trapezoid, capitate, hamate, pisiform, triquetral, lunate, and scaphoid).

zygoma   cheekbone.

Speed-Reading
At The
Keyboard

Volume 1

*By Edward Shanaphy, Stuart Isacoff
and Julie Jordan*

INTRODUCTION

The ability to read music at sight is an *earned* capacity which opens the door to infinite musical discoveries each day of one's musical life. Just imagine yourself as one of those remarkable people who can sit down and play straight through a Rachmaninoff prelude, or the score to a Gilbert & Sullivan opera, or "The Marriage Of Figaro," or "Porgy And Bess," the very first time you see the music!

Sight-reading is one of the most ignored aspects of piano pedagogy. If one is a trumpet player, or a french hornist, one would automatically become a sight reader by virtue of having to play with other instrumentalists from time to time. Ensemble playing with orchestra, bands, or chamber groups is one of the most certain ways to become a good sight-reader. However, the pianist, primarily a solo performer, is usually left to his own wits and devices to acquire this skill. Most teachers concentrate the efforts of their students toward interpretation and technique, devoting much of their effort on specific solo pieces or works. Therefore, it is to those students, and musicians who seek to improve their sight-reading capacity, that we dedicate these volumes of study.

TRAINING YOUR REFLEXES

Sight-reading has been described above as an earned capacity. It is not an inherited gift with which one is born, such as perfect pitch. It is a reflex activity which one can develop, nurture and improve, much the same as driving an automobile. The driver of an automobile is able to carry on a conversation while driving simply because of reflexes. His brain and limbs will react to road signs, signals, pedestrians, traffic, at the same time he is speaking. This is a very similar process to that of a musician reading a piece of music. He may be thinking of something totally removed from the music at hand, but his brain *and* his fingers are *automatically* responding to those signals (notes) on his music stand.

GOALS FOR THIS COURSE

The primary goal of the course is, obviously, to make you, the student, a proficient sight-reader at the keyboard, and to provide teachers with a guided course of study, and a collection of pieces to which they can direct their students. The method produces the desired result. There exists no other graduated collection of such size and scope for this express purpose. In fact, the large quantity of music provided solves one of the many short-comings that keyboard students experience: the lack of exposure to a generous cross-section of pieces. Such lack of exposure is, perhaps, the greatest reason for poor sight-reading among pianists. Many students are taught to repeat a single piece ad infinitum for perfection's sake, for what may be months (or more) on end. This precious time devoted to one single piece of music precludes the player from the enjoyment of, as well as benefits derived from playing numerous easier pieces, pieces which provide new melodies to the player's ear and familiarize him with the styles of various composers. The pieces also act as exercises for technical improvement. The volumes of music contained herein provide, therefore, a graduated sequence of piano pieces, themes, excerpts and accompaniments, designed to introduce the student's reflexes in a logical and painless way to the complexities of musical notation for piano. From simple key and time signatures to complex, from whole-note and half-note pieces to those with more intricate rhythms, this method insures a step-by-step sequence, carefully planned to make the learning process not only logical, but musically enjoyable. When you scan the volumes, and look at the simplicity of the early pieces in contrast to the more complicated selections near the end, you realize the amount of work it will take you to get there. But it is not nearly as long a process as it may seem at first glance. And as they say in the travel business, half the fun is getting there. Half the fun is listening to what you are playing whether it's a simple Mozart piece, or a dainty minuet by Bach, or a lovely Viennese waltz by Strauss, or a soaring, romantic theme from a concerto by Tchaikovsky.

All of the works selected for this course have been painstakingly reviewed and sequenced for the primary purpose of leading the student through a logical and deliberate progression in sight-reading study. They have also been selected because of their musicality. They constitute good music and are most enjoyable to play and hear. The editors believe that any of the music provided herein functions not only as lab work for such a sight-reading project, but as fine performance material as well. In this respect, your purchase of these volumes becomes doubly valuable to you.

COURSE ESSENTIALS

The first two volumes in the course contain two main elements: Flash-Pages and Reading Pieces. The Flash-Pages are designed primarily to train the eye to scan music, and the memory to retain it for a very short period; the Reading Pieces are those studies to which you will apply the *graduated reflex technique* through use of a metronome as well as guidelines and instructions within the volumes of pieces themselves.

You will also encounter a type of drill we have called "Map Tone" Exercises. These will help you to spot the most important notes in a piece at first glance — to see the trees within the forest. Your ability to discern the *crucial* notes, the ones that mold the shapes of the musical lines, will make sight-reading a great deal easier. (Professionals who are called upon to sight-read often pick out these key notes and simply "fake" the rest. They know that bringing out the *important* melodies and harmonies is 90% of the job.)

Volume three contains a wealth of accompaniment music in all styles from pop to classical. These pieces will give you experience in playing the kind of keyboard music you will most likely need to sight-read one day. The music in this volume increases in difficulty in stages. We suggest that you play through pieces in this supplemental collection as a way to break the routine of the programmed training of volumes one and two . . . and to test your progress! When you come to a piece in volume three that is just too difficult, resume your course work and return to it at a later date. You will be amazed at the development of your sight-reading ability, as measured by your progress through volume three.

An absolute essential for sight-reading study is a good metronome. It is this instrument which becomes your conductor, which dictates the tempo to which you must, at all costs, adhere. The metronome is crucial to the proper training of your sight-reading reflexes. To proceed any further without this very essential instrument would be a total waste of your time and money. Any local music store should be able to provide you with a reliable and economically priced metronome.

It is suggested that a minimum of twenty minutes be spent on a daily basis for your sight-reading regimen. It is the continuity of such study which will ensure the best results.

HOW TO USE
THE FLASH PAGES

A PICTURE IN THE MIND

Reading music at sight requires not only training of a recognition reflex, as mentioned above, but also adopting the concept of reading *musical units* (short phrases, motifs, etc.) *at a glance*. This concept requires that the musician take an "instant photograph" of a measure of music, or a short melodic line, or progression, rather than perform a note by note analysis and translation of a much larger segment of the piece. The goal is to avoid being that kind of reader whose head bobs up and down from fingers to page, page to fingers, as he or she laboriously depresses the keys in each hand, note by agonizing note.

In order to develop this musical *unit* concept, the musician must train his eye to become a scanning camera, and his mind to become the film. The following pages, therefore, are to function as over-sized flash-cards, in this case 'flash-pages', which you should take away from the piano in order to practice the concept.

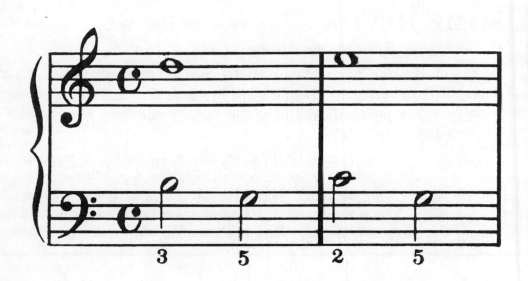

THE DRILL. . .

1) Look at the flash-page for two or three seconds, then close your eyes, and the book . . .

2) Reconstruct whatever you can in your mind of what appeared on the page.

3) Go to the piano and try to play it.

If you draw a blank on all or part of the phrase, open to the page again, take another 'picture', and continue to repeat the process until you have memorized the musical unit. As you continue this drill, your ability to retain more and more of a phrase at a glance will grow dramatically.

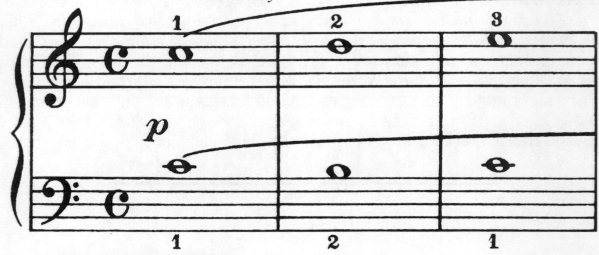

SOME HINTS. . . or, *the middle comes last:*

1) Get the top line first (the melody), then . . .

2) Try for the top line together with the bottom-most notes (bass), or as many bass notes as you can.

3) Start filling in the middle once the melody and bass have been achieved.

This concept of leaving the middle to last is precisely what every good sight-reader often does when encountering a new piece of music. The melody has priority; try to support it with as many bass notes as can be read and played, filling in the middle when and if possible.

There will be additional flash-page drills as you progress; however, you should continue to develop this concept on your own by isolating measures, phrases, melodies, chord progressions, and taking 'instant photos'. For example, when playing an easy measure, say of whole or half note duration, look ahead to the next measure and take a picture while holding those notes. Perhaps the most important rule for a sight reader is always to LOOK AHEAD.

SECTION 1

Flash Pages

Drill No. 1

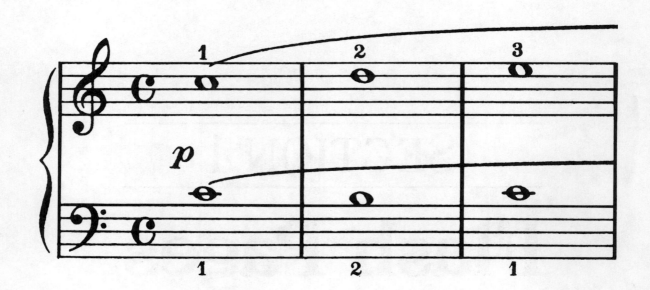

Drill No. 2

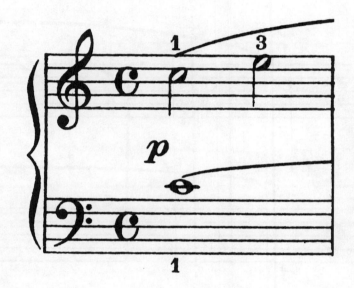

Drill No. 3

Drill No. 4

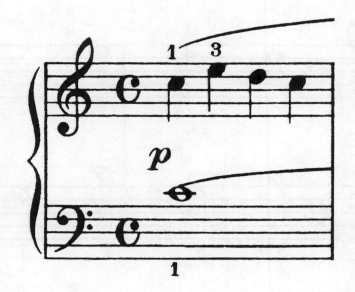

Drill No. 5

Drill No. 6

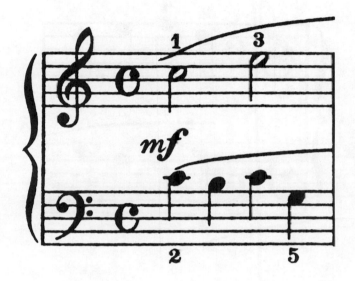

Drill No. 7

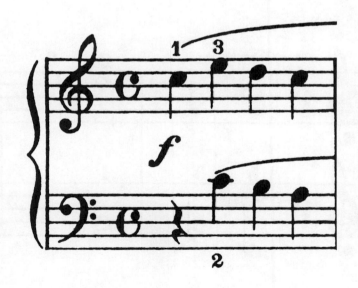

Drill No. 8

Drill No. 9

SECTION 1
Reading Pieces

How To Use
The Reading Pieces

Step One:

As you proceed to the first reading piece, you will set the metronome to a tempo within the suggested range indicated at *METRONOME #1*. (Note: if the suggested setting is too fast or too slow for your own ability, by all means set your own tempo, and make note of that tempo at the top of the page.)

Step Two:

If any measure numbers are indicated at the beginning of the piece under "Special Attention," it is to warn you that these specific measures may cause a little trouble and are worth a quick look before you proceed to play the study. (Note: you should not pre-play these trouble spots, but merely analyze in your mind what is happening in those measures.) Any good musician who is sight-reading a piece knows enough to scan the piece quickly for such trouble spots.

Step Three:

Pre-Reading the Piece: Check the key signature and time signature and get them firmly set in your mind. Look at the first few measures without playing while your metronome is ticking. Do you have a feel for how the music will sound? Approximately? (Note: under no circumstances are you to stop playing to fix a mistake, or check a fingering or replay a passage. This will defeat the entire purpose of this course, which is to sharpen the reflexes. If you hit wrong notes, let them lie! You are the only one listening. Just keep plugging ahead with the inexorable metronome, playing as many of the right notes as possible.

Step Four:

Once you have completed a study, make a pencil notation of the exact metronomic marking you used and the date, and go on to the next study. DO NOT REPEAT THE STUDY. ALWAYS MOVE AHEAD TO THE FOLLOWING STUDY. Play a sufficient number of studies to fill your twenty minutes, or whatever time you have allotted yourself in excess of twenty minutes.

Step Five:

Once you have completed a volume, return to the first reading piece in that volume and play it within the range indicated by Metronome #2. Continue in the following manner: for every *new* study you read, re-read an earlier study at the faster setting.

FINAL HINTS

You will become a good sight-reader more quickly if you cultivate and apply the good reading habits you probably already use when reading a book or magazine. Keep these basic rules in mind:

1) Fast readers don't move their lips as they read. Therefore, when reading through the music pieces, play *without pausing on every note.*

2) Just as you wouldn't point to each word in reading a sentence, be sure to read your music *without looking down at the keyboard.*

3) The key to quick and efficient reading is the ability to take in large chunks of text without moving your eyes. Practice doing the same when reading music. (Many of the "Flash Pages" are specially designed to help you do just that!)

By following these tips, you will be taking advantage of what you already know — transferring skills from ordinary book reading to music speed-reading.

Reading Piece No. 1: Whole Note Etudes

1st Reading Tempo: _50_   **Date:** _12-21-8?_

2nd Reading Tempo: _72_   **Date:** _1-7-92_

Metronome Range #1: o = 40-50
Metronome Range #2: o = 60-72
Actual Tempo: o = 88

Special Attention: "Pre-read" pieces to watch for parallel and contrary motion.   **Reminder:** Always look ahead.

Helpful Hint: C means there are 4 beats per measure, each quarter note getting one beat; in 2/2, there are two half notes getting a beat each in every measure. The result here is virtually the same.

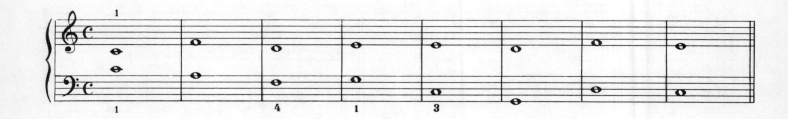

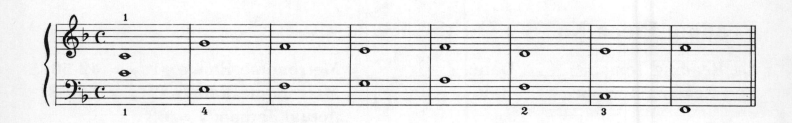

Reading Piece No. 2 : Silver Sledges *(M. Yordansky)*

1st Reading Tempo: ___52___   **Date:** ___12-21-87___   **Metronome Range #1:** ♩ = 42-52

2nd Reading Tempo: ___72___   **Date:** ___1-7-92___   **Metronome Range #2:** ♩ = 52-76

                                                                    Actual Tempo: ♩ = 76

Special Attention: Use rests in each hand to look ahead.

Reminder: *Decrescendo* ——————— means gradually softer.

Reading Piece No. 3 : On the Ice *(M. Krasyev)*

1st Reading Tempo: ___52___   **Date:** ___12-21-87___   **Metronome Range #1:** ♩ = 42-50

2nd Reading Tempo: ___72___   **Date:** ___1-7-92___   **Metronome Range #2:** ♩ = 50-63

                                                                    Actual Tempo: ♩ = 63

Special Attention: Use the rests in each hand to look ahead.

Reminder: The tenuto mark - means that the note should be played with expressive emphasis. The accent mark > means that the note should be struck percussively.

Did you read the dynamic markings?

Reading Piece No. 4 : Theme With Variations *(J. N. Hummel)*

1st Reading Tempo: _60_ **Date:** _12-21-87_

2nd Reading Tempo: _108_ **Date:** _1-9-92_

Special Attention: See Variation VII before selecting tempo.

Metronome Range #1: ♩ = **44-60**

Metronome Range #2: ♩ = **64-108**

Actual Tempo: ♩ = **180**

Reminder: All variations to be played at identical tempo.

Theme

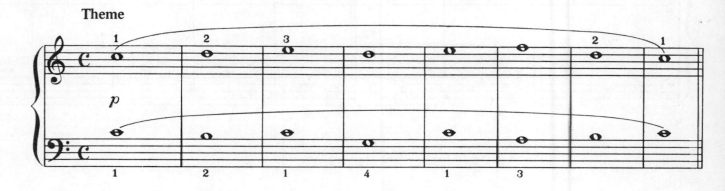

Var. I

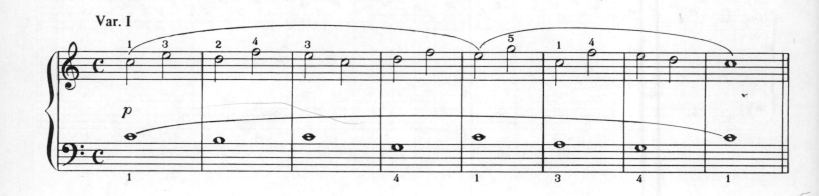

Var. II

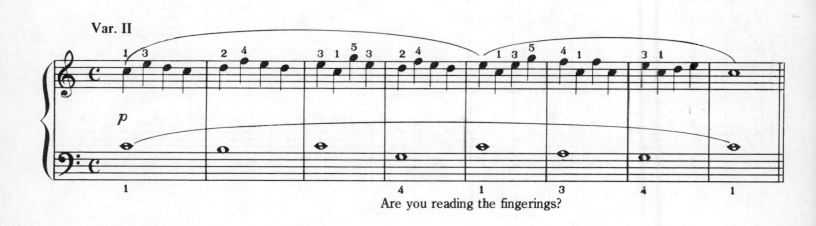

Are you reading the fingerings?

Var. III

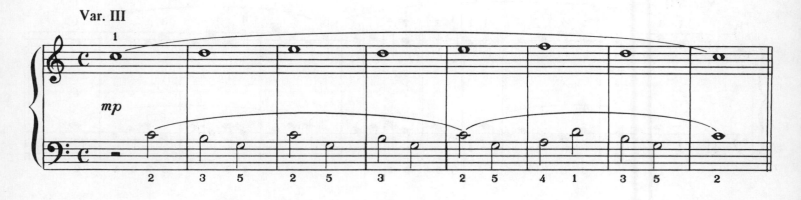

Var. IV

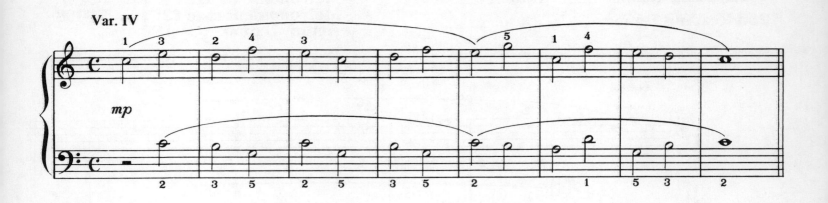

Var. V

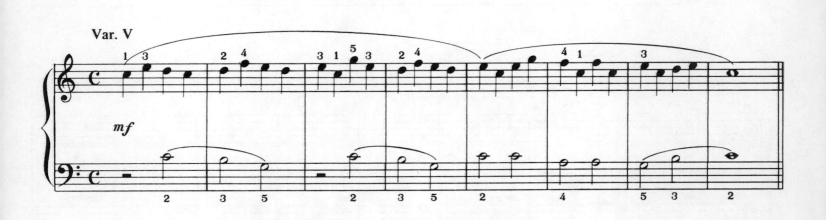

Var. VI

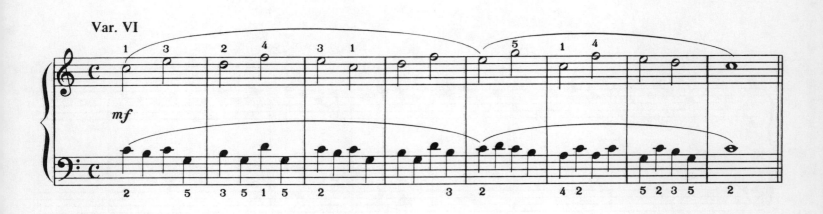

Var. VII

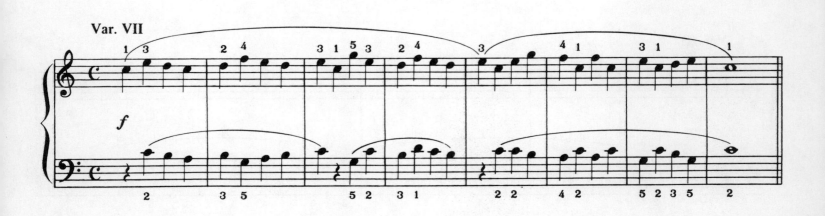

SECTION 2

Flash Pages

Drill No. 10

Drill No. 11

Drill No. 12

Don't read! Take a snapshot, close your eyes...play.

Drill No. 13

Drill No. 14

Drill No. 15

Drill No. 16

Flowing

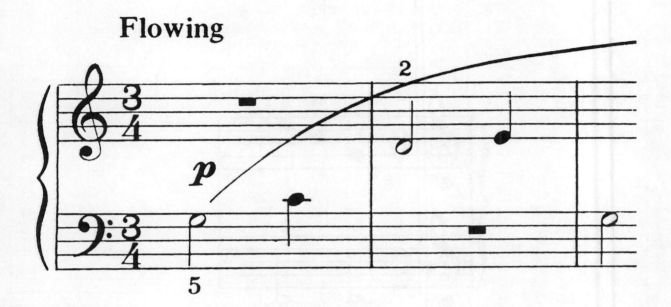

Drill No. 17

Smoothly

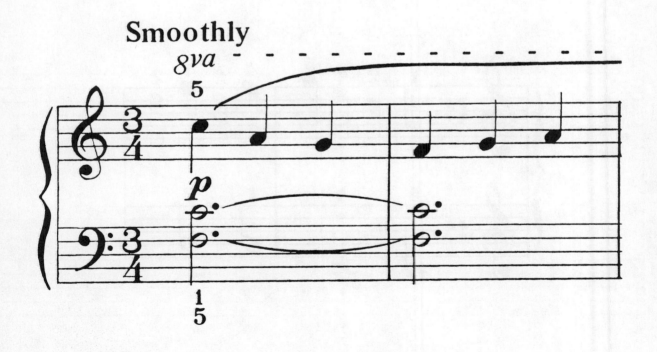

Drill No. 18

Drill No. 19

Drill No. 20

Drill No. 21

Picture both measures with your eyes shut!

Drill No. 22

Drill No. 23

Drill No. 24

Drill No. 25

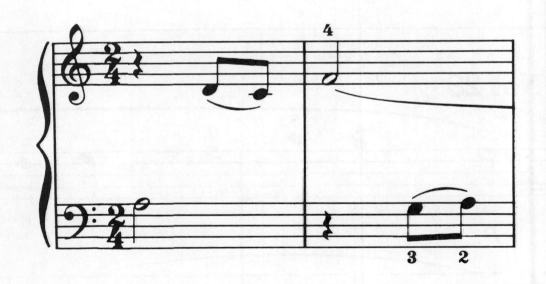

Drill No. 26

Memorize the direction of the lines (see arrows).

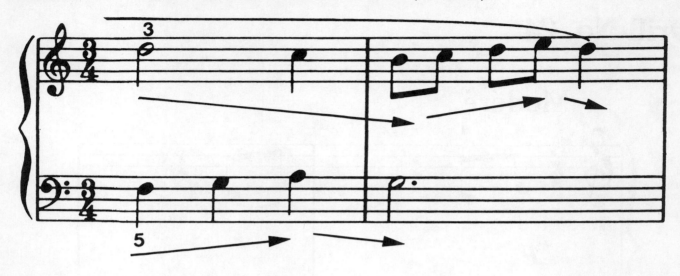

Drill No. 27

Drill No. 28

SECTION 2

Reading Pieces

Reading Piece No. 5 : Amazing Grace   *Traditional*

1st Reading Tempo: _60_   **Date:** _1-3-88_

2nd Reading Tempo: _90_   **Date:** _1-10-92_

Metronome Range #1: ♩ = 40-60
Metronome Range #2: ♩ = 60-90
Actual Tempo: ♩ = 90

Special Attention: Dotted notes (♩.) and leger line notes in right hand below staff.

Reminder: 3/4 meter (three ♩ per measure).

Moderato

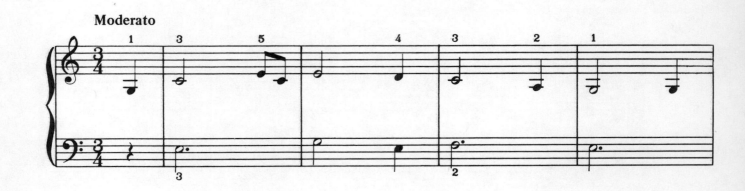

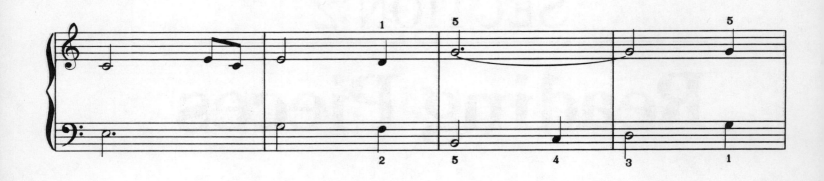

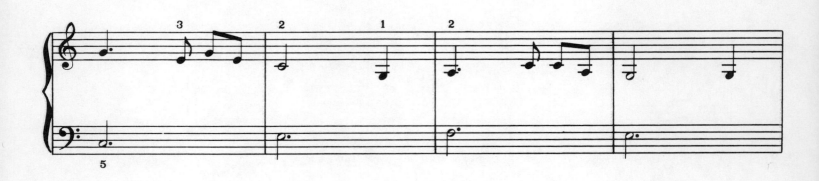

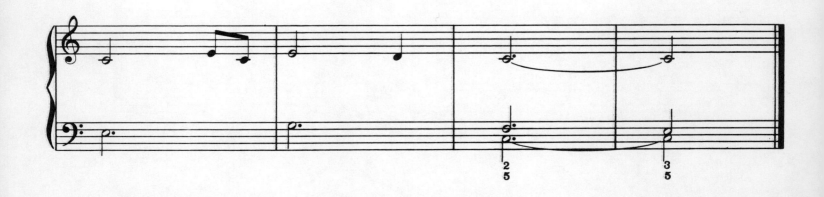

Reading Piece No. 6 : A Little Autumn Song *(Y. Abelyev)*

1st Reading Tempo: _60_ **Date:** _1-3-88_

2nd Reading Tempo: _96_ **Date:** _1-10-92_

Metronome Range #1: ♩ = **40-56**

Metronome Range #2: ♩ = **56-96**

Actual Tempo: ♩ = **96**

Special Attention: Observe the 3 2 fingering in each hand. Both hands are in treble clef.

Reminder: Two-note slurs should be played with a relaxed wrist in a down-up motion.

Moderato ♩ = 96

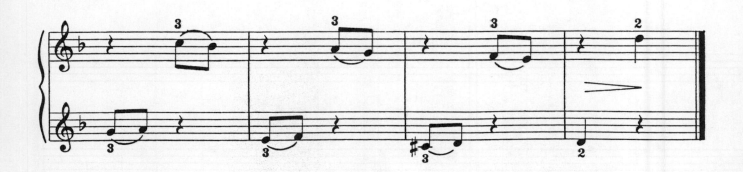

Reading Piece No. 7 : Greensleeves

1st Reading Tempo: **90** Date: **1-3-88**
2nd Reading Tempo: **126** Date: **1-10-92**

Metronome Range #1: ♩ = **60-90**
Metronome Range #2: ♩ = **104-126**
Actual Tempo: ♩ = **168**

Special Attention: Dotted notes (♩.) and accidentals (#, ♭).

Reminder: 3/4 meter (three ♩ per measure).

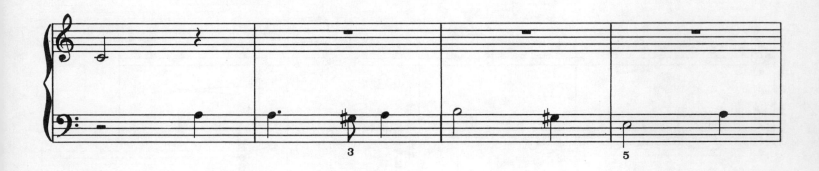

Reading Piece No. 8 : Child's Play *(E. Satie)*

1st Reading Tempo: 1-3-88 **Date:** 72

2nd Reading Tempo: 120 **Date:** 1-10-92

Metronome Range #1: ♩ = **54-72**

Metronome Range #2: ♩ = **72-120**

Actual Tempo: ♩ = **120**

Special Attention: Try to keep the music flowing between the hands as the eighth note duplets alternate from treble to bass.

Reminder: For any given pulse (e.g. the 4th and 5th systems, etc.), when smaller note values change to larger ones (such as eighth notes to half notes), remember *not* to rush on the longer note.

Hint: It is helpful to count the smallest unit as the basic pulse (i.e. eighth notes in this piece).

Reading Piece No. 9: The Merry Widow Waltz _Franz Lehar_

1st Reading Tempo: 1-3-88 **Date:** 104

2nd Reading Tempo: 138 **Date:** 1-10-92

Metronome Range #1: ♩ = 92-104
Metronome Range #2: ♩ = 116-138
Actual Tempo: ♩. = 76

Special Attention: The melody is sometimes presented in single notes spread between the hands; at other times both hands play together. Look ahead to prepare for these changes.

Reminder: In waltz time the first beat of each measure is slightly accented.

Reading Piece No. 10 : Half Note Etudes

1st Reading Tempo: _69_ **Date:** _1-3-88_

2nd Reading Tempo: _100_ **Date:** _1-10-92_

Metronome Range #1: ♩ = **59-69**

Metronome Range #2: ♩ = **72-100**

Actual Tempo: ♩ = **120**

Special Attention: Watch fingerings.

Reminder: Keys change for each etude.

Reading Piece No.11 : A Little Child On The Earth
Has Been Born *(Traditional)*

1st Reading Tempo: _66_ **Date:** _1-4-88_   **Metronome Range #1:** ♩ = **50-66**

2nd Reading Tempo: _116_ **Date:** _1-10-92_   **Metronome Range #2:** ♩ = **66-116**

Actual Tempo: ♩ = **116**

Special Attention: Notice the important fingering suggestions which vary for different melodic intervals. For instance, the interval of a third can use a 2-3 fingering (measures 2-3 R.H. from a to c), a 1-2 fingering (2nd system, measure 2 from f to a), or a 1-5 fingering (3rd system, measure 4 from a to c).

Reminder: When the basic pulse is quarter notes, try to look ahead during the longer half notes.

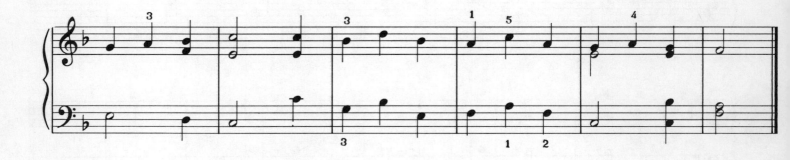

Reading Piece No. 12 : Minuet *(J. Hook)*

1st Reading Tempo: _72_ **Date:** _1-4-88_   **Metronome Range #1:** ♩ = **54-72**

2nd Reading Tempo: _120_ **Date:** _1-10-92_   **Metronome Range #2:** ♩ = **72-120**

Actual Tempo: ♩ = **120**

Special Attention: When using the fingerings indicated, both hands are in a 5-finger position, and need not move off their home keys.

Reminder: In time signatures where the quarter note receives one beat, an eighth note triplet  equals one beat. *Poco rit.* (ritardando) means slowing down a little.

3

Reading Piece No. 13: Morning (Peer Gynt Suite) *Edvard Grieg*

1st Reading Tempo: 72 **Date:** 1-4-88

2nd Reading Tempo: 88 **Date:** 10-5-93

Metronome Range #1: ♩ = 60-72

Metronome Range #2: ♩ = 88-104

Actual Tempo: ♩ = 152

Special Attention: *8va* indicates that you should play one octave higher than written. *loco* restores the music to its original octave.

Reminder: Watch for left hand switches between held chords and "walking" bass lines.

Reading Piece No. 14 : What the Little Tulip Princess Is Saying

(E. Satie)

1st Reading Tempo: 60   **Date:** 1-4-88   **Metronome Range #1:** ♩ = 52-60

2nd Reading Tempo: 88   **Date:** 10-5-93   **Metronome Range #2:** ♩ = 84-116

Actual Tempo: ♩ = 144

Special Attention: Music underneath a phrase mark ⌒ is to be played legato, that is, with a smooth but clean connection of the notes.

Reading Piece No. 15 : In May *(F. Behr)*

1st Reading Tempo: _69_ **Date:** _1-4-88_   **Metronome Range #1:** ♩ = **52-69**

2nd Reading Tempo: _88_ **Date:** _10-5 93_   **Metronome Range #2:** ♩ = **69-120**

Actual Tempo: ♩ = **120**

Special Attention: Because of the limited range of both hands (basically a five-finger position), use this as an exercise to train the eye to read whole measures. Choose a tempo that allows you to see the direction and design of both hands in one measure blocks.

Reminder: Notice that both hands play in the treble·clef.

Reading Piece No. 16: The Beautiful Bride *(Ukrainian folk song)*

1st Reading Tempo: 72 **Date:** 1-4-88

2nd Reading Tempo: 88 **Date:** 10-5-93

Metronome Range #1: ♪ = **60-72**

Metronome Range #2: ♪ = **100-120**

Actual Tempo: ♩. = **60-72**

Special Attention: Both hands are in the treble clef. Strive for an exact balance between L.H. and R.H. When played properly, this piece should sound as if it were being played by one hand only.

Reminder: *Rit.* (ritardando) means slowing down. Long slurs indicate that the music contained within them should be played legato and as one phrase, that is, one musical idea.

Reading Piece No. 17: Camptown Races *Stephen Foster*

1st Reading Tempo: _100_ **Date:** _1-4-88_
2nd Reading Tempo: _____ **Date:** _10-5-93_

Metronome Range #1: ♩ = **84-100**
Metronome Range #2: ♩ = **108-126**
Actual Tempo: ♩ = **200**

Special Attention: Keep your left hand thumb "anchored" on C in the first section of this piece. This will help your hand to "measure" the distances it must travel to strike the correct notes.

Reminder: Keep a steady count at all times in order not to be thrown by rhythmic changes in the melody.

Lively

Reading Piece No. 18 : First Lessons *C. Czerny*

1st Reading Tempo: _90_ **Date:** _1-4-88_
2nd Reading Tempo: _132_ **Date:** _0-5-93_

Metronome Range #1: ♩ = **60-90**
Metronome Range #2: ♩ = **96-112**
Actual Tempo: ♩ = **144**

Special Attention: Review right hand notes above staff (leger lines).

Reminder: Both hands are in treble clef.

Helpful Hint: Like the Flash Pages, read these in two measure segments.

Reading Piece No. 19 : The Chocolate Waltz *(E. Satie)*

1st Reading Tempo: _72_ **Date:** _1-5-88_

2nd Reading Tempo: _112_ **Date:** _10-93_

Metronome Range #1: ♩ = **56-72**

Metronome Range #2: ♩ = **72-112**

Actual Tempo: ♩ = **112**

Special Attention: When sight-reading this relatively simple waltz (with only one voice in each hand), try *visually* to *grasp* the entire measure as you play the downbeat of the triple meter. Try to recognize the "direction" of each hand, i.e. contrary, similar or oblique motion.

Reminder: "rall." means "rallentando," or to play with a slower pulse.

Reading Piece No. 20: Beautiful Dreamer *Stephen Foster*

1st Reading Tempo: _10_ **Date:** _10-93_
2nd Reading Tempo: _____ **Date:** _____

Metronome Range #1: ♪ = **60-72**
Metronome Range #2: ♪ = **84-100**
Actual Tempo: ♪ = **132**

Special Attention: This time signature indicates that there will be three groups of three eighth notes in each measure. At fast tempos, there should be a feeling of three strong beats per measure.

Reminder: Use held notes in one hand as an opportunity to concentrate on the moving line in the other hand.

SECTION 3

Flash Pages

Drill No. 29

Drill No. 30

Drill No. 31

Drill No. 32

Drill No. 33

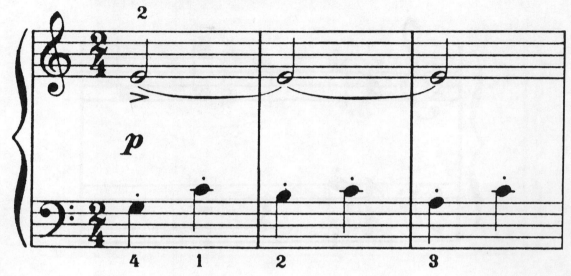

Drill No. 34

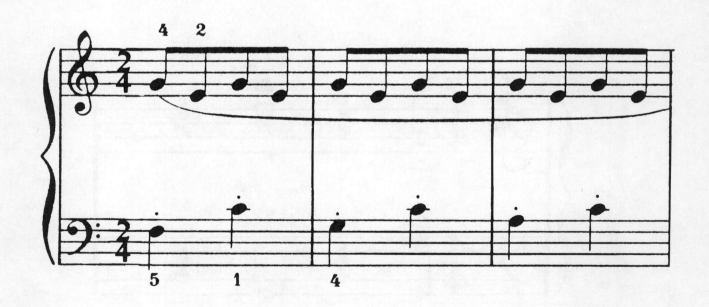

Drill No. 35

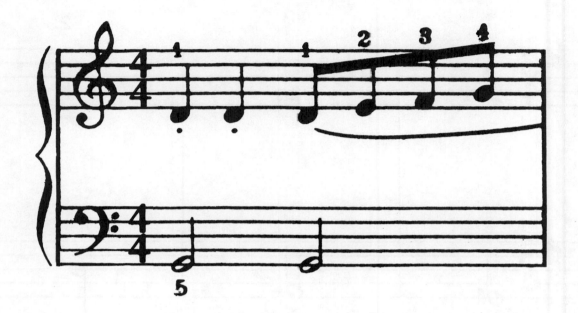

Drill No. 36

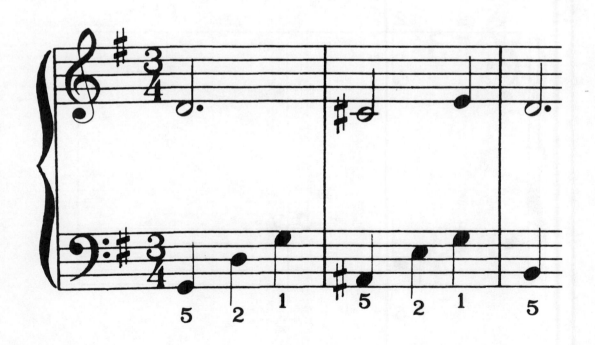

Drill No. 37

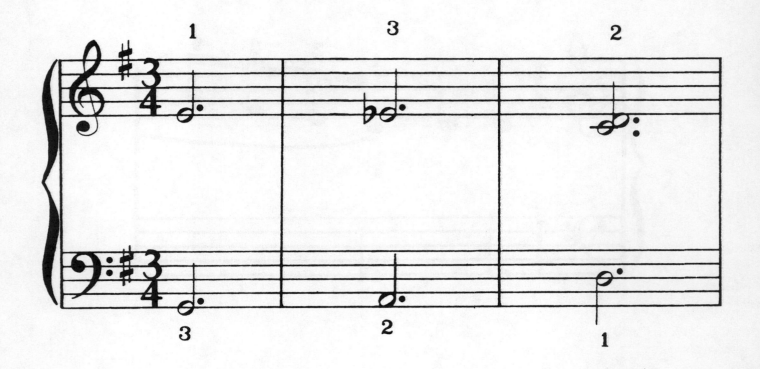

Drill No. 38

Drill No. 39

Drill No. 40

Drill No. 41

Drill No. 42

Drill No. 43

Drill No. 44

Drill No. 45

Drill No. 46

Drill No. 47

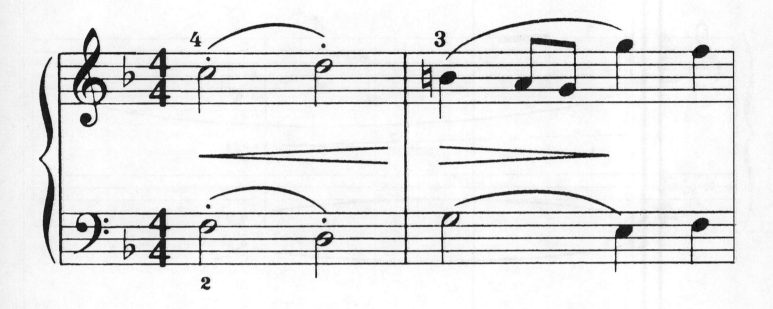

Drill No. 48

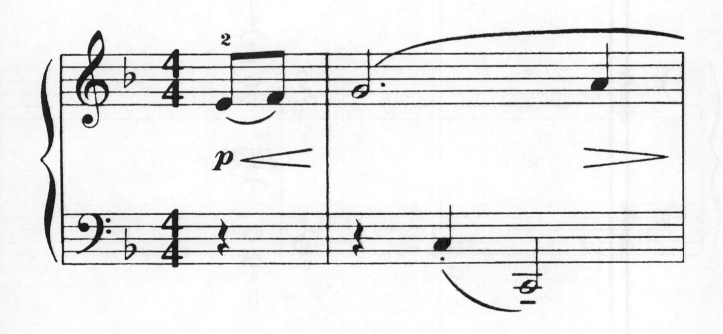

Drill No. 49

Drill No. 50

Drill No. 51

(Note left hand pattern)

Drill No. 52

Drill No. 53

Drill No. 54

Drill No. 55

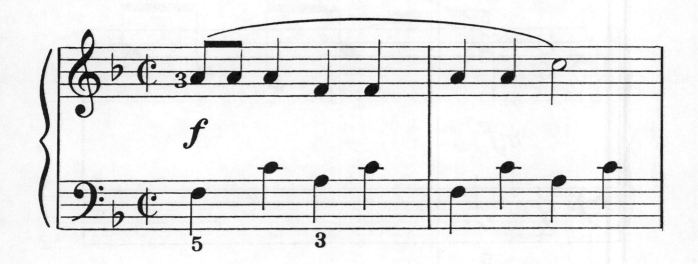

Drill No. 56

Drill No. 57

Drill No. 58

Drill No. 59

Drill No. 60

Drill No. 61

Drill No. 62

SECTION 3
Reading Pieces

Reading Piece No. 21: Etude (Simplified) *Frederic Chopin*

1st Reading Tempo: 69 **Date:** 1-5-88

2nd Reading Tempo: _____ **Date:** 10-93

Metronome Range #1: ♩ = **60-69**
Metronome Range #2: ♩ = **80-92**
Actual Tempo: ♩ = **116**

Special Attention: Watch for leger lines in the left hand part.

Reminder: Maintain the same hand position whenever possible (as, for example, when the left hand thumb can remain "anchored" on middle C).

Lento

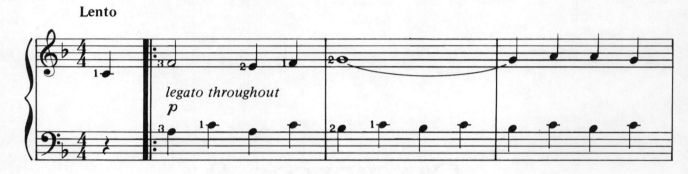

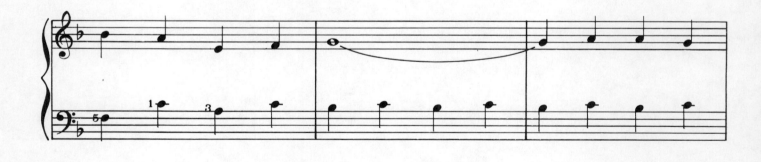

Reading Piece No. 22: Ah! Vous Dirai-Je, Maman *W. A. Mozart*

1st Reading Tempo: 84   **Date:** 1-5-88   **Metronome Range #1:** ♩ = 64-84
2nd Reading Tempo: ___   **Date:** 10-93   **Metronome Range #2:** ♩ = 96-112
                                                Actual Tempo: ♩ = 60

Special Attention: Left hand chords in 3rd and 5th system (line of music).   **Reminder:** Two beats per measure.

Reading Piece No. 23: Skip To My Lou

1st Reading Tempo: _108_   **Date:** _1-5-88_

2nd Reading Tempo: _____   **Date:** _10-93_

Metronome Range #1: ♩ = **80-108**
Metronome Range #2: ♩ = **120-168**
Actual Tempo: ♩ = **108**

Special Attention: Tricky rhythms in measures 9 and 11.

Reminder: The first beat of any measure is the "strong" beat.

Reading Piece No. 24 : The Shepherd Plays *(T. Salutrinskaya)*

1st Reading Tempo: _72_   **Date:** _1-5-88_   **Metronome Range #1:** ♩ = **52-72**

2nd Reading Tempo: _____   **Date:** _10-93_   **Metronome Range #2:** ♩ = **72-104**

                                                 Actual Tempo: ♩ = **104**

Special Attention: Note the clef changes on systems 4 and 5. Try to observe the dynamics, as they will add greatly to the expressiveness of this folk-like Russian tune.

Reminder: Cantabile means with a singing tone. A repetitive bass helps free your eyes to concentrate reading ahead in the R.H.

Reading Piece No. 25: You Tell Me Your Dream *C. N. Daniels*

1st Reading Tempo: _100_ **Date:** _1-5-88_
2nd Reading Tempo: _____ **Date:** _10-93_

Metronome Range #1: ♩ = **84-100**
Metronome Range #2: ♩ = **104-120**
Actual Tempo: ♩ = **144**

Special Attention: Watch for chords and accidentals in last two systems.
Reminder: Keep looking ahead for left-hand movement, and use correct fingering.

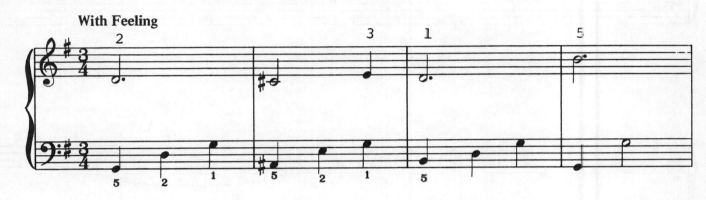

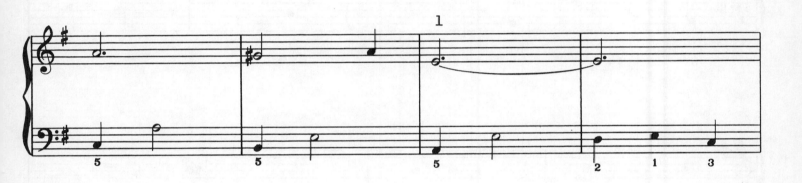

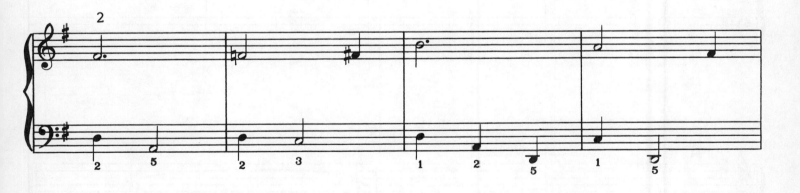

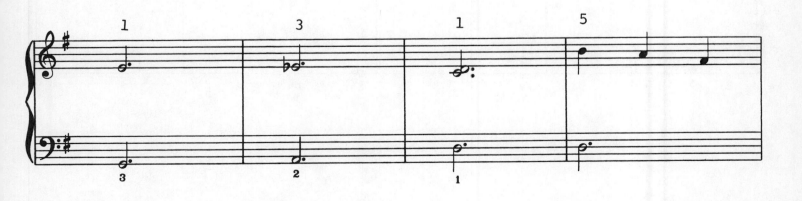

Reading Piece No. 26 : Rosamunde *(F. Schubert)*

1st Reading Tempo: _66_   **Date:** _1-5-88_

2nd Reading Tempo: _____   **Date:** _10-93_

Metronome Range #1: ♩ = **50-66**

Metronome Range #2: ♩ = **66-112**

Actual Tempo: ♩ = **112**

Special Attention: The leger lines above the bass clef (used here for the notes above "middle C") are to be played with the L.H.

Reading Piece No. 27: La Donna e Mobile *(G. Verdi)*

1st Reading Tempo: _60_ **Date:** _1-5-88_

2nd Reading Tempo: _____ **Date:** _10-93_

Metronome Range #1: ♩ = **46-60**

Metronome Range #2: ♩ = **60-138**

Actual Tempo: ♩ = **138**

Special Attention: The melody of this aria is marked by the motivic unit ♩♩♩♪♪♩ . The important part of this motive is the eighth note figure, which occurs in almost every other measure. Therefore, let the preparatory quarter notes lead to that motive; this should make the reading smoother, and should also help you visually grasp the piece in two-measure groups.

Helpful Hint: See the next to last measure before playing.

Reading Piece No. 28: Surprise Symphony *Josef Haydn*

1st Reading Tempo: _80_ **Date:** _1-6-88_   **Metronome Range #1:** ♩ = **60-80**

2nd Reading Tempo: _____ **Date:** _10-93_   **Metronome Range #2:** ♩ = **90-120**

Actual Tempo: ♩ = **176**

Special Attention: See chord in 16th measure. Also 8th note runs (right hand) in measures 18, 23, 26, 31.

Reminder: Soft staccato sound, but watch for "surprise" loud chord.

Moderato con moto

Keep playing with the beat, even if you hit wrong notes.

Reading Piece No. 29: Waltz *(D. Shostakovich)*

1st Reading Tempo: 72 **Date:** 1-6-88

2nd Reading Tempo: _____ **Date:** 10-93

Metronome Range #1: ♩ = **60-72**

Metronome Range #2: ♩ = **84-104**

Actual Tempo: ♩. = **54**

Special Attention: Although this piece is in the key of A minor (no sharps or flats), be aware of the unexpected B flats and E flats. They occur and eventually return to their natural state.

Reminder: Many times, as in this piece, dynamics follow the contour of the melody line; crescendos happen on rising lines, while decrescendos happen on falling lines.

Reading Piece No. 30: Marche Slave *(P. I. Tchaikovsky)*

1st Reading Tempo: _50_ **Date:** _1-6-88_

2nd Reading Tempo: _____ **Date:** _10-93_

Metronome Range #1: ♩ = **40-50**

Metronome Range #2: ♩ = **50-69**

Actual Tempo: ♩ = **69**

Special Attention: Look over this piece and notice how the R.H. on lines 1 and 2 is repeated one octave higher on lines 3 and 4, while the L.H. is duplicated exactly.

Reminder: Use repetitive bass notes to allow your eyes to read ahead in the melody line.

Reading Piece No. 31: Morning Has Broken

1st Reading Tempo: _88_ **Date:** _1-6-88_

2nd Reading Tempo: _____ **Date:** _10-93_

Metronome Range #1: ♩ = 66-88

Metronome Range #2: ♩ = 100-132

Actual Tempo: ♩ = 144

Special Attention: Dynamic changes in measures 12 and 18. Ritard in measure 18.

Reading Piece No. 32: Polovtsian Dance *(A. Borodin)*

1st Reading Tempo: _76_   **Date:** _1-6-88_   **Metronome Range #1:** ♩ = **46-76**

2nd Reading Tempo: _____   **Date:** _____   **Metronome Range #2:** ♩ = **76-108**

Actual Tempo: ♩ = **120**

Special Attention: The R.H. should be played with a singing legato sound, while the L.H. plays accurate syncopations.

Reminder: When the L.H. is divided into 2 voices, the rhythms of each voice are indicated separately (e.g.), and should be executed as such.

Reading Piece No. 33: Air In F *G.H. Bach*

1st Reading Tempo: _80_ **Date:** _1-6-88_
2nd Reading Tempo: _____ **Date:** _____

Metronome Range #1: ♩ = 66-80
Metronome Range #2: ♩ = 84-108
Actual Tempo: ♩ = 126

Special Attention: Watch fingering suggestions.

Reminder: When switching from ♪ to ♩ to ♩ keep the tempo even.

Helpful Hint: Keep your attention on the busy line, treble or bass.

Reading Piece No. 34 : Musetta's Waltz *(G. Puccini)*

1st Reading Tempo: _72_ **Date:** _1-6-88_
2nd Reading Tempo: _____ **Date:** _10-27-93_

Metronome Range #1: ♩ = **52-72**
Metronome Range #2: ♩ = **72-104**
Actual Tempo: ♩ = **104**

Special Attention: Look ahead to the next measure while playing.

Reminder: When a slur mark ⌒ extends from one clef to another (as in the fourth system), the continuity should be kept, and the entire phrase should sound smoothly connected (despite the change of clefs).

Reading Piece No. 35: Humoreske *(A. Dvorak)*

1st Reading Tempo: _58_ **Date:** _1-6-88_

2nd Reading Tempo: _____ **Date:** _10-29-93_

Metronome Range #1: ♩ = **46-58**

Metronome Range #2: ♩ = **58-84**

Actual Tempo: ♩ = **84**

Special Attention: Because the tempo is "poco lento" with a grazioso character, the reader may take a very comfortable tempo and try to follow the *indicated fingerings* (they are suited for a smooth reading).

Reminder: When the fingering calls for a shift (e.g. over with the second finger as in measure 3, or under with the thumb as in measure 1), try to keep the fingers close to the keys (to provide legato) without looking down at the keyboard.

Poco lento e grazioso

Reading Piece No. 36: Follow The Leader *D. Kabalevsky*

1st Reading Tempo: _69_ **Date:** _1-6-88_

2nd Reading Tempo: _____ **Date:** _____

Metronome Range #1: ♩ = 52-69

Metronome Range #2: ♩ = 80-120

Actual Tempo: ♩ = 152

Special Attention: Look over measures 9 through 16 before playing.

Reminder: Look one measure ahead for what the other hand will do. Remember the flash page exercises.

Reading Piece No. 37: Elephant Walk *D. Kabalevsky*

1st Reading Tempo: _72_   **Date:** _1-6-88_

2nd Reading Tempo: _____   **Date:** _____

Metronome Range #1: ♩ = 52-72
Metronome Range #2: ♩ = 80-120
Actual Tempo: ♩ = 126

Special Attention: Look over final two measures before playing.

Reminder: Andante means walking.

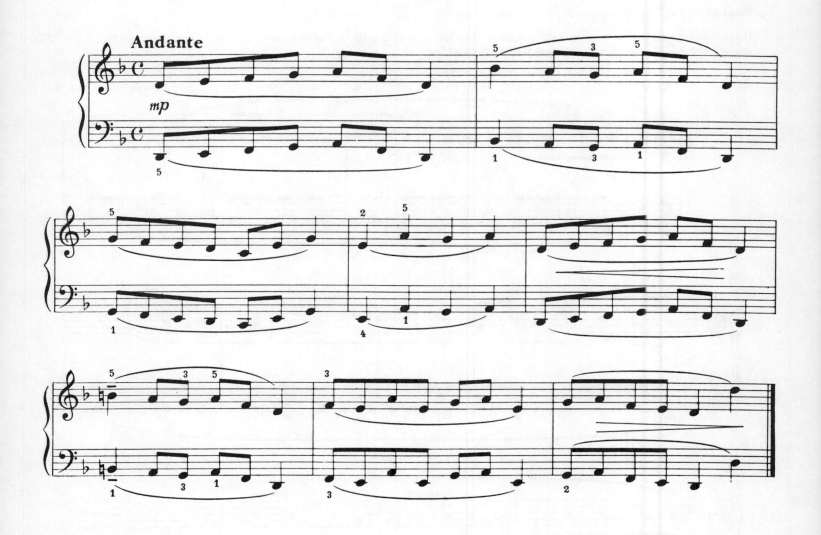

Reading Piece No. 38 : Silly Pranks *(E. Satie)*

1st Reading Tempo: _56_   **Date:** _1-6-88_

2nd Reading Tempo: _____   **Date:** _____

Metronome Range #1: ♩ = **40-56**

Metronome Range #2: ♩ = **56-96**

Actual Tempo: ♩ = **132**

Special Attention: This entire piece is written in the treble clef for *both* hands. The contrapuntal lines will be easier to read if you remember that the L.H. is playing "F" as a pedal point *every other eighth note* until the very last line.

Reminder: "Rall." means rallentando (to get slower gradually).

Hint: In a five-finger position piece remember that if you carefully place each finger over adjacent keys, and use the basic fingering (1-2-3-4-5-4-3-2-1), your reading will be much easier and often *felt* rather than read.

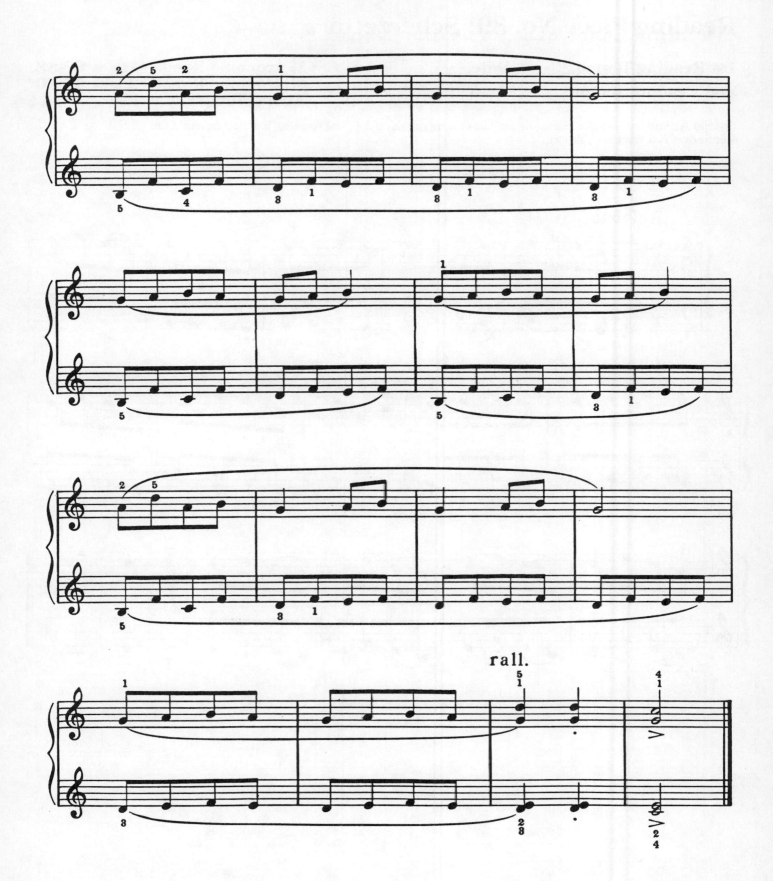

Reading Piece No. 39: Scherzetto *D. Kabalevsky*

1st Reading Tempo: 88   **Date:** 1-6-88

2nd Reading Tempo: ____   **Date:** ____

Metronome Range #1: ♪ = **60-88**
Metronome Range #2: ♩ = **56-90**
Actual Tempo: ♩ = **132**

Special Attention: Look for changes in melodic patterns (measures 3-4), and repeating motifs (measures 9-10).
Reminder: Left hand in treble clef.

Reading Piece No. 40: Allegretto *A. E. Muller*

1st Reading Tempo: _72_ **Date:** _1-6-88_

2nd Reading Tempo: _____ **Date:** _____

Metronome Range #1: ♩ = 52-72
Metronome Range #2: ♩ = 80-132
Actual Tempo: ♩ = 132

Special Attention: Look over the 4th and 5th systems before playing.

Reminder: Try to see whole phrase groups at one time.

Reading Piece No. 41 : Taking Advantage Of The Corns
On His Toes To Take His Hoop From Him *(E. Satie)*

1st Reading Tempo: _59_ **Date:** _1-6-88_   **Metronome Range #1:** ♩ = 48-59
2nd Reading Tempo: _____ **Date:** _____   **Metronome Range #2:** ♩ = 69-100
Actual Tempo: ♩ = 144

Special Attention: There should be a continuity between the hands, even though the duplets are separately and distinctly paired.

Reminder: When there is a rest in one hand (especially for 1 or 2 measures), always look ahead, and prepare for the next entrance.

SECTION 4

Flash Pages

Drill No. 63

Drill No. 64

Drill No. 65

Drill No. 66

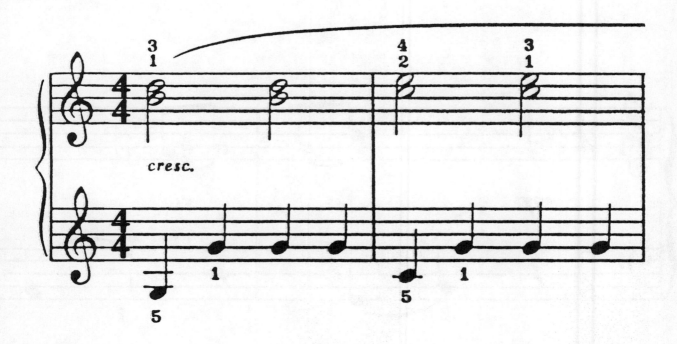

Drill No. 67

Andante grazioso

Drill No. 68

Drill No. 69

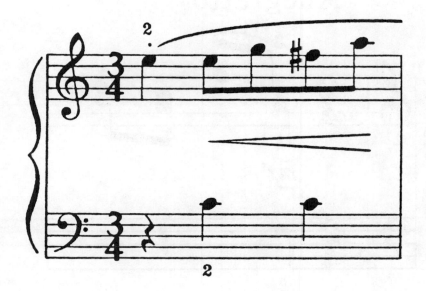

Drill No. 70

Drill No. 71

Allegretto

Drill No. 72

Drill No. 73

Drill No. 74

Drill No. 75

Drill No. 76

Drill No. 77

Drill No. 78

Drill No. 79

Drill No. 80

Drill No. 81

Drill No. 82

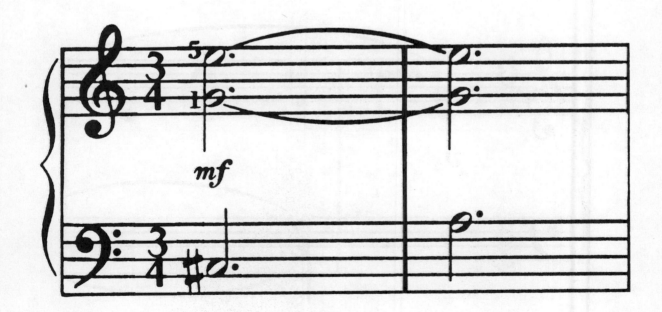

Drill No. 83

Drill No. 84

Drill No. 85

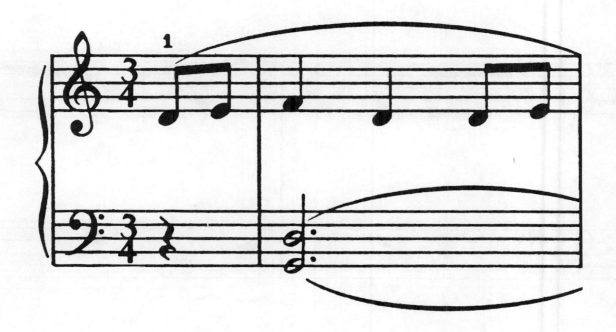

Drill No. 86

Moderato

Drill No. 87

Drill No. 88

Drill No. 89

Drill No. 90

Drill No. 91

Drill No. 92

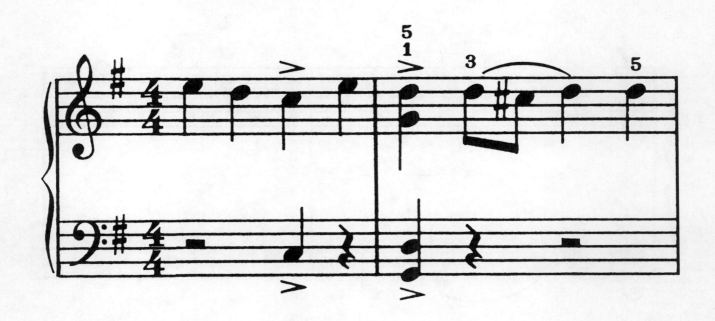

Drill No. 93

Drill No. 94

Drill No. 95

Drill No. 96

Drill No. 97

Drill No. 98

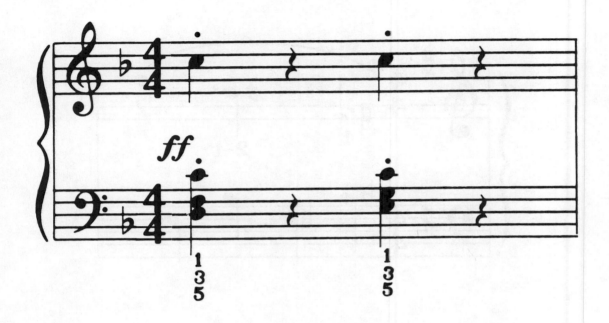

Drill No. 99

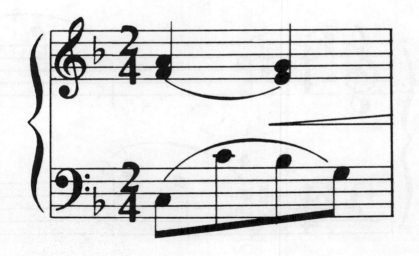

Drill No. 100

Drill No. 101

Drill No. 102

Drill No. 103

Drill No. 104

Drill No. 105

SECTION 4

Reading Pieces

Reading Piece No. 42: Barcarolle *Jacques Offenbach*

1st Reading Tempo: _144_ **Date:** _1-11-88_

2nd Reading Tempo: _____ **Date:** _____

Metronome Range #1: ♩ = 132-144
Metronome Range #2: ♩ = 152-176
Actual Tempo: ♩ = 200

Special Attention: Notice that in the first five systems of this piece the third beat of each measure anticipates the half note downbeat.

Reminder: Scale passages (systems six and seven) which exceed the melodic range of a fifth should be carefully fingered to avoid "getting stuck" or running out of fingers.

Reading Piece No. 43: Lullaby *(J. Brahms)*

1st Reading Tempo: _60_ **Date:** _1-11-88_

2nd Reading Tempo: ____ **Date:** ____

Metronome Range #1: ♩ = **46-60**

Metronome Range #2: ♩ = **60-92**

Actual Tempo: ♩ = **92**

Special Attention: The upbeat eighth note figure is part of the downbeat. Do not play the upbeat until you know "where you are going."

Reminder: Often crescendi $<$ and decrescendi $>$ are linked with the melodic design. Try to make the crescendi-decrescendi gradually, and not suddenly on one note.

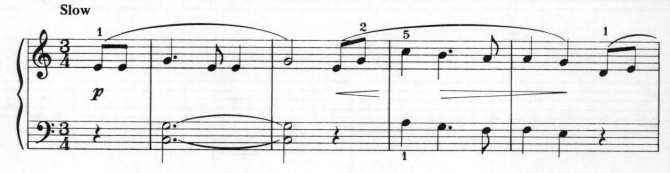

Reading Piece No. 44: Drink To Me Only

1st Reading Tempo: _100_   **Date:** _1-11-88_   **Metronome Range #1:** ♪ = **80-100**
2nd Reading Tempo: _____   **Date:** _____   **Metronome Range #2:** ♪ = **108-138**
Actual Tempo: ♪ = **160**

Special Attention: RH fingering change in third system.
Reminder: Feel two groups of three eighth notes in every measure. Strong beats are first and fourth.

Reading Piece No. 45 : Fascination *F. Marchetti*

1st Reading Tempo: _96_   **Date:** _1-11-88_

2nd Reading Tempo: _____   **Date:** _____

Metronome Range #1: ♩ = 76-96
Metronome Range #2: ♩ = 104-126
Actual Tempo: ♩ = 160

Special Attention: Watch for chords with accidental signs (#, ♭); don't forget to keep moving when you come to them.
Reminder: Accidental signs are in effect for one measure only.

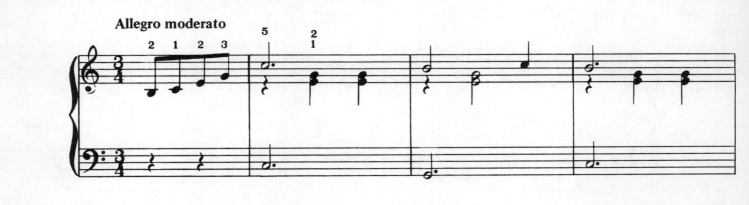

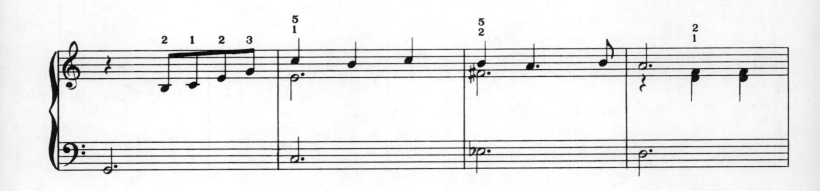

Reading Piece No. 46: Galloping *Dmitri Kabalevsky*

1st Reading Tempo: _100_ **Date:** _1-11-88_

2nd Reading Tempo: _____ **Date:** _____

Metronome Range #1: ♩ = 76-100

Metronome Range #2: ♩ = 104-132

Actual Tempo: ♩ = 200

Special Attention: At measure 18 the acceleration and building must be executed smoothly.

Reminder: In $\frac{3}{4}$ time, the first beat is stressed.

Reading Piece No. 47 : Trepak *(P. I. Tchaikovsky)*

1st Reading Tempo: _66_   **Date:** _1-11-88_

2nd Reading Tempo: _____   **Date:** _____

Metronome Range #1: ♩ = **44-66**

Metronome Range #2: ♩ = **66-144**

Actual Tempo: ♩ = **144**

Special Attention: Notice the changing clefs in the L.H.; they are: *first system – bass clef, second system – treble clef, third system – bass clef* and *fourth system – treble clef.* Reading should be easier with this in mind.

Reading Piece No. 48: I Met A Little Man *Englebert Humperdinck*

1st Reading Tempo: 132   **Date:** 1-11-88

2nd Reading Tempo: _____   **Date:** _____

Metronome Range #1: ♩ = 100-132
Metronome Range #2: ♩ = 72-88
Actual Tempo: ♩ = 144

Special Attention: Keep the continuity of the melodic line as it passes from L.H. to R.H. in the first and second systems.

Reminder: Notice the repeated four-measure phrase in systems one, two and four.

Observe all indications (dynamics, articulation, rit.) to "bring the piece to life."

Lightly

Reading Piece No. 49 : Ode to Joy *(L. V. Beethoven)*

1st Reading Tempo: _66_ **Date:** _1-11-88_

2nd Reading Tempo: _____ **Date:** _____

Metronome Range #1: ♩ = **52-66**

Metronome Range #2: ♪ = **66-112**

Actual Tempo: ♩ = **144**

Special Attention: In this famous theme, the melody is simple and is played by the R.H. in 5-finger position (D-E-F#-G-A).

Helpful Hint: For a preliminary warm-up, notice the repetitive chord pattern.

Reading Piece No. 50: Sweet Adeline *Harry Armstrong*

1st Reading Tempo: _84_ **Date:** _1-11-88_
2nd Reading Tempo: _____ **Date:** _____

Metronome Range #1: ♩ = 66-84
Metronome Range #2: ♩ = 96-112
Actual Tempo: ♩ = 132

Special Attention: Watch fingering in LH at measures 1, 9 and 15.

Reminder: Two flats in the signature indicates the key of B♭.

Moderately

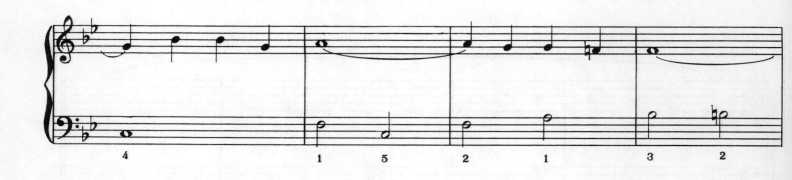

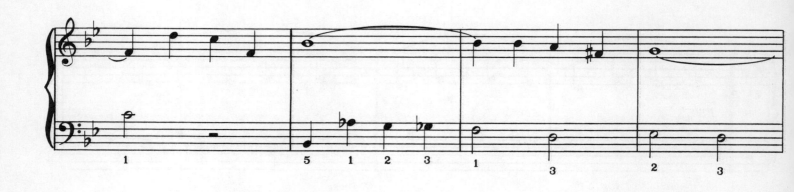

Reading Piece No. 51: Melody in F *(A. Rubinstein)*

1st Reading Tempo: _69_ **Date:** _1-11-88_

2nd Reading Tempo: _____ **Date:** _____

Metronome Range #1: ♩ = **58-69**

Metronome Range #2: ♩ = **69-100**

Actual Tempo: ♩ = **126**

Special Attention: Throughout this piece, one harmony is implied in each measure (with the exception of the measures with all half notes). Glance at the (bass) L.H. accompaniment before beginning.

Reminder: Notice the "lower-neighbor" on beat three of each measure. In systems one and three, it resolves by half step to the chord tone.

Moderato

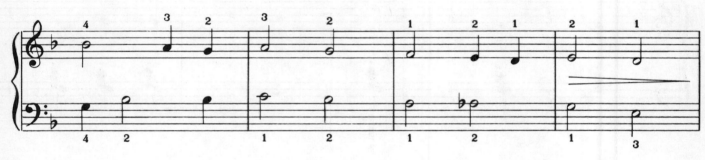

Reading Piece No. 52: Dance *Dmitri Kabalevsky*

1st Reading Tempo: 96 **Date:** 1-11-88
2nd Reading Tempo: _____ **Date:** _____

Metronome Range #1: ♩ = 80-96
Metronome Range #2: ♩ = 104-126
Actual Tempo: ♩ = 120

Special Attention: In L.H. chords, watch for places where some notes change and others don't.
Reminder: • indicates staccato: a short dry sound.

Reading Piece No. 53 : I Saw Three Ships *(traditional)*

1st Reading Tempo: 80   **Date:** 1-11-88

2nd Reading Tempo:_____   **Date:**_____

Metronome Range #1: ♪ = **66-80**

Metronome Range #2: ♪ = **96-120**

Actual Tempo: ♩. = **72**

Special Attention: The dotted quarter notes (and the opening dotted half) should be held for their full value, especially when the eighth notes occur.

Reminder: A flowing legato, appropriate for this song, can be achieved by carefully connecting the notes with the fingers and not with the pedal.

Reading Piece No. 54: Solace (Simplified) *Scott Joplin*

1st Reading Tempo: 76 **Date:** 1-11-88

2nd Reading Tempo:_____ **Date:**_____

Metronome Range #1: ♪ = **76-96**
Metronome Range #2: ♪ = **116-144**
Actual Tempo: ♩ = **108**

Special Attention: *Syncopations* are little rhythmic "surprises" that occur when accents happen at unexpected times. Follow the counting in the music for help.

Reminder: Keep counting, even when notes are being held rather than struck.

Moderate

Reading Piece No. 55: Valsette *Rhené Baton*

1st Reading Tempo: _88_   **Date:** _1-11-88_

2nd Reading Tempo: _____   **Date:** _____

Metronome Range #1: ♩ = 72-88

Metronome Range #2: ♩ = 96-132

Actual Tempo: ♩ = 160

Special Attention: Watch clef changes in LH.

Reminder: ▬ = full weight on the note.

Tempo di Valse moderato

Reading Piece No. 56: March of the Dwarfs *Edvard Greig*

1st Reading Tempo: _84_ **Date:** _1-11-88_

2nd Reading Tempo: _____ **Date:** _____

Metronome Range # 1: ♩ = 63-84
Metronome Range #2: ♩ = 84-120
Actual Tempo: ♩ = 120

Special Attention: The R.H. in measures 3-5 and 7-9 utilizes a sequential pattern with a pedal point on the thumb.

Reminder: The contrast between the staccato and legato markings gives a piece its character.

Moderate

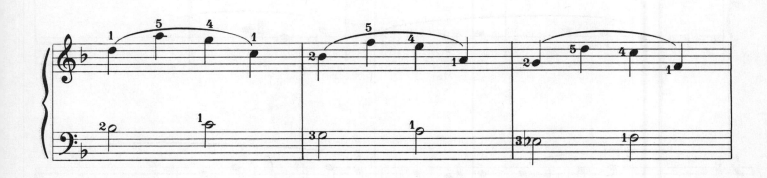

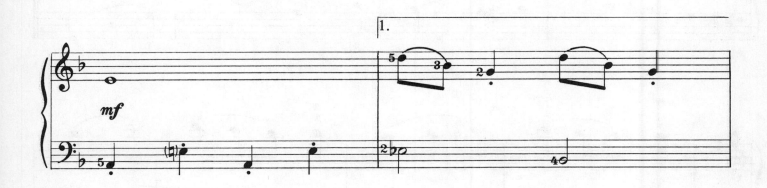

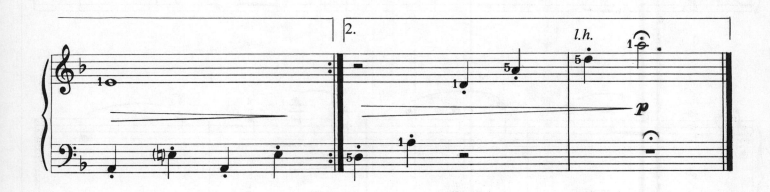

Reading Piece No. 57 : Minuet *Joseph Haydn*

1st Reading Tempo: 66   **Date:** 1-16-88   **Metronome Range #1:** ♩ = 54-69
2nd Reading Tempo: ___   **Date:** ___   **Metronome Range #2:** ♩ = 69-108
Actual Tempo: ♩ = 132

Special Attention: This two-voice piece has single notes in each hand *except* at measures 9, 11, 13, 15 where you should look for double
notes in the R.H.

Reading Piece No. 58: Piano Concerto No. 2 *Sergei Rachmaninoff*

1st Reading Tempo: _88_ **Date:** _1-16-88_

2nd Reading Tempo: _____ **Date:** _____

Metronome Range #1: ♩ = **66-88**
Metronome Range #2: ♩ = **88-116**
Actual Tempo: ♩ = **132**

Special Attention: The accidentals in this piece are significant to the colorful harmonies; stress these chromatic or appogiatura effects.

Reminder: The melodic phrases begin on the second beats of measures 1, 4 and 8; try to hear *long* melodic lines over the bar line.

Moderato

Reading Piece No. 59 : Theme from Peter and the Wolf *(S. Prokofiev)*

1st Reading Tempo: _80_ **Date:** _1-16-88_ **Metronome Range #1:** ♩ = 52-80

2nd Reading Tempo: _____ **Date:** _____ **Metronome Range #2:** ♩ = 100-120

Actual Tempo: ♩ = 168

Special Attention: Take note of the finger-switching indicated in the right hand. The character of this well-known melody is dependent upon the observance of the phrasing.

Reminder: F is automatically sharp in measures 5 and 6.

Reading Piece No. 60 : Allegretto *(L. V. Beethoven)*

1st Reading Tempo: _56_ **Date:** _1-16-88_
2nd Reading Tempo: _____ **Date:** _____

Metronome Range #1: ♪ = **44-58**
Metronome Range #2: ♪ = **58-84**
Actual Tempo: ♪ = **132**

Special Attention: This well known Allegretto from Beethoven's Seventh Symphony is transcribed here entirely in the *bass clef* for *both* hands.

Reminder: When you have a rest (as the quarter rest ⌐ at the end of the second system), immediately let the hand move and set up for the following notes or positions.

Hint: Double notes are not as difficult to read if you let the previous double note (whether it be a second, third or fifth) be your point of reference. This will allow you to *feel* more for directional movement.

Reading Piece No. 61: Give My Regards To Broadway

1st Reading Tempo: _100_ **Date:** _1-16-88_ **Metronome Range #1:** ♩ = 72-100

2nd Reading Tempo: _____ **Date:** _____ **Metronome Range #2:** ♩ = 100-152

Actual Tempo: ♩ = 152

Special Attention: Use the given fingering as an effective aid to sight-reading.

Reminder: Although the tune is written in ⁴⁄₄ time, much of the motion is "by the half measure": by the half note pulse.

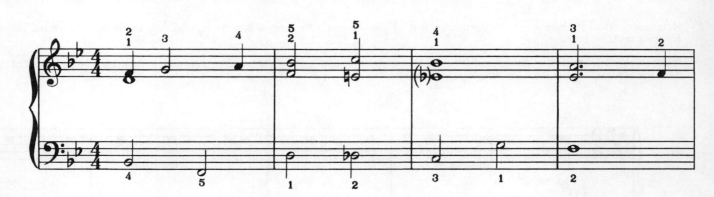

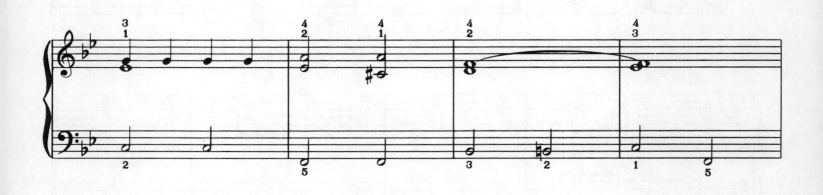

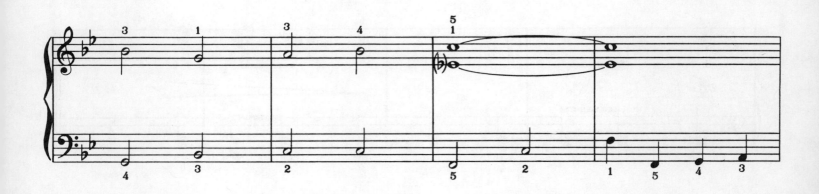

Reading Piece No. 62 : Pavane *Maurice Ravel*

1st Reading Tempo: 52 **Date:** 1-18-88

2nd Reading Tempo: _____ **Date:** _____

Metronome Range #1: ♩ = 52-66

Metronome Range #2: ♩ = 66-80

Actual Tempo: ♩ = 80

Reminder: The "rit." in measure six means that you are free to *broaden* the tempo (which coincides with the expansive dynamic markings in measure seven), until the "a tempo" indication of measure eight, where you resume the original tempo.

Slow

Reading Piece No. 63 : Eating His Bun *(E. Satie)*

1st Reading Tempo: 72 **Date:** 1-18-88

2nd Reading Tempo:_____ **Date:**_____

Metronome Range #1: ♩ = **52-72**

Metronome Range #2: ♩ = **80-116**

Actual Tempo: ♩ = **72**

Special Attention: The distinctly *different articulation* for each hand is easier when you realize that the L.H. or R.H. staccato pattern is always a repetition.

Hint: Concentrate on the moving legato line after you initially recognize the staccato notes.

Reading Piece No. 64: Balletto *Georg Simon Lohlein*

1st Reading Tempo: _72_ **Date:** _1-18-88_

2nd Reading Tempo: _____ **Date:** _____

Metronome Range #1: ♪ = 72-80
Metronome Range #2: ♪ = 84-100
Actual Tempo: ♩ = 88

Special Attention: See measure 4 before setting tempo.
Reminder: *Allegretto* indicates a light, bouncy feel.

Allegretto

Reading Piece No. 65: Minuet *Wolfgang Amadeus Mozart*

1st Reading Tempo: _66_ **Date:** _1-18-88_

2nd Reading Tempo: _____ **Date:** _____

Metronome Range #1: ♩ = **44-66**
Metronome Range #2: ♩ = **66-112**
Actual Tempo: ♩ = **126**

Special Attention: Two-note slurs are played long – short. Notice the measure with parallel slurs before beginning.
Reminder: Key is Bᵇ major. "See" each measure in one harmonic unit.

Reading Piece No. 66: Folk Song *Ludwig Van Beethoven*

1st Reading Tempo: _66_ **Date:** _1-21-88_

2nd Reading Tempo: _____ **Date:** _____

Metronome Range #1: ♩ = **56-80**
Metronome Range #2: ♩ = **92-104**
Actual Tempo: ♩ = **120**

Helpful Hint: Think of 4 sixteenth notes (♫♫) per beat in order to play the dotted rhythm correctly.

Reminder: Take all repeats.

Reading Piece No. 67: Minuet *Wolfgang Amadeus Mozart*

1st Reading Tempo: 1-23-88 **Date:** 69

2nd Reading Tempo: _____ **Date:** _____

Metronome Range #1: ♩ = **50-69**
Metronome Range #2: ♩ = **72-88**
Actual Tempo: ♩ = **116**

Special Attention: Allow your eyes to see whole groups sectioned off by the phrase-marks: especially measures 5-6, 6-7, 13-14, and 14-15.
Reminder: :‖ indicates "repeat."

Reading Piece No. 68: Minuet *Georg Philipp Telemann*

1st Reading Tempo: _72_ **Date:** _1-23-88_

2nd Reading Tempo: _____ **Date:** _____

Metronome Range #1: ♩ = 60-72
Metronome Range #2: ♩ = 80-120
Actual Tempo: ♩ = 132

Special Attention: Be careful of skips in the LH.

Reminder: The *Minuet* was a graceful and delicate dance.

Reading Piece No. 69: Study for Beginners *C. Czerny*

1st Reading Tempo: _72_ Date: _1-23-88_

2nd Reading Tempo: _____ Date: _____

Metronome Range #1: ♩ = 58-72

Metronome Range #2: ♩ = 72-120

Actual Tempo: ♩ = 168

Special Attention: Double thirds in R.H.

Reminder: L.H. plays in treble clef.

Reading Piece No. 70: Bouree *Georg Philipp Telemann*

1st Reading Tempo: _76_ **Date:** _1-23-88_
2nd Reading Tempo: _____ **Date:** _____

Metronome Range #1: ♩ = **58-76**
Metronome Range #2: ♩ = **76-132**
Actual Tempo: ♩ = **144**

Special Attention: Two-note slurs should be played with a slight "down-up" motion. Relax and lift wrist slightly as the second note of slur is played, before playing the next repeated notes.
Reminder: Look at the triplet in the fourth system before beginning.

Reading Piece No. 71: Music Box *Béla Bartók*

1st Reading Tempo: 66 **Date:** 1-24-88
2nd Reading Tempo: ____ **Date:** ____

Metronome Range #1: ♩ = 46-66
Metronome Range #2: ♩ = 72-92
Actual Tempo: ♩ = 108

Helpful Hint: If tied rhythms present counting problems, play without ties at first.
Special Attention: Play piece through without shifting hand positions.
Reminder: A four-beat pulse should be felt even when half notes and tied notes appear.

Reading Piece No. 72 : Berceuse *(E. Satie)*

1st Reading Tempo: _80_ **Date:** _1-24-88_

2nd Reading Tempo: _____ **Date:** _____

Metronome Range #1: ♩ = **58-80**

Metronome Range #2: ♩ = **92-108**

Actual Tempo: ♩ = **69**

Special Attention: Double thirds can easily be recognized; they fluctuate from 2 consecutive line pairs (‡) to two consecutive space pairs (‡). As they occur in this piece, try to sight-read the double thirds using the visual spacing as a guide.

Reminder: In a lullaby or song form such as this piece, scan the form for musical symmetry. This will be seen either in phrasing, voicing, or melodic variation, as the verses are often repeated or interchanged between the hands.

Reading Piece No. 73 : Woman Is Fickle from "Rigoletto" *(G. Verdi)*

1st Reading Tempo: _58_ **Date:** _1-24-88_

2nd Reading Tempo: _____ **Date:** _____

Metronome Range #1: ♩ = 46-80

Metronome Range #2: ♩ = 80-138

Actual Tempo: ♩ = 138

Special Attention: Grace notes are played before the beat.

Reminder: Play this 3/4 time with strong first beats.

Reading Piece No. 74 : Minuet in C *Wolfgang Amadeus Mozart*

1st Reading Tempo: 66   **Date:** 1-26-88

2nd Reading Tempo: _____   **Date:** _____

Metronome Range #1: ♩ = 66-88
Metronome Range #2: ♩ = 88-120
Actual Tempo: ♩ = 160

Special Attention: Note double 3rds in L.H. and double 6ths in R.H.
Reminder: Watch for sections where the harmonic movement is slow, and read two measures at a time.

SECTION 5

Flash Pages

Drill No. 106

Drill No. 107

Drill No. 108

Drill No. 109

Drill No. 110

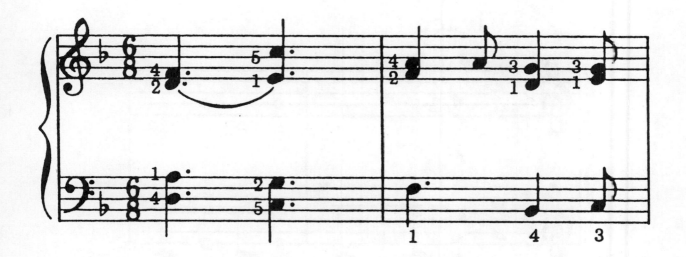

Drill No. 111

Drill No. 112

Drill No. 113

Drill No. 114

Drill No. 115

Drill No. 116

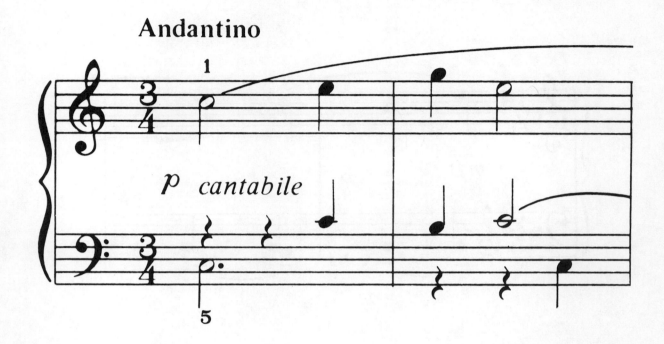

Drill No. 117

Drill No. 118

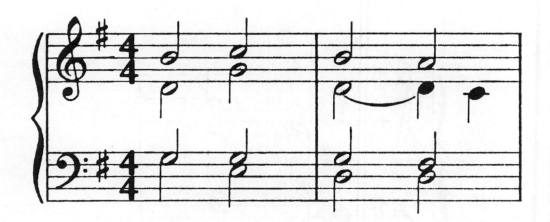

Drill No. 119

53

Drill No. 120

Drill No. 121

Drill No. 122

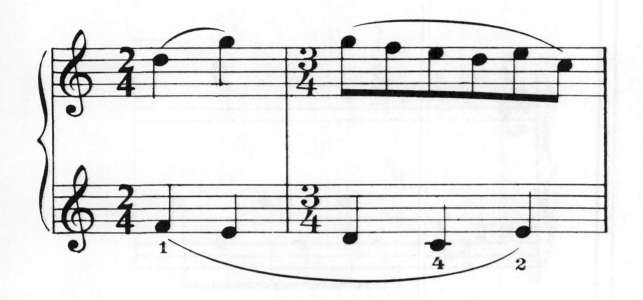

Drill No. 123

Drill No. 124

Drill No. 125

Drill No. 126

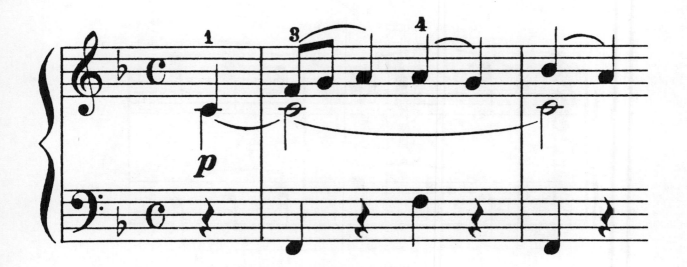

Drill No. 127

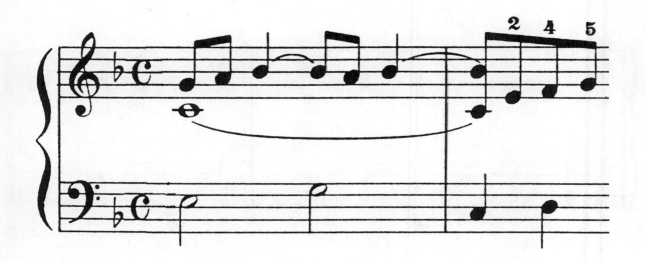

Drill No. 128

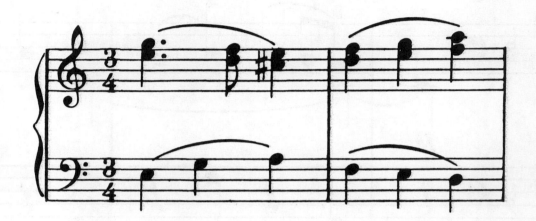

Drill No. 129

Drill No. 130

Drill No. 131

SECTION 5
Reading Pieces

Reading Piece No. 75: Prelude Op. 28 No. 7 (Simplified) *(F. Chopin)*

1st Reading Tempo: _56_   **Date:** _1-26-88_

2nd Reading Tempo: _____   **Date:** _____

Metronome Range #1: ♩ = **56-66**

Metronome Range #2: ♩ = **69-84**

Actual Tempo: ♩ = **92**

Special Attention: In order to give this piece its proper lilt, think in terms of two-bar phrases. . . . This means that you will have a strong downbeat every two measures, instead of every measure.

Reminder: Observe the bass note ties.

Reading Piece No. 76 : Waltz from Sleeping Beauty _(P. I. Tchaikovsky)_

1st Reading Tempo: _92_ **Date:** _2-1-88_   **Metronome Range #1:** ♩ = **56-92**
2nd Reading Tempo: _____ **Date:** _____   **Metronome Range #2:** ♩ = **92-144**
                                                     Actual Tempo: ♩ = **144**

Special Attention: Prepare the entire measure as you are playing the L.H. pattern; i.e. have clusters of thirds and seconds "under the fingers" as you play the single note downbeat.

Reminder: A waltz is a slow dance characterized mainly by the accompaniment pattern consisting of a low bass note on the first beat and two chords in the middle register on the second and third beats. Remember to sustain this _waltz_ characteristic throughout, particularly in measures 21-28 as the pattern is distributed between the two hands.

Tempo di Valse

Reading Piece No. 77 : Good Christian Men, Rejoice *(John Mason Neale)*

1st Reading Tempo: _88_ **Date:** _2-1-88_

2nd Reading Tempo: _____ **Date:** _____

Metronome Range #1: ♪ = **66-88**

Metronome Range #2: ♪ = **96-112**

Actual Tempo: ♪ = **176**

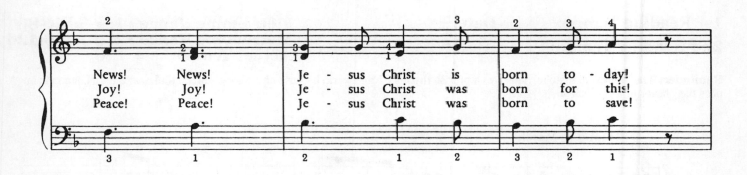

News! News! Je - sus Christ is born to - day!
Joy! Joy! Je - sus Christ was born for this!
Peace! Peace! Je - sus Christ was born to save!

Ox and ass be - fore Him bow, and
He hath ope'd the heav'n - ly door, and
Calls you one and calls you all, to

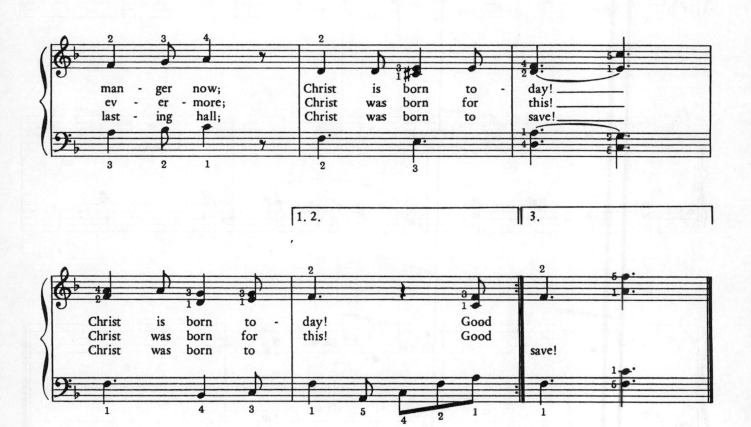

man - ger now; Christ is born to - day! _____
ev - er - more; Christ was born for this! _____
last - ing hall; Christ was born to save! _____

| 1. 2. | 3. |

Christ is born to - day! Good
Christ was born for this! Good
Christ was born to save!

Reading Piece No. 78: Toreador Song *Georges Bizet*

1st Reading Tempo: _80_ **Date:** _2-1-88_

2nd Reading Tempo: _____ **Date:** _____

Metronome Range #1: ♩ = **60-80**
Metronome Range #2: ♩ = **80-126**
Actual Tempo: ♩ = **126**

Reminder: The "tempo di marche" indicates a precise rhythmic framework; because of the song's origin (*Carmen*) the L.H. staccato implies the "flavor of a Spanish shop."

Tempo di Marche

Reading Piece No. 79: Song *Henry Purcell*

1st Reading Tempo: 69   **Date:** 2-1-88
2nd Reading Tempo: ___   **Date:** ___

Metronome Range #1: ♩ = 54-69
Metronome Range #2: ♩ = 76-104
Actual Tempo: ♩ = 120

Special Attention: RH rhythm is a bit tricky at measures 5 and 7.
Reminder: ♩. is held for three full beats in 3/4 time.

Reading Piece No. 80: Three Easy Pieces on Five Notes

Igor Stravinsky

1st Reading Tempo: _66_ **Date:** _2-1-88_
2nd Reading Tempo: _____ **Date:** _____

Metronome Range #1: ♩ = 46-66
Metronome Range #2: ♩ = 66-104
Actual Tempo: ♩ = 104

Special Attention: Changing meter [³⁄₄ ²⁄₄] should be noted in the second system.   **Reminder:** L.H. plays in treble clef, too.

Reading Piece No. 81: Miniature Rondo *Daniel Gottlob Turk*

1st Reading Tempo: _60_ **Date:** _2-1-88_

2nd Reading Tempo: _____ **Date:** _____

Metronome Range #1: ♩ = **50-76**

Metronome Range #2: ♩ = **76-104**

Actual Tempo: ♩ = **144**

Special Attention: L.H. alternates between 𝄞 and 𝄢 clefs.   **Reminder:** Look for contrasting dynamic markings: "P," "F," "P," "F."

Reading Piece No. 82 : Chorale *Robert Schumann*

1st Reading Tempo: _60_ **Date:** _2-1-88_

2nd Reading Tempo: _____ **Date:** _____

Metronome Range #1: ♩ = **60-72**
Metronome Range #2: ♩ = **80-96**
Actual Tempo: ♩ = **138**

Special Attention: Look for common tones in chords, so you can concentrate on reading the "moving voices."
Reminder: The fermata sign (𝄐) means: "hold."

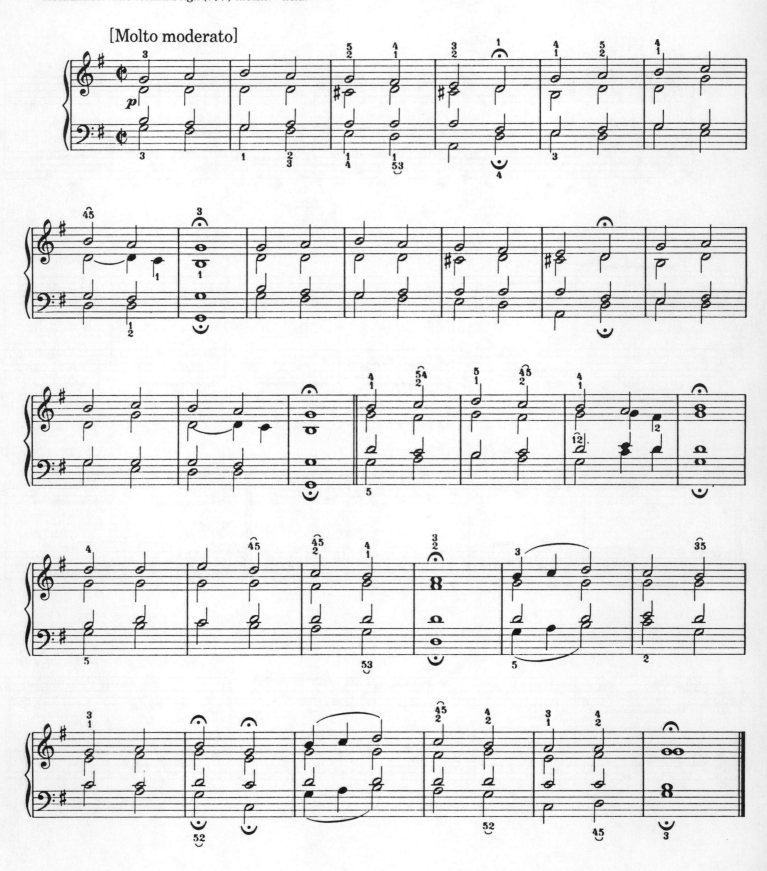

Reading Piece No. 83: German Dance *Franz Joseph Haydn*

1st Reading Tempo: _60_ **Date:** _2-1-88_

2nd Reading Tempo: _____ **Date:** _____

Metronome Range #1: ♩ = 50-66
Metronome Range #2: ♩ = 66-116
Actual Tempo: ♩ = 116

Special Attention: L.H. accompaniment has pedal point of thumb on "A" in first two lines, and broken octave on "D" in last two lines.
Reminder: L.H. plays first two lines in treble clef.

Reading Piece No. 84 : Sleepers Awake from Cantata No. 40

(J. S. Bach)

1st Reading Tempo: 52 **Date:** 2-2-88

2nd Reading Tempo: _____ **Date:** _____

Metronome Range #1: ♩ = **44-63**

Metronome Range #2: ♩ = **63-116**

Actual Tempo: ♩ = **116**

Special Attention: Before playing, look over the phrasing of line 1 and the rhythm of line 4. The two-beat phrases should be played with a slight expressive emphasis on the first note of each phrase:

Be sure to observe the rests in the L.H. of the first line.

Reminder: In baroque music of contrapuntal nature, it is extremely important that you try to observe the note values of the inner voices.

Reading Piece No. 85: Quarter Note Etudes

1st Reading Tempo: _56_ **Date:** _2-2-88_

2nd Reading Tempo: _____ **Date:** _____

Metronome Range #1: ♩ = 40-50

Metronome Range #2: ♩ = 60-72

Actual Tempo: ♩ = 88

Special Attention: Create your own fingerings, by looking ahead.

Reading Piece No. 86 : Minuet *(C. Reinecke)*

1st Reading Tempo: ___40___   **Date:** ___2-8-88___

2nd Reading Tempo: _____   **Date:** _____

Metronome Range #1: ♩ = **40-50**

Metronome Range #2: ♩ = **58-69**

Actual Tempo: ♩ = **92**

Special Attention: Be sure to hold the dotted half notes in the bass while playing repeated eighth notes (e.g. m. 3-4, 7, 9-10, 13-14, etc.). Observe key changes. Be aware of the accidentals in the center section. Bring out the melody line as it occurs in both hands.

Reminder: *Dolce* means sweetly.

Reading Piece No. 87: Oh, Had I A Cave *Franz Josef Haydn*

1st Reading Tempo: _66_ **Date:** _2-8-88_

2nd Reading Tempo: _____ **Date:** _____

Metronome Range #1: ♩ = **56-66**

Metronome Range #2: ♩ = **76-88**

Actual Tempo: ♩ = **112**

Special Attention: This folk song arrangement alternates between block chords and eighth note motion. Be sure to maintain an even pulse throughout.

Reminder: Clef changes occur in the left hand part. Always review a piece quickly before sight-reading, and notice "tricky" sections.

1. Oh had I a cave on some
2. Fals - est of wo - man - kind,

wild dis - tant shore,
can'st thou de - clare

Where the winds
All thy

howl to the wave's dash - ing roar;
plight - ed vows fleet - ing as air!

There would I weep my woes, There seek my ___
To thy new lov - er hie, Laugh o'er thy ___

lost re - pose, Till grief ___ my ___ eyes should close,
per - ju - ry ___ Then in ___ thy ___ bos - om try

Ne'er to wake more.
What peace is there.

Reading Piece No. 88: Baroque Fanfare *(J. Mouret)*

1st Reading Tempo: _66_ **Date:** _2-8-88_ **Metronome Range #1:** ♩ = **46-66**

2nd Reading Tempo: _____ **Date:** _____ **Metronome Range #2:** ♩ = **66-132**

Actual Tempo: ♩ = **132**

Special Attention: This piece should be played regally, with the original scoring for trumpets in mind. A slightly detached touch will simulate the tonguing which occurs in the playing of brass instruments.

Reminder: *Fine* indicates the end of a piece after a return from a repeat.

SECTION 6

"Map Tone" Exercises

Good sight-readers look at a music score the way navigators search the night sky. Within the jumble of countless tiny stars, a navigator can spot important shapes, and use them to find his bearings. Key stars define those broad outlines and serve as focal points in the map of the constellations.

Pianists can similarly find important notes within the outlines of a piece of music, to be used as guideposts or central points in the maps of their musical "constellations."

The following map-tone exercises are designed to help you pick out key notes in a long phrase so that you may begin to play "shapes" instead of individual pitches. First play the exercise at a moderate tempo — whatever feels comfortable without allowing you to spend too much time on each note. Then, play the piece that follows.

When playing the actual piece, be sure to keep playing, even if you fumble on some of the notes. Look for the outlines of the music, and the patterns being formed. You should find before long that you are "seeing" shapes and map-tones as you read each new piece of music. This is a key to your growth as a sight-reader.

Drill No. 132   Map Tone Exercise

Reading Piece No. 89 : Burleske *From Leopold Mozart's Note Book*

1st Reading Tempo: 126 (♩)   **Date:** 5-25-88

2nd Reading Tempo: _____   **Date:** _____

Metronome Range #1: ♪ = 48-69
Metronome Range #2: ♪ = 69-120
Actual Tempo: ♪ = 144

Special Attention: Octaves in L.H. should be played before beginning, to help your tactile memory of what an octave "feels" like.

Reminder: Try to read "upbeat" melodic unit in one phrase, as marked throughout (16th notes leading to an eighth note).

Drill No. 133   Map Tone Exercise

Reading Piece No. 90 : Minuet and Trio *Johann Sebastian Bach*

1st Reading Tempo: _88_ **Date:** _5-25-88_

2nd Reading Tempo: _____ **Date:** _____

Metronome Range #1: ♩ = **46-63**

Metronome Range #2: ♩ = **63-108**

Actual Tempo: ♩ = **108**

Special Attention: First two lines are in contrary motion. Note the switch to parallel motion.

Reminder: Key is "G minor."

Drill No. 134   Map Tone Exercise

Reading Piece No. 91: Russian Folk Song *Ludwig van Beethoven*

1st Reading Tempo: _66_ **Date:** _2-4-90_

2nd Reading Tempo: _____ **Date:** _____

Metronome Range #1: ♩ = **50-66**
Metronome Range #2: ♩ = **80-96**
Actual Tempo: ♩ = **120**

Special Attention: Articulation () changing to legato phrasing.

Drill No. 135   Map Tone Exercise

Reading Piece No. 92 : Evening Song *Daniel Gottlob Turk*

1st Reading Tempo: _46_ **Date:** _2-4-90_
2nd Reading Tempo: _____ **Date:** _____

Metronome Range #1: ♪ = **46-60**
Metronome Range #2: ♪ = **60-104**
Actual Tempo: ♩ = 80

Special Attention: The exact phrasing *pattern* should be looked at before beginning.

Reminder: Look "a measure ahead" especially when the R.H. and L.H. alternate.

Drill No. 136   Map Tone Exercise

Reading Piece No. 93: A Farewell *Henry Purcell*

1st Reading Tempo: _50_ **Date:** _2-4-90_

2nd Reading Tempo: _____ **Date:** _____

Metronome Range #1: ♪ = 50-63
Metronome Range #2: ♪ = 63-88
Actual Tempo: ♩ = 88

Special Attention: Note whether the hands move in similar or contrary motion.
Reminder: Beware of the 16th note pulse throughout the piece.

Drill No. 137   Map Tone Exercise

Reading Piece No. 94 : Study *Carl Czerny*

1st Reading Tempo: _63_ **Date:** _1-7-92_
2nd Reading Tempo: _____ **Date:** _____

Metronome Range #1: ♪ = **63-80**
Metronome Range #2: ♪ = **80-114**
Actual Tempo: ♪ = **144**

Special Attention: As hands alternate in playing "scales," try to have the "resting" hand prepared and ready to play.
Reminder: "Feel" the steps rather than looking down.

Drill No. 138   Map Tone Exercise

Reading Piece No. 95: Le Petit Rien *Francois Couperin*

1st Reading Tempo: 56   **Date:** 1-7-92

2nd Reading Tempo: _____   **Date:** _____

Metronome Range #1: ♩ 48-69
Metronome Range #2: ♩ = 69-92
Actual Tempo: ♩ = 112

Special Attention: L.H. alternates between 𝄞 and 𝄢 clefs.
Reminder: Try to keep your eyes one measure ahead of your hands, noting that the melodic range within each measure is almost always within the five-finger position.

SECTION 7

Flash Pages

Drill No. 139

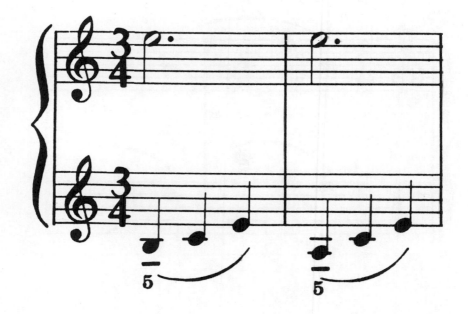

Drill No. 140

Drill No. 141

Drill No. 142

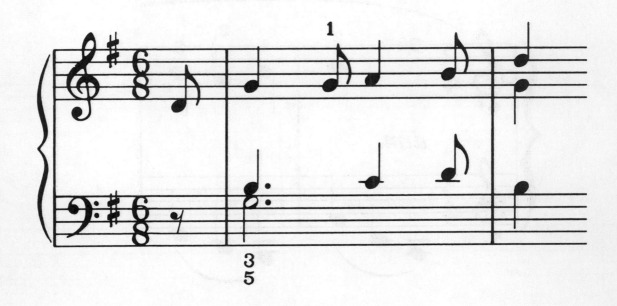

Drill No. 143

Drill No. 144

Drill No. 145

Drill No. 146

Drill No. 147

Drill No. 148

Drill No. 149

Drill No. 150

Drill No. 151

Drill No. 152

Drill No. 153

Drill No. 154

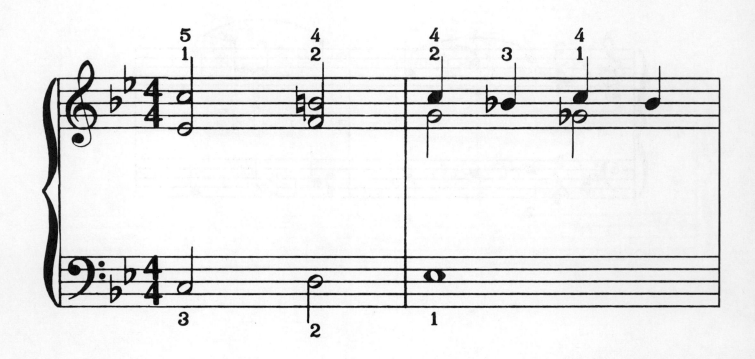

Drill No. 155

Drill No. 156

Drill No. 157

Drill No. 158

Drill No. 159

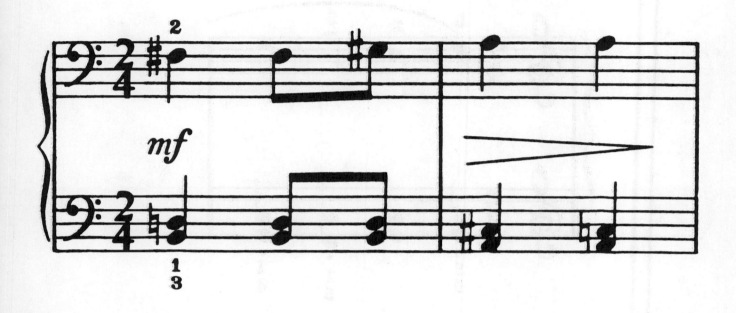

Drill No. 160

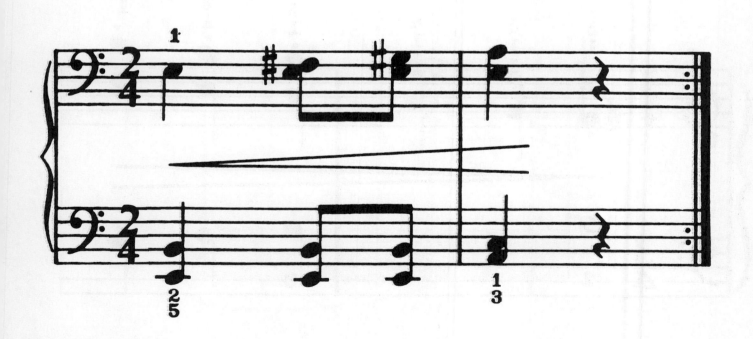

Drill No. 161

Drill No. 162

Drill No. 163

Drill No. 164

Drill No. 165

Drill No. 166

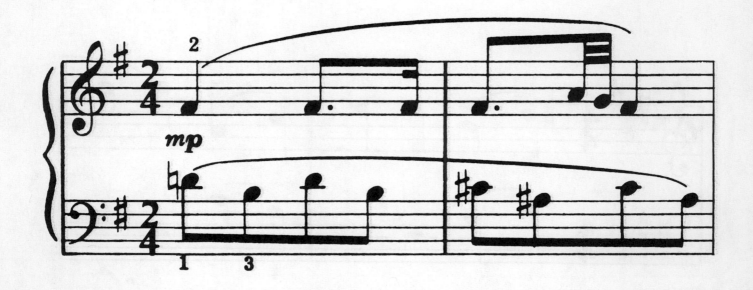

Drill No. 167

Drill No. 168

Drill No. 169

Drill No. 170

SECTION 7
Reading Pieces

Reading Piece No. 96: Andantino *Georg Frederik Handel*

1st Reading Tempo: _63_   **Date:** _1-7-92_

2nd Reading Tempo: _____   **Date:** _____

Metronome Range #1: ♪ = 63-80
Metronome Range #2: ♪ = 80-104
Actual Tempo: ♪ = 138

Special Attention: Octave leaps in L.H. should be played before beginning.

Reminder: Key is D minor.

Andantino

Reading Piece No. 97: A Regal Dance *Daniel Gottlob Turk*

1st Reading Tempo: _56_ **Date:** _1-7-92_

2nd Reading Tempo: _____ **Date:** _____

Metronome Range #1: ♩ = 48-69
Metronome Range #2: ♩ = 69-112
Actual Tempo: ♩ = 112

Special Attention: Clef change in L.H. from treble-bass-treble-bass etc.

Reminder: The third beat (♫ or ♫♫) of almost every measure is used as a "pick-up" or lead into the downbeat.

Therefore, look ahead to the following downbeat *before* playing the third beat of each measure.

Reading Piece No. 98: Landler *Ludwig van Beethoven*

1st Reading Tempo: _66_ **Date:** _1-7-92_

2nd Reading Tempo: _____ **Date:** _____

Metronome Range #1: ♩ = 52-69
Metronome Range #2: ♩ = 69-132
Actual Tempo: ♩ = 132

Special Attention: Leger line notes below the bass clefs are C, G, E♭: try to play the L.H. line first with the leaping intervals.
Reminder: Key is "C Minor."

Reading Piece No. 99: Air *Henry Purcell*

1st Reading Tempo: 66 **Date:** 1-7-92

2nd Reading Tempo: _____ **Date:** _____

Metronome Range #1: ♩ = 52-66
Metronome Range #2: ♩ = 66-96
Actual Tempo: ♩ = 112

Special Attention: Half note and dotted half note should be held in L.H.

Reminder: Notice the ♩♫♩ rhythmic pattern throughout.

Reading Piece No. 100 : Gavotte *Daniel Gottlob Turk*

1st Reading Tempo: _60_ **Date:** _1-7-92_

2nd Reading Tempo: _____ **Date:** _____

Metronome Range #1: ♩ = **50-69**
Metronome Range #2: ♩ = **69-108**
Actual Tempo: ♩ = **126**

Special Attention: Leger lines (especially in L.H.) should be looked at first.

Reminder: Try to read in "half measures."

Reading Piece No.101: Lullaby *Johann Philipp Kirnberger*

1st Reading Tempo: 80   **Date:** 1-1-92

2nd Reading Tempo: ____   **Date:** ____

Metronome Range #1: ♪ = 69-88
Metronome Range #2: ♪ = 100-138
Actual Tempo: ♩. = 69

Special Attention: Tricky LH leaps in measures 13-14.
Note: At actual tempo you may hit clinkers in measures 9 through 14. Don't stop! Keep going!

Reading Piece No.102: Entrée *Leopold Mozart*

1st Reading Tempo: 63 **Date:** 1-7-92
2nd Reading Tempo: _____ **Date:** _____

Metronome Range #1: ♩ = 52-76
Metronome Range #2: ♩ = 76-116
Actual Tempo: ♩ = 138

Special Attention: Accidentals (F#, G#): the raised 6th and 7th degrees of "A minor."
Reminder: This 2-voice piece should be read always observing the similar and contrary motion between the hands.

Reading Piece No.103: The Doll's Lament *Cesar Franck*

1st Reading Tempo: _60_ **Date:** _1-7-92_

2nd Reading Tempo: _____ **Date:** _____

Metronome Range #1: ♩ = 48-66
Metronome Range #2: ♩ = 66-100
Actual Tempo: ♩ = 100

Special Attention: "Alberti-bass" type of L.H. accompaniment.
Reminder: Try to "feel" for triadic intervals (i.e. 3rds and 5ths) without looking at keyboard.

Reading Piece No.104: Carnival *Francois Couperin*

1st Reading Tempo: 63   **Date:** 1-7-98

2nd Reading Tempo: ____   **Date:** ____

Metronome Range #1: ♪ = 56-76
Metronome Range #2: ♪ = 80-104
Actual Tempo: ♪ = 144

Special Attention: L.H. ostinato figure throughout (16th note pattern using the same motive). Hold dotted quarter with 5th finger of L.H. as directed.